THIS FIELD GUIDE BELONGS TO:

DINOSAUR FIELD GUIDE

REVISED AND UPDATED

BY DR. THOMAS R. HOLTZ, JR.
and
DR. MICHAEL BRETT-SURMAN

ILLUSTRATED BY ROBERT WALTERS

SCHOLASTIC
SYDNEY AUCKLAND NEW YORK TORONTO LONDON MEXICO CITY
NEW DELHI HONG KONG BUENOS AIRES PUERTO RICO

A note to parents: This book is appropriate for ages 8 and up.
Jurassic World is rated M.
Consult www.classification.gov.au for further information.

Designed by Hayley Richards | Edited by Hannah Janssen

First published in 2015.

This edition published by Scholastic Australia in 2025.

Scholastic Australia Pty Limited
PO Box 579 Gosford NSW 2250
ABN 11 000 614 577
www.scholastic.com.au

Part of the Scholastic Group
Sydney • Auckland • New York • Toronto • London • Mexico City
New Delhi • Hong Kong • Buenos Aires • Puerto Rico

ISBN 978-1-76172-053-6

Printed in China.

CONTENTS

WHY ARE DINOSAURS SO POPULAR?

Hollywood has been featuring dinosaur-inspired creatures in movies for years, from the many versions of Sir Arthur Conan Doyle's *The Lost World* to *The Beast from 20,000 Fathoms*, *Godzilla* and *Jurassic World*. What could be more exciting than seeing such amazing creatures on the big screen? Yet Hollywood is not the only reason that dinosaurs are so popular.

The award-winning book *The Complete Dinosaur* suggests dinosaurs are popular because they represent 'adventure, power, time travel, science, mystery, [and] lost worlds'. But what truly sets dinosaurs apart from other popular movie creatures is that dinosaurs were REAL. They were not part of some backdrop; they actually ruled our planet for more than 150 million years—that's 75 times longer than our own human species! Even though many dinosaur movies are loaded with inaccuracies (they are, after all, not documentaries, but entertainment!), they often spark our desire to know more. And that's why we've written this book: to tell you more about these amazingly popular creatures.

There are now over 1,200 named species of Dinosauria, and the number grows by about 40 each year! So how did we narrow that 1,200 down to the entries in this book? We wanted to give you a sample from every dinosaur group, and to include several that are familiar—some that have been around since being discovered in the 1800s, some featured in the *Jurassic World* movies, several that were named during our lifetime, and some brand-new ones.

Since the 'Dinosaur Renaissance' began in 1975, the number of professional dinosaur palaeontologists (people who work on dinosaurs full-time at the professional level) has risen from about 20 to over 200. This has led to an explosion of new explorations and discoveries. At one time, North America was the centre for new finds. Now China and Argentina lead the world in finding and naming new dinosaur species. With about 40 new species named per year, scientists learn something new about dinosaurs literally each month. The field of vertebrate palaeontology is one of the most interdisciplinary of the sciences. Each year it will see new growth, new students, and new adventures. Care to join us?

Finally, there is one dark side to the sometimes 'overpopularity' of dinosaurs. They now have a commercial value that makes the unethical and illegal collecting of fossils financially rewarding in some cases. For every dinosaur fossil with scientific value that gets collected as a 'trophy', or winds up in a 'non-permanent' collection, the whole world and all future citizens run the risk of losing a key to our planet's history. In the words of fictional character Indiana Jones (regrettably an archaeologist—not a palaeontologist), 'It belongs in a museum'.

Dr. Thomas R. Holtz, Jr.
& Dr. Michael Brett-Surman

WHEN WAS THE AGE OF DINOSAURS?

The Age of Dinosaurs began about 252 million years ago (MYA), during a time known as the Mesozoic Era. Now, to us humans, who have only been around for about 1.5 million years, 252 million years may seem like a long time ago. But it really isn't that long when you consider it as a part of what scientists call Geologic Time, or the time measured from today back to the birth of Earth—about 4.5 *billion* years ago (BYA)!

The first 89 percent of Earth's history, from 4.5 billion to 541 million years ago, is called Precambrian (pree-CAIM-bree-in) Time. The oldest fossils show up in the early Precambrian about 3.75 billion years ago. These earliest fossils were of bacteria, the simplest known living things. More complex fossils, including traces of worm-like animals, show up much later in Precambrian Time. Because early life did not have hard parts, the fossil record is very sparse in the Precambrian. However, at around 541 million years ago animals developed shells, bones, teeth, and other hard parts. From this time onward, fossils become common. Scientists refer to the time from 541 million years ago to today as the Phanerozoic (FAN-uh-ro-ZO-ick), or 'visible life', Eon. This eon is divided into three eras: Paleozoic, Mesozoic and Cenozoic.

A GEOLOGIC TIME SCALE

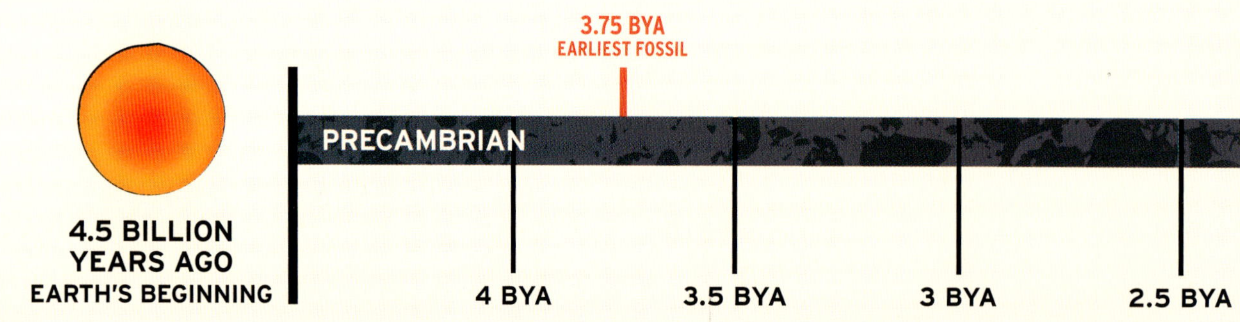

PALEOZOIC ERA

PAY-lee-oh-ZO-ick ee-RA

541–252 MILLION YEARS AGO

The first era of visible life is called the Paleozoic, or 'ancient life', Era. This is when trilobites (an extinct group of sea-dwelling relatives of insects, crustaceans, and spiders) lived, fishes ruled the seas, and the first plants, insects, and amphibians (animals with backbones that live on land but must be in water to reproduce) colonised the planet. It was late in the Paleozoic that descendants of the amphibians developed shelled eggs, evolved, and split into the two major groups of dominant land vertebrates (backboned animals) that have ruled until today. One group is called the synapsids, which includes the mammals (humans among them) and our protomammal ancestors. The other, and far larger, group is called the reptiles. Reptiles include turtles, lizards and snakes, crocodilians, dinosaurs, birds, and various other extinct groups.

During the Paleozoic a series of collisions between continents produced the supercontinent of Pangaea (pan-JEE-ah), which means 'all Earth'. Pangaea was mostly in the Southern Hemisphere. All of Earth's landmasses were pushed together, surrounded by a single ocean—Panthalassa (pan-tha-LAS-ah), or 'all sea'. The Paleozoic Era ended with the most sweeping extinction known in Earth's history, which may have been caused by the biggest series of volcanic eruptions in the Phanerozoic Eon, the remains of which are found in Siberia. It is estimated that up to 95 percent of all animal species went extinct.

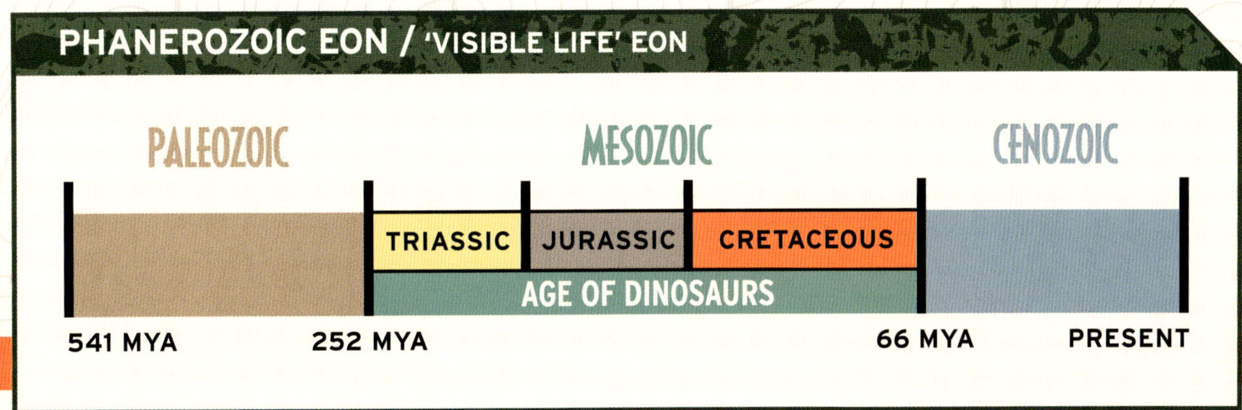

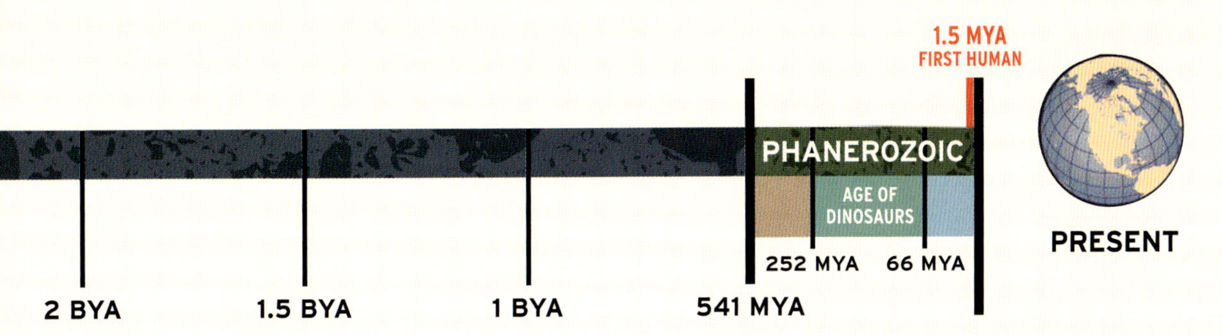

MESOZOIC ERA

MES-oh-ZO-ick ee-RA

252–66 MILLION YEARS AGO

The second era of the Phanerozoic Eon was the Mesozoic Era, or Age of Dinosaurs. The supercontinent of Pangaea began to break apart and a new ocean formed in the split between North America and Africa. This new area became the Atlantic Ocean. Many continents started to drift northward. North America travelled across the equator into its current position. It was possible to walk from New York to London. South America began to separate from Africa. Antarctica was still connected to Australia and India.

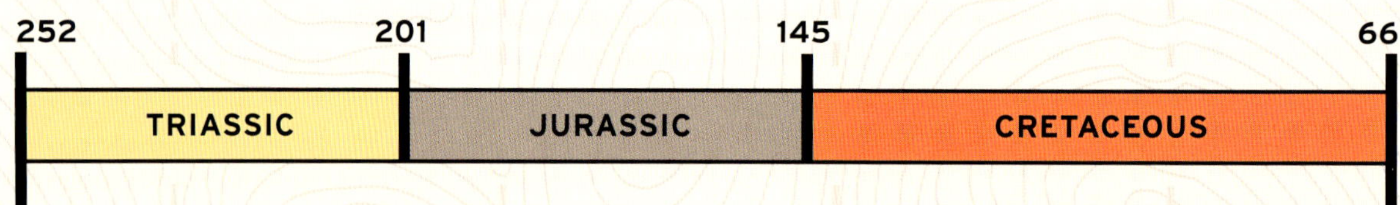

TRIASSIC PERIOD / 252–201 MYA

The first of the three geologic periods within the Mesozoic is the Triassic (try-AS-ick). This was a very interesting time. At its beginning, most of the ecologically dominant synapsids (protomammals) were replaced by reptiles. Dinosaurs, winged pterosaurs, crocodilians, lizards and turtles all first appeared during the Late Triassic, as did the first mammals.

CEOLOPHYSIS
PAGE 55

PROCOMPSOGNATHUS
PAGE 106

AETOSAURUS
PAGE 137

JURASSIC PERIOD / 201–145 MYA

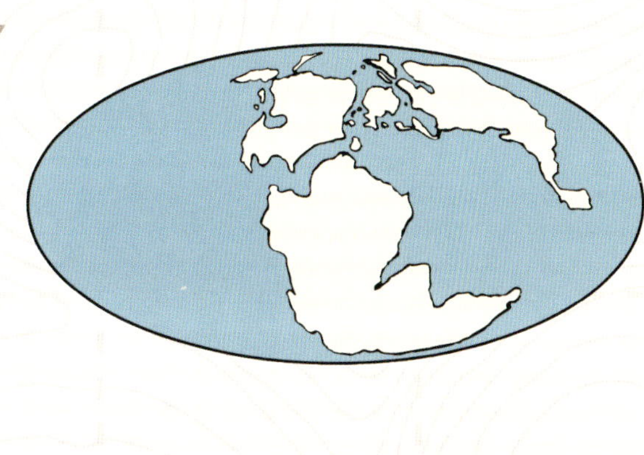

The second period of the Mesozoic is called the Jurassic (joo-RAS-ick). This was the 'age of giants'. Sauropods, or long-necked plant-eaters, became the largest land animals of all time. Theropods, or meat-eaters, became the most diverse (having the largest number of species) group of land predators, and the first birds appeared from one of these theropod groups. Ornithischians (the main group of plant-eating dinosaurs) were mostly represented by the armoured ankylosaurs and the plated stegosaurs.

STEGOSAURUS
PAGE 118

MEGALOSAURUS
PAGE 91

CAMARASAURUS
PAGE 48

DILOPHOSAURUS
PAGE 62

CRETACEOUS PERIOD / 145–66 MYA

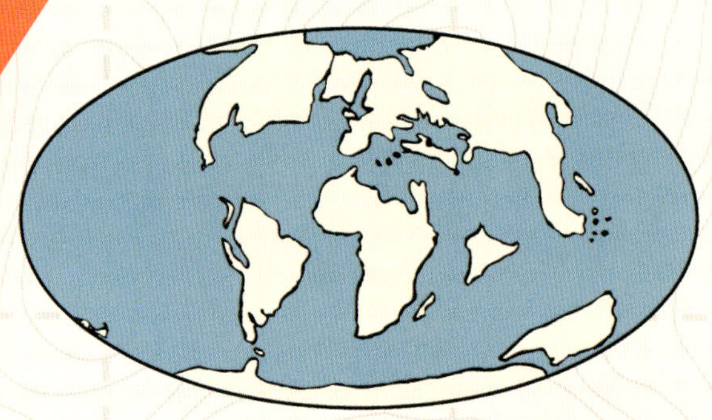

The third, longest, and final period of the Mesozoic is called the Cretaceous (kri-TAY-shus). Sauropod species declined in the Northern Hemisphere but flourished in the Southern Hemisphere — especially the titanosaurs. Theropods experienced their greatest diversity of groups, from tyrannosaurs to birds. The bird groups expanded and diversified into the seabirds, predators, waterfowl, and the flightless runners and swimmers. The plated dinosaurs went extinct, but the armoured dinosaurs split into three groups. Ornithopods (two-legged herbivores) also diversified and finally resulted in the most elegant of dinosaurs (the duckbills with their crests) and the most elaborate dinosaurs (the ceratopsians with their frills of bone up to 3m long). The final group of dinosaurs also appeared: the pachycephalosaurs, or boneheads. As far as we can tell from the fossil record, the largest number of dinosaur species occurred at this time. Then it all ended about 66 million years ago in the fourth-largest extinction event in Earth's history (the three larger extinction events were in the Paleozoic Era).

TOROSAURUS
PAGE 122

CORYTHOSAURUS
PAGE 59

TYRANNOSAURUS
PAGE 126

PACHYCEPHALOSAURUS
PAGE 100

EXTINCTION!

The reasons for the extinction of the Mesozoic dinosaurs (excluding birds) are very complex and still debated by scientists. Entire scientific books have been written on this subject, with more on the way! Basically there are currently two competing theories—the asteroid theory and the gradual decline theory.

ASTEROID THEORY

The asteroid theory states that an asteroid hit the Yucatán Peninsula in the country of Mexico. The resulting fireball and explosion covered Earth with ash that blocked sunlight for years and caused an ecological disaster.

GRADUAL DECLINE THEORY

The gradual decline theory states that dinosaurs were already near the end of an extinction event when the asteroid finished off the remaining dinosaurs.

Both theories have major problems and unanswered questions. The timing of the asteroid impact is most important. Did it hit before, during, or after dinosaurs had reached the point of no return? The studies continue.

CENOZOIC ERA

SEN-oh-ZO-ick ee-RA

66 MILLION YEARS AGO–PRESENT

The final era, which we are in now, is called the Cenozoic, or 'recent life', Era. It began with the continents continuing to split apart (except for India, which crashed into Asia, forming the Himalaya Mountains). Australia separated from Antarctica. North America finally separated from Asia first, then Europe. Mountain-building continued with the formation of the Rocky Mountains, the Andes, and the Alps. The great inland sea across North America retreated, and the Great Plains were formed.

Life as we know it began to take over the Earth. Grasslands appeared for the first time, as well as great forests of oak. Mammals were everywhere, and getting larger. Birds could be found on each of the seven continents. The climate continued to get warmer.

Then, about 3 million years before today, the climate shifted and temperatures dropped. An Ice Age gripped Earth, and continent-sized glaciers reshaped the landscape. As the glaciers pushed the surface rocks before them (like a titanic snow shovel), they piled up the debris. One of these piles is now known as Long Island, New York!

As temperatures fluctuated between an ice-covered world at one extreme and warm intervals with retreating glaciers at the other, a new two-legged species of mammal appeared. It was the human race, the most dangerous predators ever to evolve.

Is the Ice Age over? Or are we just in one of the many temporary warm spells? Will the glaciers return, or will human industrial activities (adding pollutants to the atmosphere) send us back to the higher temperatures common in the Cenozoic?

PLANT LIFE DURING THE AGE OF DINOSAURS

Some people think of plants as a passive backdrop in our environment, not evolving or changing. This is far from the truth. Plants are the basis of the food system and have important and dynamic interactions with animals. The evolution of plants is tightly entwined with the evolution of the animals that feed on them.

Being a plant-eating dinosaur wasn't easy. During the Mesozoic Era, or Age of Dinosaurs, plants were harder to digest than modern plants are and provided little nutrition. After a herd of herbivorous, or plant-eating, dinosaurs passed through an area, eating everything in their path, the plant life may have taken a year to grow back. This means that plant-eaters either kept moving around one large region or migrated from region to region. All that extra walking would require more energy, which would require eating more plants, which would require more walking, and so on.

During the Mesozoic Era, there were no grasslands, lush jungles, or fields of grain. There were, however, club mosses (lycopsids), horsetails (sphenopsids), ferns, seed ferns, cycads, and big trees—the cycadeoids, conifers (cone-bearing trees), and ginkgos. From the Late Triassic (when dinosaurs first appeared) until the Late Cretaceous (when flowering plants started to dominate), these were the only plants a dinosaur could eat. Most of the plants we see today—the angiosperms—did not arrive until the Cretaceous Period.

Plant-eating dinosaurs quickly became the largest animals ever to walk the Earth. This is because they were the first to be able to feed high up in the trees, where the foliage was, without actually having to climb or fly.

Because the world of the Late Triassic and Jurassic was dominated by cycads and conifers, which were poor in nutrients, plant-eaters developed larger gut areas so they could digest the plants longer to get more nutrients out of them. This left the relatively smaller ornithischians (such as the ornithopods, stegosaurs, and ankylosaurs) to specialise in eating ground cover.

A new food source appeared during the Cretaceous that changed both the landscape and dinosaur evolution. Angiosperms are far more efficient at reproducing and recovering from being eaten than ferns, cycads, and conifers. This meant that angiosperms were better and quicker at growing back in areas cleared by dinosaurs—and they began to push out the older plant groups.

As angiosperms evolved from ground cover into tree-sized plants, so the once smaller plant-eaters evolved into sauropod-sized giants. This new, rapidly growing food source may have been the reason why ornithischians, especially the ornithopods and ceratopsians, began their diversification.

HOW DINOSAURS ARE DUG UP

So you want to discover a new dinosaur? How do you start? Well, you can't just go into your backyard, start digging, and expect to find fossils. Digging up fossils is actually a five-part process.

PART 1: INVESTIGATION

Before you begin searching for fossils, you need to know where to look. The first step is to find out where sedimentary rocks of the Mesozoic Era (or the Age of Dinosaurs) are now located on the surface of the Earth. This requires a trip to the library. You can research popular books (see the reading list in the back of this book) and old scientific papers by area of interest, geologic formation and fossil group.

PART 2: PREPARATION

Once you know where to look, you need to make sure you have permission to dig on the land (on private or public land), and to collect whatever you may find. This permission needs to come from Traditional Owners on native title, pasturalists and local councils. It is illegal to dig in any national parks.

Check with your state museum or interest group to find which sites are cleared for fossicking.

Never do any field work on your own, always bring an adult to accompany you. Make sure you both know basic first aid and can be easily in contact with emergency services. Wear suitable clothing to reduce risks: long pants, enclosed shoes, a hat, sunglasses, safety glasses and sunscreen.

In your field kit on a day trip, the least you will need is: water, lunch, geologic and topographic maps of the local area, a ruler, a camera, a notebook and pencils, and a first aid kit.

PART 3: EXPLORATION

Assuming you find a dinosaur (which, of course, you are going to give to a school or museum), do not dig it up! First, you must take pictures of the specimen (with the ruler beside it to show size), then map the specific location and the general area.

Accurately plot your location on your maps (ideally using GPS, or global positioning satellite, equipment). Next is the most important part—get a professional vertebrate palaeontologist to help unearth your find.

DINOSAURS COME IN LITERALLY ALL SIZES, AND EACH DIFFERENT SIZE, AND METHOD OF PRESERVATION, REQUIRES A DIFFERENT TECHNIQUE.

There is no one-way-fits-all method of excavating fossils—different types of fossil bone even require different glues. Any data lost while digging (for example, ancient pollen samples) is gone forever! This is why a professional is needed. The Society of Vertebrate Paleontology (available at vertpaleo.org) can supply the names of palaeontologists in each state and country.

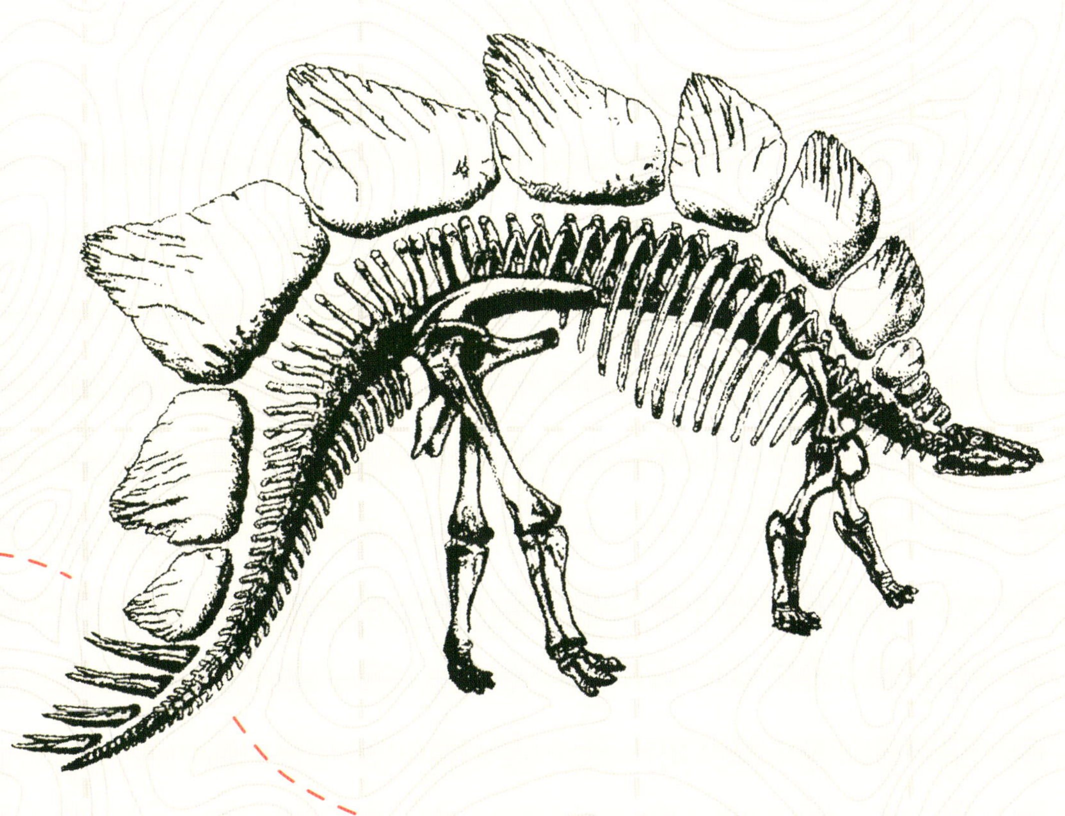

PART 4: EXCAVATION

Before digging, set up a grid system around the specimen so you can take more pictures and map exactly where each bone is found. Gradually clear away the surface sediments all around the specimen until there is at least 1 metre of space around each bone. Do not hurry. As each bone is exposed, you'll need to clean it, apply polyvinyl acetates (as shown to you by the palaeontologist), and take pictures of each bone.

Using tools provided by the palaeontologist, keep digging around the specimen until it is sitting on a pedestal of sediment. Apply a covering of toilet paper or aluminum foil as a separator so the specimen will not stick to the next layer—plaster of Paris reinforced by burlap or a substitute of various linen products.

Then turn the specimen over and repeat the process until it is completely covered. Then take sediment samples from underneath the specimen (where the rock has not been exposed to the air) and seal them in an airtight container. These will be your pollen samples. Label all plaster jackets, boxes and containers.

The size of the resulting block of rock and plaster will determine how much reinforcing is needed to lift it without breaking it. Wooden planks are generally used for blocks under 200 kilograms. (A full description of field techniques can be found in the books listed at the end of this book.)

IF YOU ARE NOT SURE ABOUT YOUR TECHNIQUE, THEN STOP AND WAIT FOR THE PROFESSIONAL TO HELP.

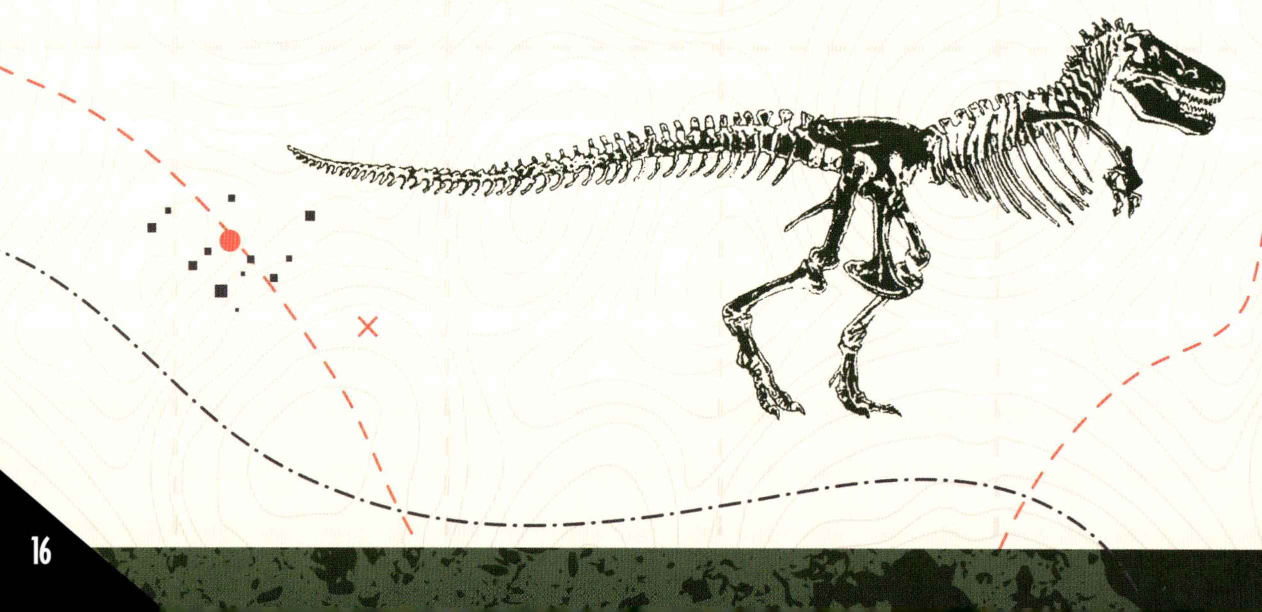

IN THE FIELD,

NEAR SHELL, WYOMING, USA

Raptor hand

A dinosaur bone, jacketed with plaster on one side, has just been rolled over so that a jacket can be put on the other side. The bone must be photographed again before it is completely covered.

A dinosaur thighbone has been jacketed with plaster and reinforced with a wooden plank. Other bones are being jacketed.

Raptor foot

This is the pubis of an immature sauropod dinosaur inside a field jacket of plaster of Paris and burlap.

Bones of a sauropod dinosaur are exposed and conserved. One person is applying a layer of plaster of Paris and burlap to protect the bones for shipment back to the museum.

PART 5: TRANSPORTATION

Here's where things start getting expensive. You'll need to get your fossils back to the lab. In general, a truck will do the job, but depending on your location, you may need a helicopter!

Make sure your find is securely packed to withstand the bumps and jolts of the ride home. Keep records of everything packed up and everything shipped. Clean the excavation site and backfill all holes.

AS SPELUNKERS, OR CAVE EXPLORERS, SAY, 'TAKE ONLY PICTURES, LEAVE ONLY FOOTPRINTS'.

Write up everything you did, who did what, and what pictures were taken, then put all the information in your field book. Give credit where credit is due.

This is a very simplified explanation. That is because it would take a book to describe all the finer details of excavation and how they vary depending upon what is found.

Fossil footprints require a different procedure, and so do microvertebrates like lizards and mammals. It is best to go on an expedition run by a school or museum before going off on your own.

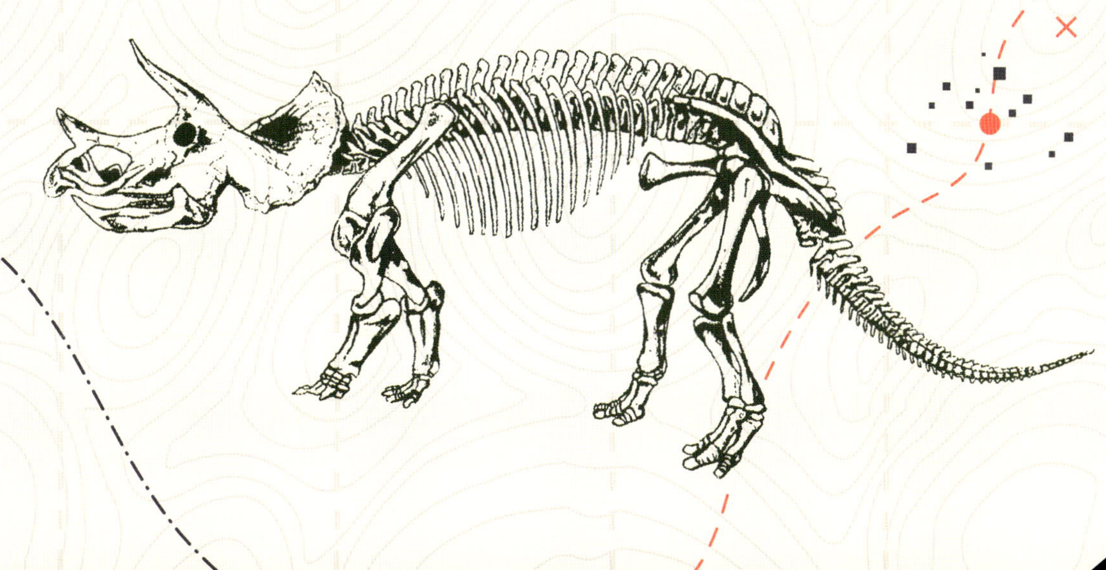

HOW DINOSAURS ARE PREPARED

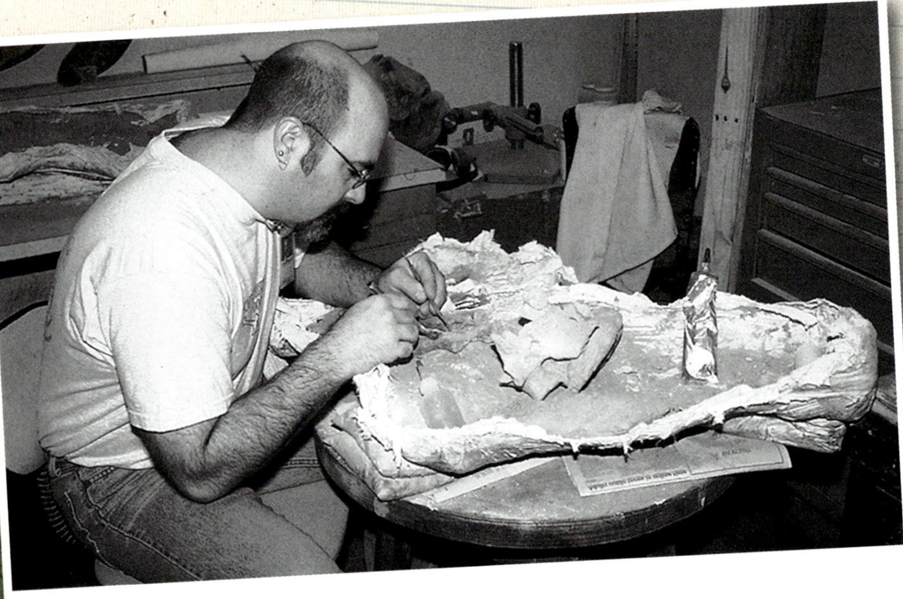

Once a specimen is back in the lab, the preparator opens the plaster of Paris field jacket, then gently removes the surrounding rock from the fossil using dental drills and scrapers. Many of these instruments are the same ones used by dentists and artists. (Shown is preparator Steve Jabo of the National Museum of Natural History in Washington, D.C.)

There are many different kinds of glues and preservatives. Which one to use depends on how the bone is preserved and on the chemicals that may be present within.

To conserve large fossil bones in museum collections, new plaster jackets are lined with foam to keep the bone from rubbing against the hard plaster. Foam is also added into open spaces, making the fit between the bones and the jacket nice and snug. Metal rods are used to add strength to the jacket. The preparator then glues and fills any cracks in the bones.

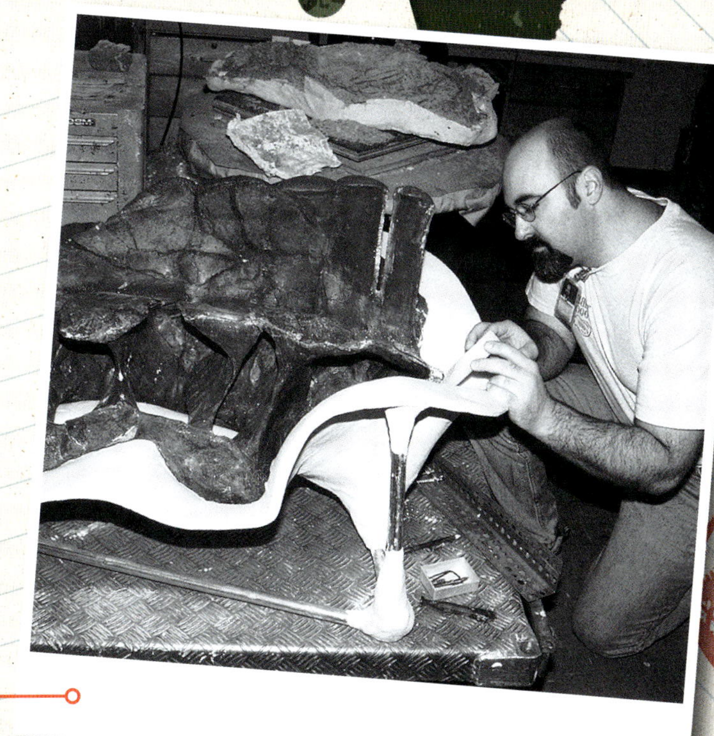

To protect the largest specimens that will not fit into museum storage drawers, metal-reinforced plaster jackets lined with foam are custom-made into protective 'clamshells'. These shells allow specimens to be flipped over for study while keeping them supported from below. A catalogue number is written on each jacket to identify the bones within.

To mount a skeleton, each bone must be individually fitted onto a metal frame. Extra metal bars and plates are sometimes added for increased strength. Preparators must know about metal welding and casting techniques, in addition to their knowledge of chemicals, preservatives, preparation methods and moulding.

The main support for a mount of an entire dinosaur is a metal 'backbone', to which the other bones will be attached.

All fossil bones need periodic cleaning and regluing. Changes in temperature or humidity, or vibrations from traffic, can cause new cracks to appear. The conservation of fossils is an ongoing process that is necessary to preserve our natural heritage for future generations.

HOW DINOSAURS ARE CLASSIFIED

What if you found a dinosaur fossil? How would you figure out what type of dinosaur it was? First you would have to compare your fossil's features to the features of other dinosaurs it most closely resembled. In other words, you would have to 'classify' your dinosaur.

Scientists have developed a complex system for classifying all living things. Each species is part of a larger group. For example, lions and tigers are part of the cat family (or Felidae), and the cat family and the dog family (or Canidae) are both part of the shearing-toothed mammal group (or Carnivora). Likewise, the dinosaurs *Edmontosaurus* and *Parasaurolophus* are both part of the duckbilled dinosaur family (or Hadrosauridae), and the hadrosaurs and horned dinosaurs are both part of the bird-hipped dinosaurs (or Ornithischia).

Other dinosaurs in this book can be classified under other families based on their similarities and shared ancestry. And all of these families can be classified under the largest group of all—**DINOSAURIA.**

WHAT IS A DINOSAUR:

To a scientist, a dinosaur is any descendant of the most recent common ancestor of *Iguanodon* and *Megalosaurus*. The following pages will show you one possible way to classify dinosaurs. It is accepted by many palaeontologists today. Note, however, that new discoveries sometimes suggest new relationships between groups of dinosaurs. In years to come, therefore, depending on new discoveries, the classifications on the next pages may change quite a bit!

WHAT IS *NOT* A DINOSAUR:

Keep in mind that not all ancient creatures were dinosaurs. For example, marine reptiles were not dinosaurs (see pages 132–135). Neither were pterosaurs (see pages 143–148). And neither were various groups of extinct furry mammals—such as woolly mammoths and saber-toothed cats—and their relatives.

DINOSAURIA

ALL DINOSAURS

Members of this group have limbs aimed directly beneath the body, an open space in the hip socket, and a special grasping hand (at least in the earliest forms). Dinosauria is divided into two groups: Saurischia and Ornithischia. Each group of dinosaurs evolved in its own way, and over time the groups became very different from each other.

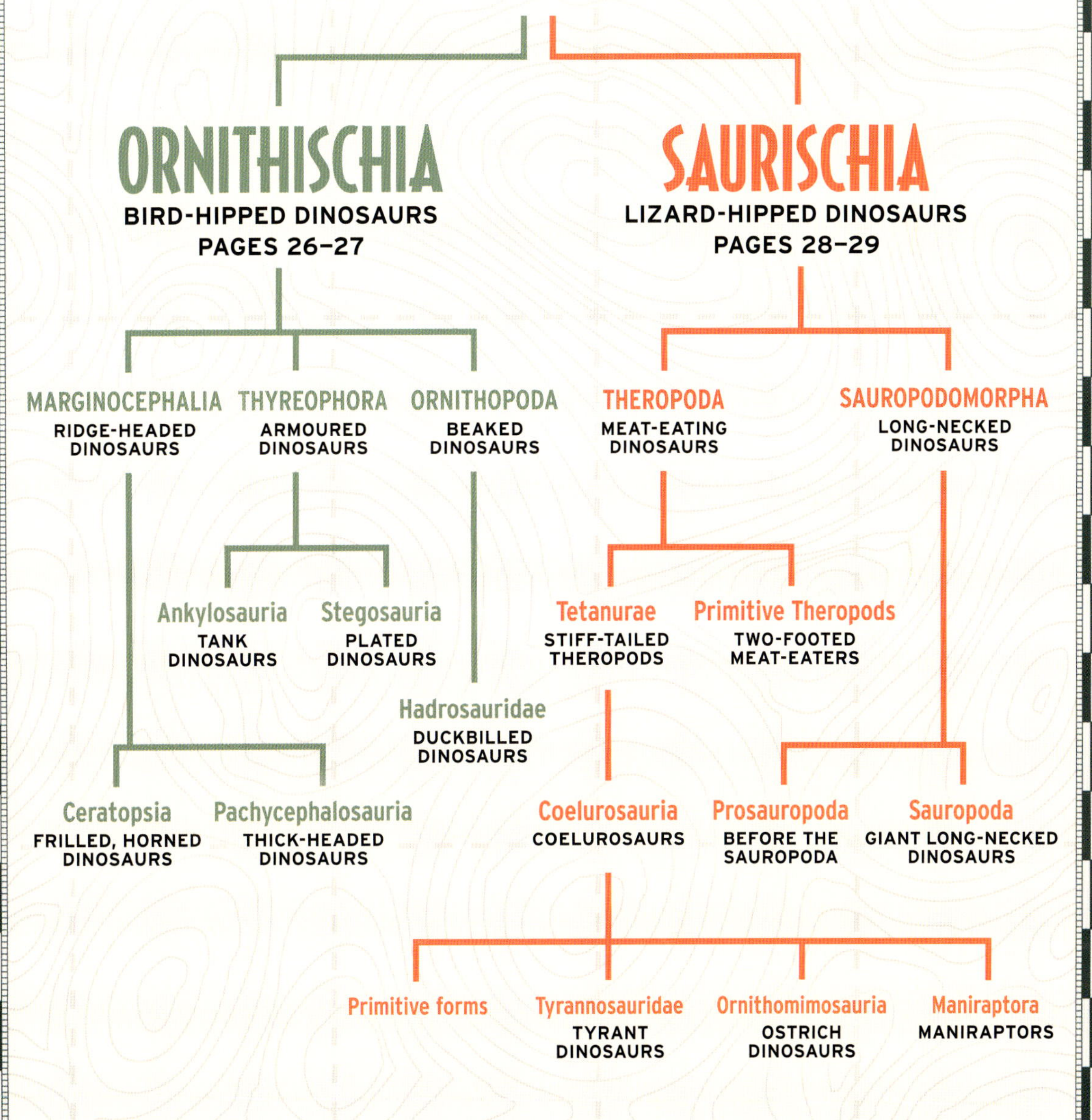

ORNITHISCHIA

BIRD-HIPPED DINOSAURS

These dinosaurs have a backward-pointing pubis bone in their hips, which made room for the extra guts needed to digest plants, and an extra bone in the front of their lower jaw, which formed the bottom part of their beak. As far as palaeontologists know, most ornithischians were herbivores, or plant-eaters. Ornithischia includes three major groups: THYREOPHORA, MARGINOCEPHALIA and ORNITHOPODA.

MARGINOCEPHALIA

RIDGE-HEADED DINOSAURS

Thyreophorans have bony armour in their skin to protect them from attackers. Most can be put into one of two groups:

THYREOPHORA

ARMOURED DINOSAURS

Marginocephalians are a group of ornithischians with a shelf of bone on the back of the skull. They include two major groups:

Ankylosauria

TANK DINOSAURS

Ankylosaurs are tank-like dinosaurs. Examples include club-tailed forms, like *Ankylosaurus*, and clubless ones, like *Edmontonia, Gargoyleosaurus, and Gastonia.*

ANKYLOSAURUS
PAGE 38

Ceratopsia

FRILLED, HORNED DINOSAURS

Early members of the frilled dinosaurs (such as *Archaeoceratops)* lacked horns, while the later, heavily built quadrupedal ceratopsians (such as *Centrosaurus)* had horns.

CENTROSAURUS
PAGE 53

Pachycephalosauria

THICK-HEADED DINOSAURS

Pachycephalosaurs are thick-headed reptiles with solid domes of bone. They include *Prenocephale, Homalocephale* and *Pachycephalosaurus.*

PRENOCEPHALE
PAGE 83

SAURISCHIA

LIZARD-HIPPED DINOSAURS

NEXT PAGE

GASPARINISAURA
PAGE 72

ORNITHOPODA

BEAKED DINOSAURS

Ornithopods were ornithischians with special teeth, some with multiple rows of teeth, to help them chew. Many primitive ornithopods (such as *Dryosaurus*, *Gasparinisaura* and *Thescelosaurus)* were relatively small and walked only on their hind legs, while more advanced ones (such as *Altirhinus*, *Iguanodon* and *Muttaburrasaurus)* were much larger and spent a lot of time walking on all fours.

Stegosauria

PLATED DINOSAURS

Stegosaurs are plated dinosaurs with rows of armoured plates and spikes down their backs. Examples include *Kentrosaurus*, *Stegosaurus* and *Wuerhosaurus.*

Hadrosauridae

DUCKBILLED DINOSAURS

Hadrosaurs are the largest and most specialised of all the ornithopods. This group includes *Edmontosaurus*, *Corythosaurus*, *Hadrosaurus*, *Parasaurolophus* and *Prosaurolophus.*

ORNITHISCHIA

BIRD-HIPPED DINOSAURS

PREVIOUS PAGE

APATOSAURUS
PAGE 40

THEROPODA

MEAT-EATING DINOSAURS

These dinosaurs are a very diverse group. All theropods walked on their hind legs, and, so far as we know, all had a wishbone.

CARNOTAURUS
PAGE 51

Tetanurae

STIFF-TAILED THEROPODS

Tetanurines generally have bigger hands than ceratosaurs. They include the giant carnosaurs (such as *Allosaurus* and *Giganotosaurus*), the crocodile-snouted spinosaurids (such as *Spinosaurus* and *Suchomimus*), and more primitive forms (such as *Metriacanthosaurus*).

Primitive Theropods

TWO-FOOTED MEAT-EATERS

Primitive theropods are all two-footed meat-eaters. They include giants such as the abelisaurs (including *Abelisaurus* and *Carnotaurus*) and smaller, more slender hunters such as *Procompsognathus*.

SPINOSAURUS
PAGE 116

Coelurosauria

COELUROSAURS

Coelurosaurs are the most advanced and diverse group of tetanurines. They have various specialised features of the skeleton, and (apparently) a very unusual feature of the skin. Recent discoveries show that most (if not all) coelurosaurs had feathers during at least part of their life! There are many groups of coelurosaurs:

Primitive forms

such as little *Compsognathus* and *Sinosauropteryx*.

COMPSOGNATHUS
PAGE 56

Tyrannosauridae

TYRANT DINOSAURS

These are giant two-fingered hunters, such as *Gorgosaurus* and *Tyrannosaurus*.

GORGOSAURUS
PAGE 76

Ornithomimosauria

OSTRICH DINOSAURS

These are small-headed, long-necked runners, such as *Gallimimus* and *Pelecanimimus*.

GALLIMIMUS
PAGE 70

SAURISCHIA

LIZARD-HIPPED DINOSAURS

These dinosaurs have longer necks than ornithischians and some have hands that were much better for grasping. In most saurischians, the pubic bone in the pelvis points forward. Saurischia is divided into the SAUROPODOMORPHA, which were plant-eaters, and the THEROPODA, which were mostly meat-eaters.

SAUROPODOMORPHA

LONG-NECKED DINOSAURS

These dinosaurs had very long necks and small heads. This allowed them to feed higher in the bushes and trees than other dinosaurs.

Prosauropoda

BEFORE THE SAUROPODA

Prosauropods are primitive, or early, sauropodomorphs. They were plant-eaters that could walk on their hind legs or on all fours. Prosauropods include *Plateosaurus.*

PLATEOSAURUS
PAGE 105

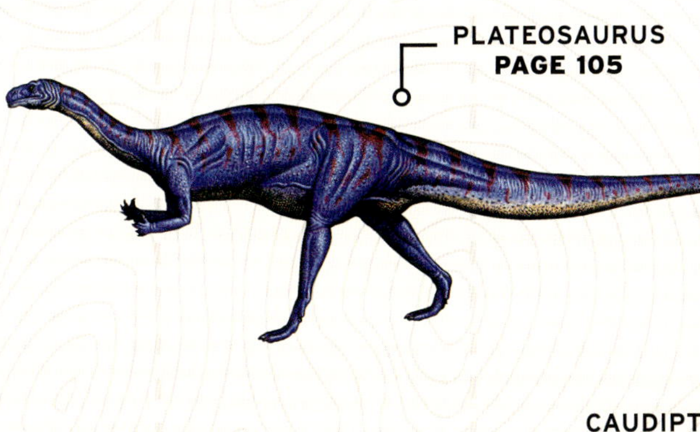

Sauropoda

GIANT LONG-NECKED DINOSAURS

Sauropods came later than the prosauropods and were so large they could walk only on all fours. Sauropods include *Apatosaurus, Argentinosaurus, Brachiosaurus* and *Jobaria.*

JOBARIA
PAGE 85

CAUDIPTERYX
PAGE 52

Maniraptora

MANIRAPTORS

Includes: long-necked, plant-eating Therizinosauria ('sloth dinosaurs'), such as *Beipiaosaurus;* short-skulled, beaked Oviraptorosauria ('egg thieves'), such as *Caudipteryx;* large-brained, big-eyed Troodontidae ('troodonts'), including *Troodon;* Dromaeosauridae ('raptors'), such as *Velociraptor;* strange, short-armed Alvarezsauria ('alvarezsaurs'), including *Shuvuuia;* and Avialae (birds), such as *Archaeopteryx.*

ARCHAEOPTERYX
PAGE 43

HOW DINOSAURS ARE NAMED

Have you ever wondered how dinosaurs are named? Let's say you dig up a new dinosaur. What would you do then? You can't just call your local newspaper and announce the new name. It would not be considered valid by scientists around the world.

Instead, to properly name your discovery, you must follow a scientific procedure guided by international laws. Specifically, your new dinosaur must meet the requirements set up by the International Committee of Zoological Nomenclature (ICZN):

1. **First, you must write a scientific paper that explains the unique features of the dinosaur you found. The paper will explain to the world exactly why your dinosaur is new to science.**
2. **You must have your paper published in a peer-reviewed scientific journal or book.**
3. **The original specimen that you dug up (known as the type specimen) must be conserved by a museum that is expected to exist beyond the lifetime of its current employees, such as the museums that meet the National Standards for Australian Museums and Galleries.**
4. **The type specimen must also be made available for study by other scientists.**

But before you write your paper, how do you decide on the name itself?

Your new dinosaur's name must follow the International Code of Zoological Nomenclature, a set of rules that govern all scientific names for living or extinct organisms. Your dinosaur's scientific name will composed of two parts. The first part, called the genus, usually refers to a feature of the dinosaur (such as *Tyrannosaurus,* or 'tyrant lizard'). The genus name may be used alone to refer to all the species in a particular genus. The second part of the name, called the specific epithet (referring to the species), can refer back to the genus (like *Tyrannosaurus rex*-rex meaning 'king', so the name means 'king of the tyrant lizards). The species name can also refer to a place, person, or icon. For example, *Lambeosaurus lambei* was named after Lawrence Lambe, a famous Canadian palaeontologist, or *Anzu wyeli* named after Anzû, a bird-like demon in Ancient Mesopotamian mythology.

A good scientific paper is written so that it can be read by palaeontologists who have not yet been born. You might think of it as a set of directions on how to repeat what you did, so that the steps you took can be repeated and tested by others in the future.

Because palaeontologists are also educators it is our job to find new discoveries about the deep past—and then tell the world!

DRAWING DINOSAURS

Any time you see an extinct dinosaur drawn with flesh on the bone and skin on the flesh, you are seeing an added bit of 'science fiction'. Like the best science fiction, these drawings are based on fact, but a lot of educated guesswork goes into them. Bob Walters' illustrations in this book represent various ideas about what dinosaurs (and other ancient beasts) looked like. In order to draw dinosaurs, Bob—and artists like him—go through the following steps:

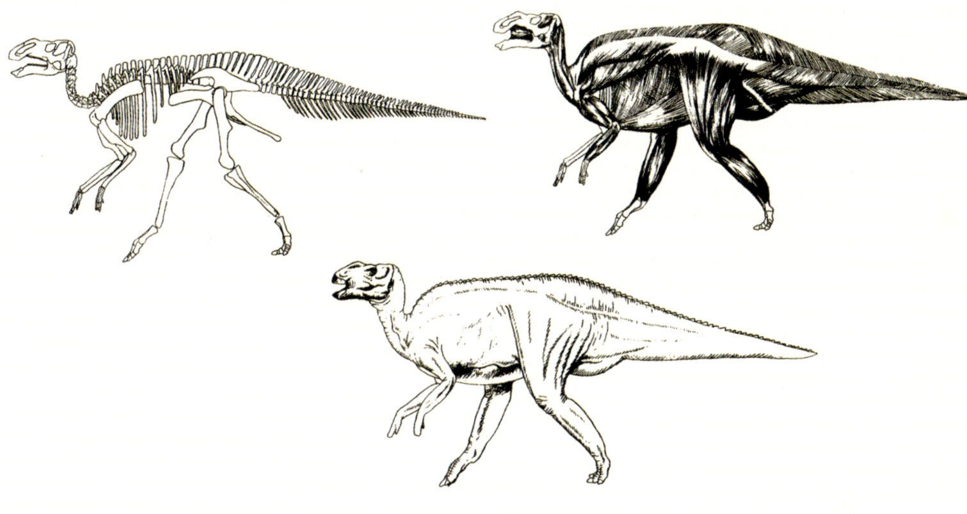

1. They reconstruct the skeletons of the dinosaur. Missing bones are restored based on comparisons with closely related dinosaurs.
2. They fill in the muscles of the skeleton. These are based on muscle scars found on bones, and/or on comparisons with living animals.
3. They place skin over the muscles.

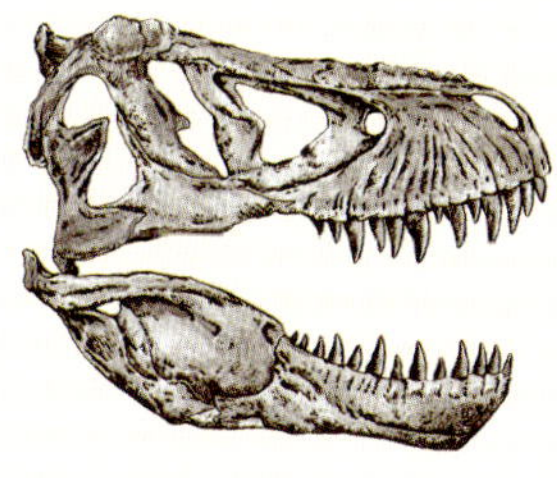

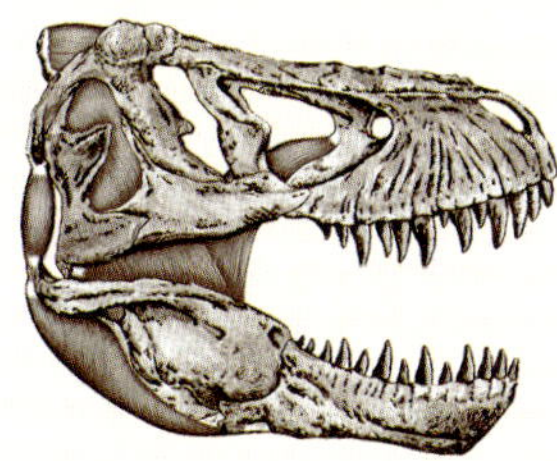

4 They 'clothe' the skin in scales and/or feathers. All dinosaurs had scales on parts of their bodies, but the exact shape and pattern of the scales is known for only a few species. In the late 1990s it was discovered that some (if not all) of the small, swift meat-eating dinosaurs had feathers, or hair-like 'protofeathers'. Scientists currently have specific knowledge of some of the feathers found on small meat-eaters from only one geological formation in China. For now, the shape and size of these features in all other creatures is based on living species.

5 They add colour to the scales and/or feathers. Colours and patterns used by artists are pure speculation, because nature is full of all different coloured animals. (For example, the skeletons of lions, tigers, and leopards are nearly identical, but they have totally different colours and colour patterns. Without seeing the living great cats, we would never know of a lion's mane, a tiger's stripes, or a leopard's spots.)

BUT REMEMBER: Although we know what the skeletons of *Tyrannosaurus* and *Velociraptor* looked like, we will never know for sure how their outsides appeared. Unless, of course, *Jurassic World* turns out to be more than a story . . .

DINOSAURS

Dinosaurs are a group of reptiles that ruled the earth for over 180 million years. They evolved diverse shapes and sizes, from the tyrant *Tyrannosaurus* to the turkey-sized *Compsognathus,* and were able to survive in a variety of ecosystems.

IN *JURASSIC WORLD*

CARNIVORE

HERBIVORE

OMNIVORE

ABELISAURUS

a-BEL-ih-SOAR-us

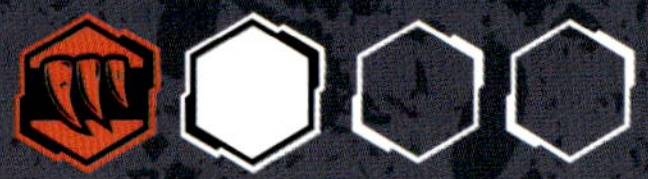

LOCATION:

Rio Negro Province, Argentina

WHAT WE KNOW:

YEAR NAMED: 1985

DIET: CARNIVORE
Other dinosaurs (titanosaurs, hadrosaurs, and small ornithopods)

SIZE: Perhaps about 7.9m long, perhaps 2m high at the hips

WEIGHT: 1,400–3,000kg

FRIENDS: None

ENEMIES: *Aucasaurus*

Abelisaurus ('[Roberto] Abel's lizard') was one of the top predators in South America at the end of the Age of Dinosaurs. While *Tyrannosaurus* and its kin dominated the northern continents during the Late Cretaceous, the abelisaurs ruled South America, India, and Madagascar.

Like the tyrannosaurs, abelisaurs had big skulls with knobby snouts. Unlike the tyrannosaurs, however, abelisaurs had teeth that were fairly small. The rounded snout of *Abelisaurus* and its relatives probably helped it to hold on to what it was biting. Its fused skull roof made its head hard enough to be used as a weapon in fights between rival abelisaurs. By pushing each other with their heads, one *Abelisaurus* could try to defeat the other without having to face attack by claws or jaws.

Abelisaurus is known at present only from a single giant skull, over 85cm long.

FUN FACT!

POSSIBLE RELATIVES OF *ABELISAURUS* ARE KNOWN FROM SPAIN AND FRANCE.

MORE SPECIES OF FOSSIL DINOSAURS HAVE BEEN FOUND IN ARGENTINA THAN ANY OTHER COUNTRY IN THE SOUTHERN HEMISPHERE.

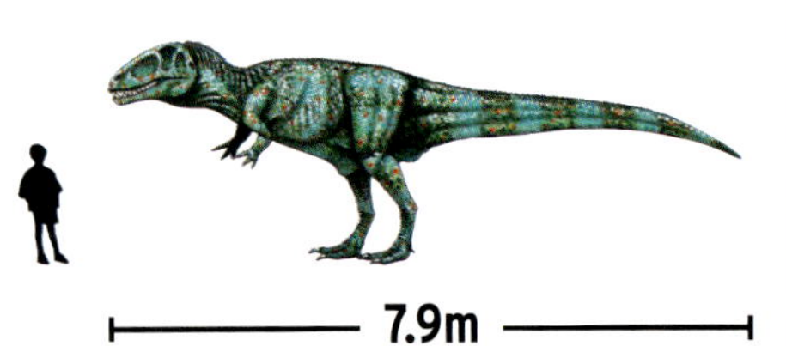

COMPARISON IS WITH A 1.2M TALL CHILD

TIME PERIOD:

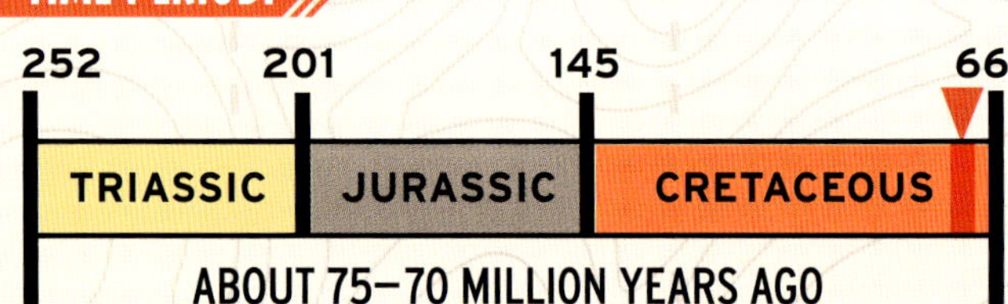

ABOUT 75–70 MILLION YEARS AGO

ALLOSAURUS

AL-oh-SOAR-us

LOCATION:

Colorado, Montana, New Mexico, Oklahoma, South Dakota, Utah, Wyoming, USA; Portugal

WHAT WE KNOW:

YEAR NAMED: 1877

DIET: CARNIVORE
Other dinosaurs

SIZE: 12m long, about 3m high at the hips

WEIGHT: 1,500kg

FRIENDS: None

ENEMIES: *Stegosaurus, Torvosaurus, Ceratosaurus, Saurophaganax*

FUN FACT!

THE FIRST FOSSIL OF *ALLOSAURUS* EVER FOUND–THE BROKEN HALF OF A BACKBONE–WAS CALLED A PETRIFIED HORSE HOOF BY ITS DISCOVERERS!

Allosaurus ('other lizard') was the most common predator of the Late Jurassic and probably one of the most dangerous. Like most meat-eating dinosaurs, its jaws were filled with serrated teeth shaped like blades. Computer studies suggest that *Allosaurus* attacked by using its upper jaw like a battle axe to hack at its victim, then it used its lower jaw to bite out a slice of meat.

It might have been easy for an *Allosaurus* to kill a fairly defenceless dinosaur like *Camptosaurus*, but *Stegosaurus* could certainly put up a fight, and the sauropods (giant long-necks) were so huge that they could easily crush even an adult *Allosaurus*.

We know that *Allosaurus* led a dangerous life. The *Allosaurus* on display at the Smithsonian Institution has a smashed shoulder blade, many broken ribs, and a lower jaw so damaged that palaeontologists didn't realise it was an *Allosaurus* jaw for over 100 years! But these were tough dinosaurs: their bones show that they lived long enough for their wounds to heal.

ALLOSAURUS IS THE OFFICIAL STATE DINOSAUR OF UTAH.

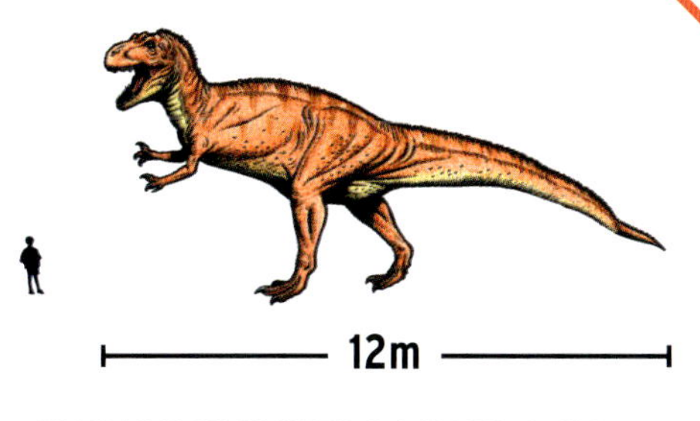

COMPARISON IS WITH A 1.2M TALL CHILD

TIME PERIOD:

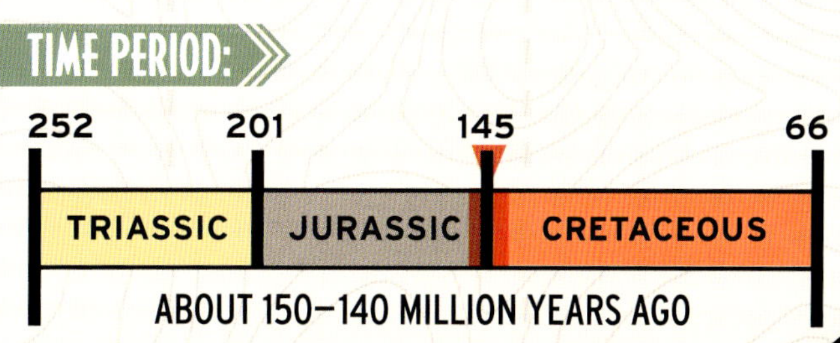

ABOUT 150–140 MILLION YEARS AGO

ALTIRHINUS

al-tee-RYE-nus

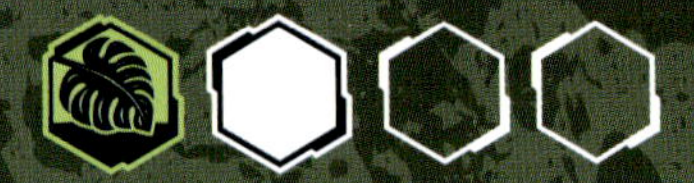

LOCATION:
Mongolia

WHAT WE KNOW:

YEAR NAMED: 1998

DIET: HERBIVORE
Possibly early flowering plants, cycads and ginkgos

SIZE: 8m long, 2m high at the hips

WEIGHT: 1,100kg

FRIENDS: *Psittacosaurus*

FUN FACT!
WITH ITS EXPANDED NOSE, *ALTIRHINUS* MAY HAVE BEEN THE FIRST DINOSAUR TO 'HOOT' LIKE A WOODWIND INSTRUMENT.

COMPARISON IS WITH A 1.2M TALL CHILD

Altirhinus ('high nose') had an enlarged beak and mouth to help it eat tough plants. This expanded nose may also have improved *Altirhinus's* sense of smell and helped it recognise the same species during mating season. (Among the *Altirhinus*, a big nose was considered very attractive!)

Altirhinus is referred to as being 'more than an *Iguanodon*, but less than a hadrosaur' because the body is like *Iguanodon's*, but the skull is closer to that of the duckbills. In fact, *Altirhinus* is a good example of how difficult it sometimes is to classify finds. For years, this dinosaur was known as *Iguanodon orientalis*. Named by a Russian scientist in 1952, *Iguanodon orientalis*—which was found in Mongolia—was thought to be in the same genus as the original *Iguanodon*, which was found in Britain. Although the bodies of the two are similar, the skulls are very different. It was not until 1998 that David Norman, an authority on the family *Iguanodontidae*, revised the taxonomy of *Iguanodon* and finally gave *I. orientalis* its new name—*Altirhinus kurzanovi*.

THE FIRST *ALTIRHINUS* SKULL TO BE DISCOVERED WENT ON A WORLD TOUR IN THE LATE 1990S.

TIME PERIOD:

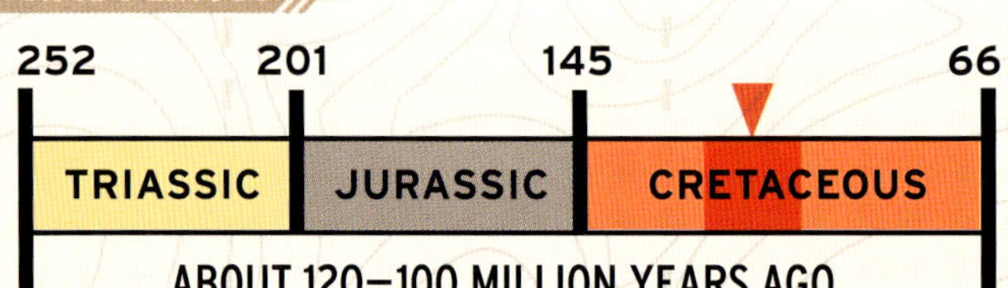

ABOUT 120–100 MILLION YEARS AGO

AMARGASAURUS

a-MAHR-gah-SOAR-us

LOCATION:

Patagonia, Argentina

WHAT WE KNOW:

YEAR NAMED: 1991

DIET: HERBIVORE
Conifers, cycads, ginkgos

SIZE: 9m long, 2.5m high at the hip

WEIGHT: 9,000kg

FUN FACT!

SOME *AMARGASAURUS* NECK SPINES ARE 50CM LONG.

9m

COMPARISON IS WITH A 1.2M TALL CHILD

Amargasaurus ('lizard from La Amarga [geologic formation]') is one of the most unusual sauropods known to science. Its most distinguishing feature is the tall double row of spines, like two sails, coming out of the back of its neck. These sails served many functions—at a price. They made the dinosaur look much bigger than it was, possibly keeping predators away. The sails could also be used—under certain conditions—like a solar panel, gathering heat when facing into the sun and losing heat when in the shade. Unfortunately, the sails were also very restrictive and would severely limit the range of motion in *Amargasaurus's* head and neck. They were also very fragile and would get seriously damaged if bitten.

THE FIRST MOUNTED AMARGASAURUS SKELETON IN THE WORLD IS IN BUENOS AIRES, ARGENTINA.

TIME PERIOD:

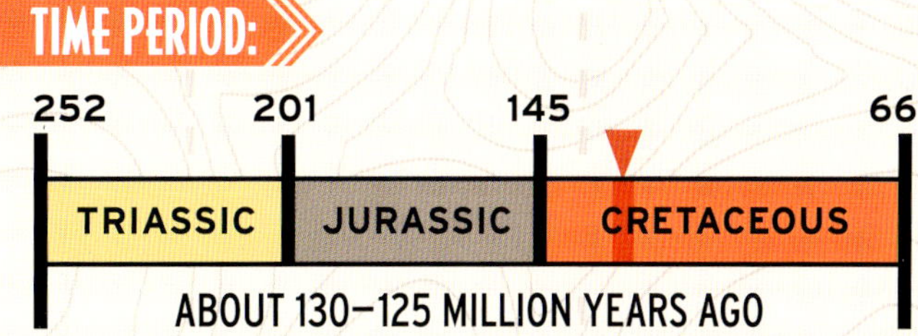

ABOUT 130–125 MILLION YEARS AGO

ANKYLOSAURUS

ANG-ki-lo-SOAR-us

LOCATION:

Montana,
Wyoming, USA;
Alberta, Canada

WHAT WE KNOW:

YEAR NAMED: 1908

DIET: HERBIVORE
Flowering plants like magnolias, possibly small insects

SIZE: 7.5m long, 1.2m high at the hips

WEIGHT: 4,000kg

FUN FACT!

***ANKYLOSAURUS* WAS THE LAST OF THE THYREOPHORA ('SHIELD-BEARERS', A GROUP THAT INCLUDES THE ANKYLOSAURS AND STEGOSAURS). THE EARLIEST WAS *SCUTELLOSAURUS*.**

Ankylosaurus ('fused lizard') is the name-bearer for the group of dinosaurs known as the Ankylosauria, or 'tank dinosaurs'. They're called 'tanks' because the upper parts of their bodies are covered with various types of armour that are fused together.

The armour of ankylosaurs can be either solid or hollow. It is found on top of their bodies and tails, and also all around the skull—imagine putting on a helmet and having your skin grow over it! This extreme level of defence was necessary because no ankylosaur could outrun a theropod, or meat-eating dinosaur. In 1998, another new species of ankylosaur was named. It was called *Animantarx* ('living fortress').

In *Ankylosaurus,* the last half of the tail has been modified into a giant war club, with the last tail bones fused together. When this club was swung from side to side, it was at the same level as the knees of theropods like *Tyrannosaurus*. How's that for strategically placed weaponry!

ANKYLOSAURUS HAD EIGHT SINUS CAVITIES, AS COMPARED TO ONLY FOUR IN *NODOSAURS* (AND ALSO IN HUMANS).

COMPARISON IS WITH A 1.2M TALL CHILD

TIME PERIOD:

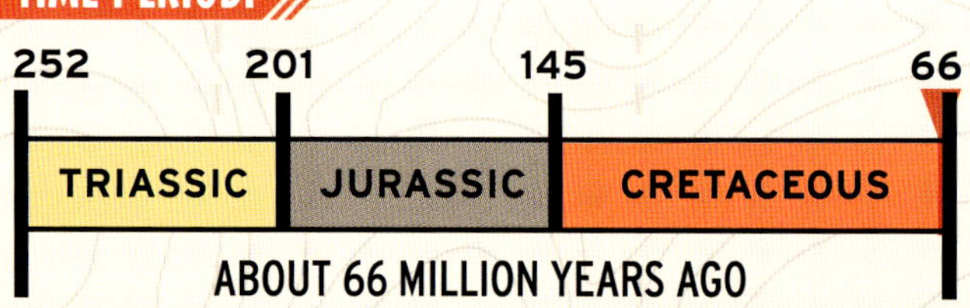

ABOUT 66 MILLION YEARS AGO

ANZU

AHN-zoo

LOCATION:

Montana, North Dakota, South Dakota, USA; Saskatchewan, Canada

WHAT WE KNOW:

YEAR NAMED: 2014

DIET: OMNIVORE
Possibly small reptiles and mammals, plants, eggs, insects

SIZE: 3.5m long, about 1.5m high at the hips

WEIGHT: About 300 kg

***ANZU* IS THE BIGGEST OVIRAPTOROSAUR KNOWN FROM NORTH AMERICA, BUT ITS CHINESE COUSIN *GIGANTORAPTOR* WAS ABOUT AS BIG AS *GORGOSAURUS*.**

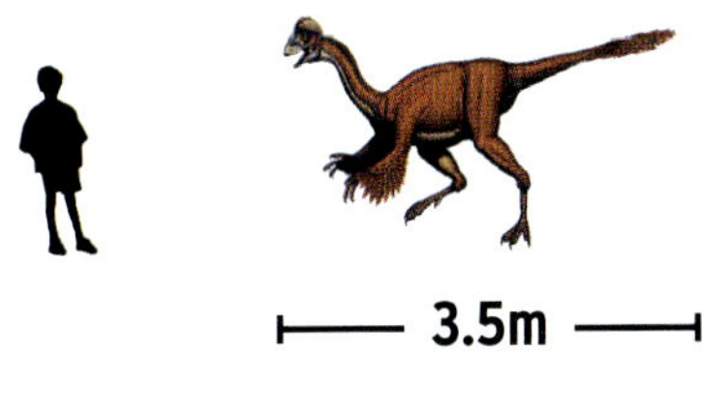

Anzu (named after a feathered demon of Mesopotamian mythology) is one of the bird-like oviraptorosaurs (egg thief reptiles), the same group that *Caudipteryx* belongs to. Its jaws had no teeth. Instead, *Anzu* had a horny beak, like a bird or turtle.

Figuring out the diet of oviraptorosaurs is difficult. Were they meat-eaters, plant-eaters or a little bit of both? Study of the function of the jaws of *Anzu* and its relatives suggest that it mostly ate plants, but maybe did gulp down eggs, mammals, amphibians, baby dinosaurs, and other small animals as well.

Many oviraptorosaurs had tall crests on their heads, and *Anzu* is no exception. These crests may have been used to show off to mates or rivals.

Although *Anzu* was named in 2014, fossils of it have been studied since 1999. A skeleton is on display at the Carnegie Museum of Natural History in Pittsburgh, Pennsylvania.

ANZU LIVED ALONGSIDE TRICERATOPS AND TYRANNOSAURUS.

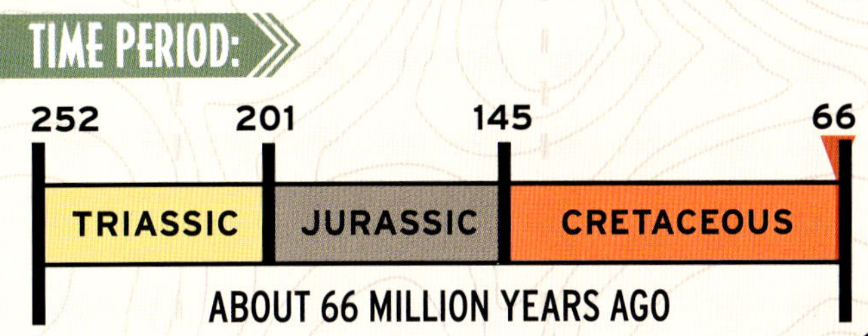

APATOSAURUS

a-PAT-oh-SOAR-us

LOCATION:

From Oklahoma, USA to Canada along the Rocky Mountains

WHAT WE KNOW:

YEAR NAMED: 1877

DIET: **HERBIVORE**
Cycads, ginkgos, ferns, conifers

SIZE: About 21m long, 3m high at the hips

WEIGHT: 22,000kg

FRIENDS: *Diplodocus, Camarasaurus*

ENEMIES: *Allosaurus, Ceratosaurus, Torvosaurus*

FUN FACT!

APATOSAURUS **LAID SOME OF THE LARGEST EGGS OF ANY DINOSAUR.**

APATOSAURUS WAS ONCE CONSIDERED TO BE A DIFFERENT ANIMAL FROM THE SAUROPOD CALLED *BRONTOSAURUS*. NOW WE KNOW THEY ARE THE SAME DINOSAUR.

Apatosaurus ('deceptive lizard') looks very much like *Diplodocus,* its closest relative. On the inside, however, it is very different. *Apatosaurus* is very massive, with thick bones and a stocky body. *Diplodocus* is slender, with thinner bones. *Apatosaurus* was one of the very first dinosaurs to have a picture of its completely restored skeleton published in newspapers. This happened in the 1880s, and the dinosaur's immense size made world headlines.

One feature that *Apatosaurus* has in common with other closely related sauropods, or giant plant-eaters, is that the openings in the skull for the nasal passages are on top of its head, behind its eyes (normally these openings are located at the end of the snout, as in the *Ornithischia,* the other major group of plant-eating dinosaurs). Palaeontologists once thought this meant the actual nostrils were right on top of the head, too. But studies of the details of the front of the skull show that like most animals (including cats and dogs and you and me) the nostrils were on the front of the face. This way it was easier for *Apatosaurus* to sniff its food before eating it.

The study of *Apatosaurus* has had a major influence on the study of all dinosaurs. In the 1970s, a study of its skeleton was used to show how sauropods lived on land, and not in the water as had been assumed for many decades. In 1979, it was learned that the wrong head had been mounted on every *Apatosaurus* skeleton in museums since the 1880s (the older mounts had heads based on *Camarasaurus*). In the 1990s, a study

of *Apatosaurus* bones showed that its head and neck were not held vertically as had been portrayed in many illustrations. The science of how a body can or cannot function is called functional morphology, and *Apatosaurus* is one of the best dinosaurs for use in this study because of its large size.

JURASSIC WORLD APPEARANCE

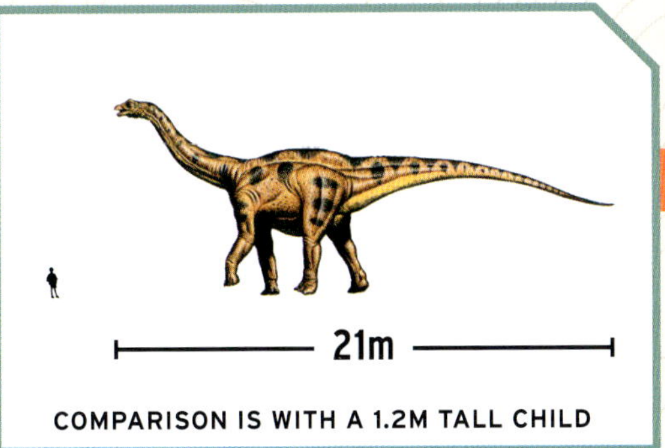

COMPARISON IS WITH A 1.2M TALL CHILD

TIME PERIOD:

252	201	145	66
TRIASSIC	JURASSIC	CRETACEOUS	

ABOUT 154–150 MILLION YEARS AGO

ARCHAEOCERATOPS

AHR-kee-oh-SERRA-tops

LOCATION:

Gansu Province, China

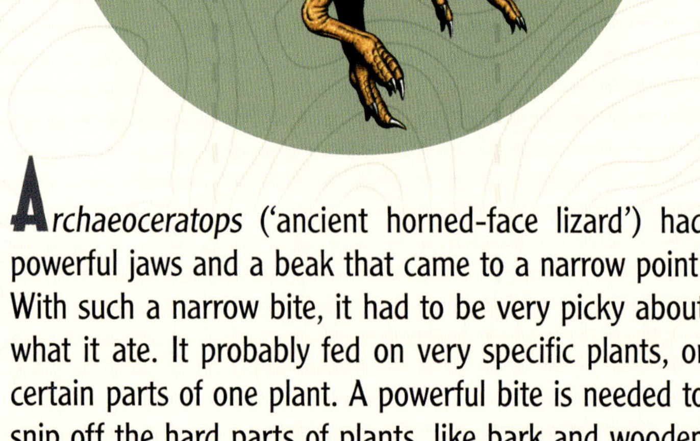

WHAT WE KNOW:

YEAR NAMED: 1997

DIET: **HERBIVORE**
Plants

SIZE: 72cm long, 35cm high at the hips

WEIGHT: 4.5kg

FRIENDS: Other ceratopsians and small ankylosaurs

ENEMIES: Juveniles of any theropods, or meat-eating dinosaurs

Archaeoceratops ('ancient horned-face lizard') had powerful jaws and a beak that came to a narrow point. With such a narrow bite, it had to be very picky about what it ate. It probably fed on very specific plants, or certain parts of one plant. A powerful bite is needed to snip off the hard parts of plants, like bark and wooden branches. It is also very helpful for defensive purposes.

Archaeoceratops is an early horned dinosaur, but not the earliest. In 2006, a much earlier relative named *Yinlong* was described. It was from 160 million years ago, in the Jurassic Period. It shows that primitive members of the horned dinosaur group were around for a very long time.

EVEN THOUGH *ARCHAEOCERATOPS'S* SKULL WAS THE SAME SIZE AS A DOG'S, IT HAD MUCH MORE POWERFUL JAWS.

FUN FACT!

THIS SMALL DINOSAUR MIGHT HAVE BEEN ABLE TO OUTRUN A TEACHER. (HOW FAST CAN *YOUR* TEACHER RUN?)

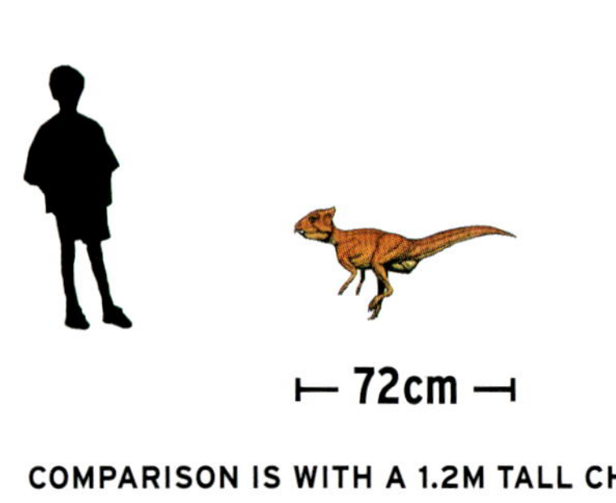

COMPARISON IS WITH A 1.2M TALL CHILD

TIME PERIOD:

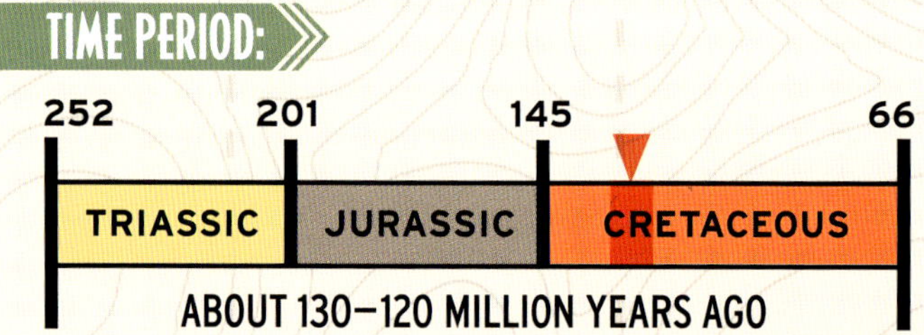

ABOUT 130–120 MILLION YEARS AGO

ARCHAEOPTERYX

AHR-kee-OP-ter-icks

LOCATION:

Germany; possibly Portugal

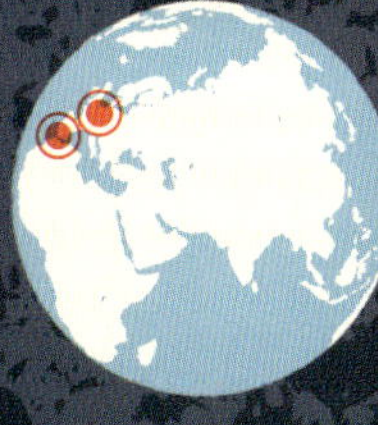

Archaeopteryx ('ancient wing') is one of the oldest and most primitive known birds. It is also one of the most important fossils ever found.

Archaeopteryx shows a mixture of features found in birds (like a wishbone, feathers and backward-facing pubis bone in the hips), as well as features found in primitive reptiles but lost in modern birds (like teeth, clawed fingers and a long, bony tail). As more dinosaur skeletons were found (especially those of smaller meat-eaters), palaeontologists began to notice that they shared many of the same features with the much smaller *Archaeopteryx*. These features included wishbones, feathers, and a backward-facing pubis bone. Scientists figured out that *Archaeopteryx* and other birds are the descendants of small meat-eating dinosaurs, and in fact (using the modern system of classification), birds are a type of dinosaur themselves!

WHAT WE KNOW:

YEAR NAMED: 1861

DIET: CARNIVORE
Small mammals and reptiles

SIZE: Almost 50cm long, 19cm high at the hips, wingspan about 61 cm

WEIGHT: 0.5–1kg

FUN FACT!

ALL KNOWN SKELETONS OF THIS EARLY BIRD WERE FOUND IN ROCKS FORMED FROM SOFT LIMY MUD. IT WAS THIS VERY FINE MUD THAT PRESERVED THE IMPRESSIONS OF THEIR FEATHERS. IF *ARCHAEOPTERYX* HAD BEEN PRESERVED IN ANOTHER ENVIRONMENT, WE MIGHT NEVER HAVE KNOWN IT HAD FEATHERS!

THE SHAPE OF THE FEATHERS ON ARCHAEOPTERYX'S WINGS SHOW THAT IT WAS CAPABLE OF FLYING, BUT PROBABLY NOT WELL.

⊢ 50cm ⊣

COMPARISON IS WITH A 1.2M TALL CHILD

TIME PERIOD:

252 | 201 | 145 | 66

TRIASSIC | JURASSIC | CRETACEOUS

ABOUT 150–140 MILLION YEARS AGO

BARYONYX

BAR-ee-ON-icks

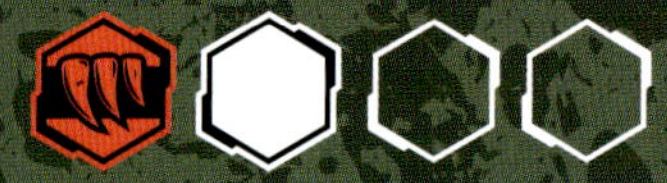

LOCATION:

Surrey, England

WHAT WE KNOW:

YEAR NAMED: 1986

DIET: CARNIVORE
Other dinosaurs (including *Iguanodon*) and fish

SIZE: 10m long, 2.5m high at the hips

WEIGHT: 2,000kg

FRIENDS: None

ENEMIES: *Neovenator*

BARYONYX WAS THE FIRST SPINOSAUR KNOWN FROM A NORTHERN CONTINENT.

FUN FACT!

BARYONYX **WAS GIVEN THE NICKNAME 'CLAWS' BECAUSE OF ITS GIANT THUMB CLAW.**

Baryonyx ('heavy claw') was discovered by an amateur fossil hunter, William J. Walker, who came across its enormous thumb claw in a clay pit in Surrey, England. Further digging by palaeontologists revealed one of the largest meat-eating dinosaurs ever found in Great Britain.

Baryonyx is a spinosaur, a member of the same group as the northern African dinosaurs *Spinosaurus* and *Suchomimus*. *Baryonyx* was smaller than these relatives but was still a big predator. It had a long, narrow snout filled with teeth that were cone-shaped—a real difference from the blade-shaped teeth of typical meat-eating dinosaurs.

Because of the shape of its snout and teeth (both of which are similar to those of modern crocodiles and alligators), some palaeontologists think that *Baryonyx* ate lots of fish. Others, however, think that it ate other dinosaurs. In fact, both ideas are supported by the original *Baryonyx* specimen from Surrey. In the guts of this dinosaur, palaeontologists found the partially digested scales of large fish as well as the partially digested bones of a young *Iguanodon*. This strongly supports the idea that *Baryonyx* ate both fish and dinosaurs!

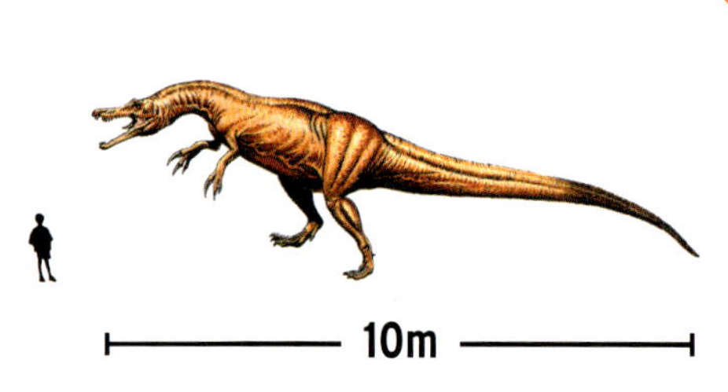

COMPARISON IS WITH A 1.2M TALL CHILD

TIME PERIOD:

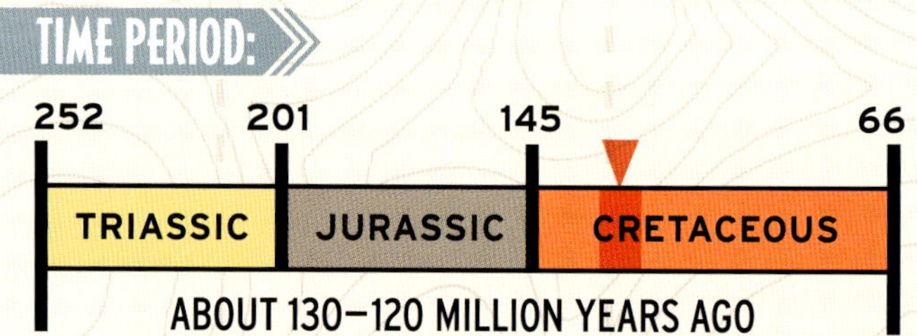

BEIPIAOSAURUS

bay-pyow-SOAR-us

LOCATION:

Liaoning Province, China

WHAT WE KNOW:

YEAR NAMED: 1999

DIET: **HERBIVORE**
Conifers, cycads, ginkgos, the earliest flowering plants

SIZE: 2.2m long, just under 0.88m high at the hips

WEIGHT: 85kg

FUN FACT!

BEIPIAOSAURUS IS THE SMALLEST KNOWN THERIZINOSAUR. ITS GIANT RELATIVE *THERIZINOSAURUS* WAS ALMOST AS BIG AS *T. REX* AND HAD CLAWS ALMOST 90CM LONG!

2.2m

COMPARISON IS WITH A 1.2M TALL CHILD

Beipiaosaurus ('Beipiao lizard') is one of the therizinosaurs, a very strange group of theropods. Therizinosaurs (also known as 'sloth dinosaurs') have very short, heavy feet, wide bellies, long necks, big claws and small heads. Their teeth are leaf-shaped, like those of plant-eating dinosaurs, which makes them plant-eating members of a family of meat-eating dinosaurs!

Beipiaosaurus is known from one partial skeleton from the Yixian Formation in northeastern China. The volcanic ash that formed the mud of this formation was so fine-grained that it preserved very small details of the animals buried in it.

Fossils show that *Beipiaosaurus's* body was covered with long, slender filaments. These filaments were a sort of protofeather, a body cover that eventually evolved into true feathers in birds and some other dinosaurs (such as *Caudipteryx*). The protofeathers of *Beipiaosaurus* might have been used for insulation or for display, or both.

BEIPIAOSAURUS IS THE FIRST THERIZINOSAUR KNOWN TO HAVE PROTOFEATHERS.

TIME PERIOD:

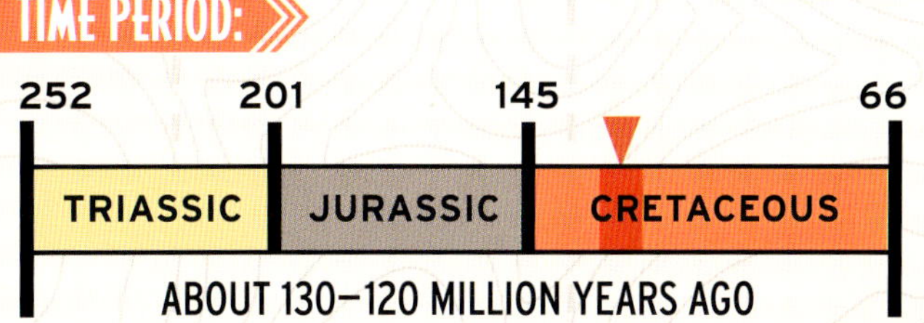

BRACHIOSAURUS

BRAK-ee-oh-SOAR-us

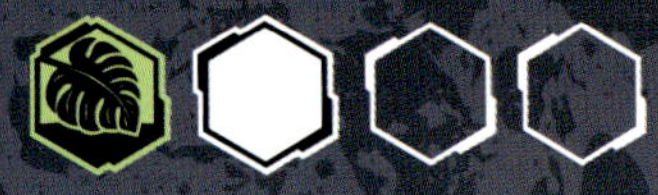

LOCATION:

Colorado, Oklahoma, Utah, Wyoming, USA

WHAT WE KNOW:

YEAR NAMED: 1903

DIET: HERBIVORE
Conifers, cycads, ginkgos

SIZE: 24m long, 7m high at the hips

WEIGHT: 30,000kg

FRIENDS: *Camarasaurus, Apatosaurus*

ENEMIES: *Allosaurus, Ceratosaurus, Torvosaurus*

FUN FACT!

BRACHIOSAURUS WAS ONE OF THE FEW DINOSAURS THAT WAS LITERALLY TOO BIG TO ATTACK!

COMPARISON IS WITH A 1.2M TALL CHILD

Brachiosaurus ('arm lizard') is one of the most spectacular dinosaurs ever discovered. It gets its name from the great height of its humerus, or upper arm bone—which is longer than most humans are tall! Originally discovered in 1900 in Colorado, *Brachiosaurus* was named in 1903 by Elmer Riggs of the Field Museum in Chicago.

TIME PERIOD:

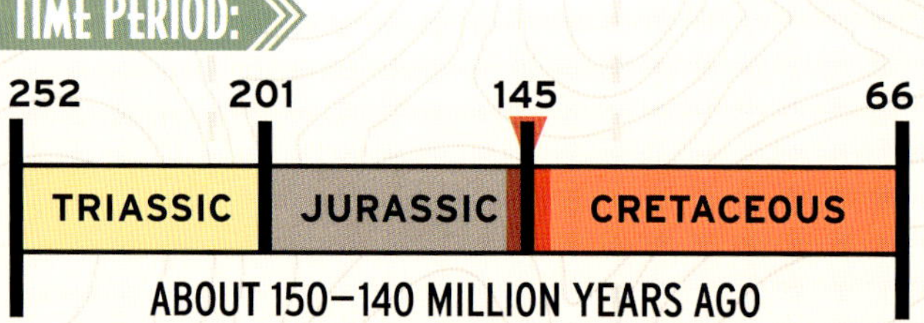

ABOUT 150–140 MILLION YEARS AGO

For almost a century, *Brachiosaurus* was considered the tallest of all dinosaurs. It was over 15m tall, and no other animal came close. Imagine going to the fifth floor of a building and looking down at the footpath.

Now imagine your feet are at street level and this is how tall you are! Get the idea? Today, however, there is a new contender for the title of tallest dinosaur. It is *Sauroposeidon,* named in 2000. Scientists believe it would stand 18m tall!

New studies by computer specialists suggest that *Brachiosaurus* may not have carried its neck angled up as high as was once thought. It may have carried the neck more at a 45- to 60-degree angle. Although this changes its height, it does not change its length—or our wonder at this gigantic, graceful dinosaur.

BRACHIOSAURUS LIVED IN THE UNITED STATES DURING THE JURASSIC PERIOD, AND A VERY SIMILAR DINOSAUR, *GIRAFFATITAN*, LIVED IN AFRICA. BECAUSE THESE DINOSAURS WOULD HAVE BEEN TERRIBLE SWIMMERS, SCIENTISTS KNOW THAT AFRICA AND NORTH AMERICA WERE CONNECTED DURING THE JURASSIC PERIOD.

KAM-ah-ra-SOAR-us

LOCATION:

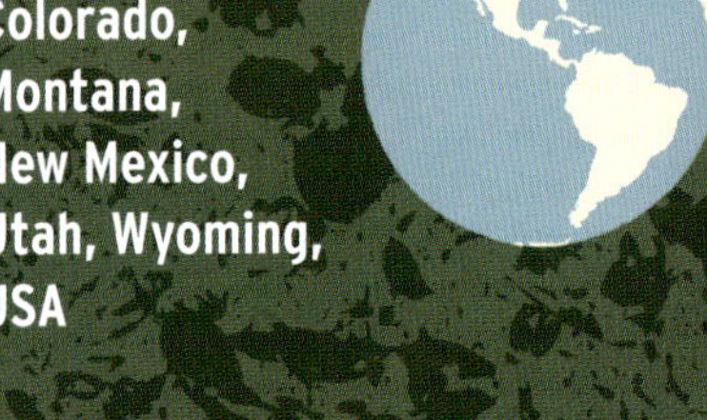

Colorado, Montana, New Mexico, Utah, Wyoming, USA

WHAT WE KNOW:

YEAR NAMED: 1877

DIET: HERBIVORE
Conifers, cycads, ginkgos

SIZE: 15m long, 2.1m high at the hips

WEIGHT: 20,000kg

THIS DINOSAUR WAS PART OF THE FAMOUS 'BONE WARS' OF THE 1870S BETWEEN EDWARD DRINKER COPE AND OTHNIEL C. MARSH, TWO SCIENTISTS WHO COMPETED TO NAME THE MOST DINOSAURS.

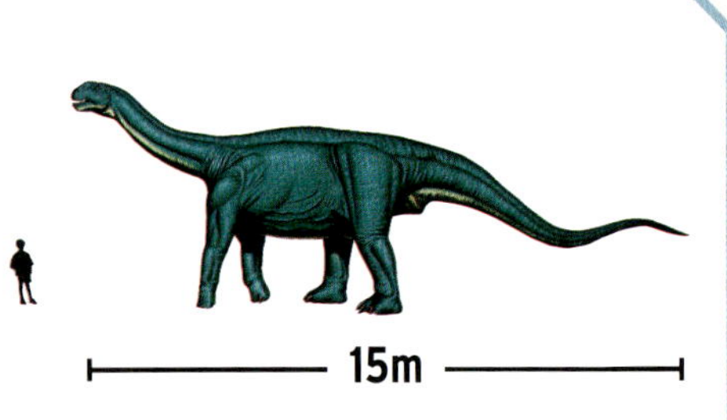

COMPARISON IS WITH A 1.2M TALL CHILD

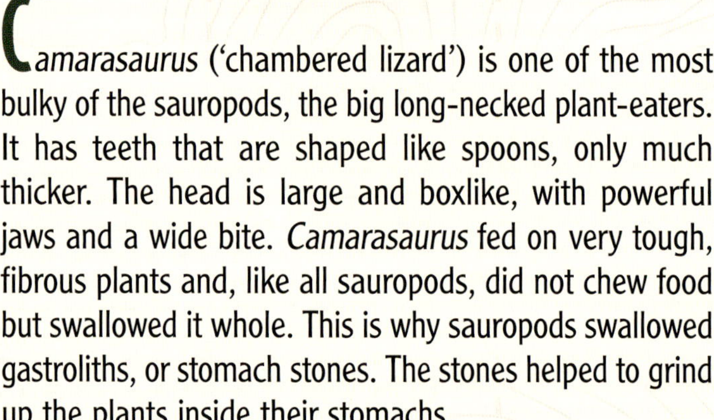

Camarasaurus ('chambered lizard') is one of the most bulky of the sauropods, the big long-necked plant-eaters. It has teeth that are shaped like spoons, only much thicker. The head is large and boxlike, with powerful jaws and a wide bite. *Camarasaurus* fed on very tough, fibrous plants and, like all sauropods, did not chew food but swallowed it whole. This is why sauropods swallowed gastroliths, or stomach stones. The stones helped to grind up the plants inside their stomachs.

The name *Camarasaurus* comes from the chambers that can be seen in its vertebrae. These hollow chambers serve to lighten the skeleton and give it strength. Some scientists believe that these chambers also housed an air-sac system similar to that in birds. Air sacs are part of the respiratory system and are connected to the lungs. This would have greatly helped the air flow through the lungs. Gigantic animals like sauropods would have benefitted from a more efficient system of breathing, because carrying around over twenty-five tons of weight would require a lot of oxygen.

CAMARASAURUS IS ONE OF THE VERY FEW DINOSAURS FOR WHICH JUVENILE SKELETONS HAVE BEEN FOUND ALONG WITH ADULTS.

TIME PERIOD:

252 | 201 | 145 | 66

TRIASSIC | JURASSIC | CRETACEOUS

ABOUT 154–150 MILLION YEARS AGO

CAMPTOSAURUS

KAMP-toe-SOAR-us

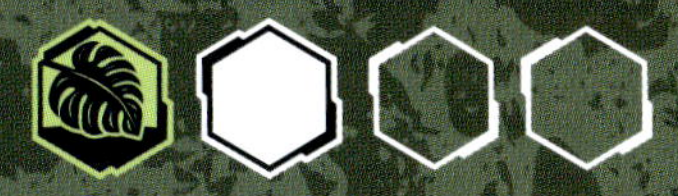

LOCATION:

Colorado, Montana, Oklahoma, Utah, Wyoming, USA

WHAT WE KNOW:

YEAR NAMED: 1885

DIET: HERBIVORE
Conifers, cycads, ginkgos, horsetails

SIZE: 4.5m long, 1.5m high at the hips

WEIGHT: 1,000kg

FUN FACT!

THE ORIGINAL SPECIMENS USED TO NAME TWO SPECIES OF *CAMPTOSAURUS* WERE ON DISPLAY AT THE SMITHSONIAN INSTITUTION IN WASHINGTON, D.C.

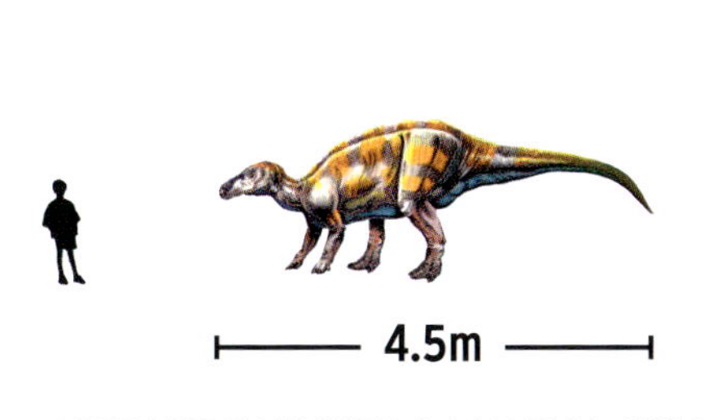

Camptosaurus ('bent lizard') is one of the ornithopods, or beaked dinosaurs. It gets its name from the fact that its thighbone is very slightly bent outward. This is common in many small bipedal dinosaurs. It is an adaptation to get the thighbone out and away from the rib cage while walking, increasing the freedom of movement. A quick escape was *Camptosaurus's* best defence against predators.

Camptosaurus is important in the study of the ornithopods because it represents the first step in a series of adaptations that eventually resulted in the hadrosaurs (duckbilled dinosaurs). In it we can see the first adaptations for carrying a large, heavy body (a thicker, wider pelvis) and the first indications of a staggered row of teeth (instead of a single row).

As far as we can tell, *Camptosaurus* was rare. Few specimens have been found, and no complete specimens. This may be because it lived in the Morrison Formation, along the Rocky Mountains. This formation is famous for its predators. A relatively small dinosaur like *Camptosaurus* would have made a good meal, and its remains would have been easily scavenged.

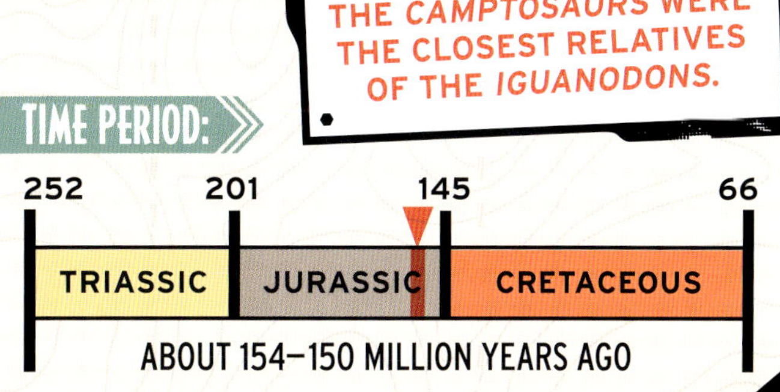

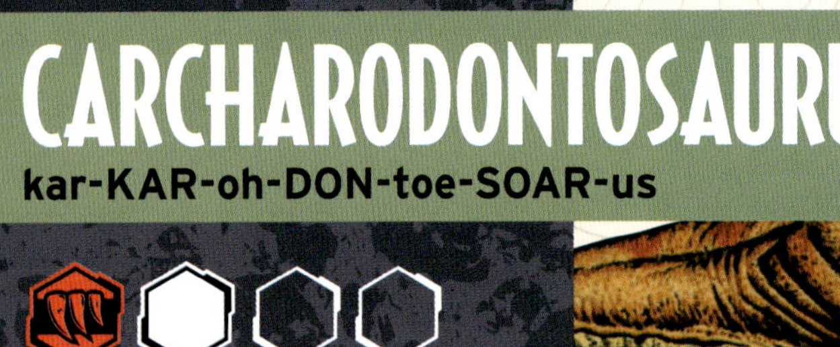

CARCHARODONTOSAURUS

kar-KAR-oh-DON-toe-SOAR-us

LOCATION:

Egypt;
Morocco;
Niger

WHAT WE KNOW:

YEAR NAMED: 1931

DIET: CARNIVORE
Other dinosaurs (titanosaurs)

SIZE: About 12m long, 3.6m high at the hips

WEIGHT: 6,000kg

FRIENDS: None

ENEMIES: *Spinosaurus, Deltadromeus*

FUN FACT!

CARCHARODONTOSAURUS HAD A VERY NARROW SKULL. BECAUSE ITS EYES FACED SIDEWAYS, IT WOULDN'T HAVE BEEN ABLE TO FOCUS WELL ON THINGS RIGHT IN FRONT OF IT, BUT IT COULD HAVE SEEN ALMOST ALL ITS SURROUNDINGS AT ONCE.

Carcharodontosaurus ('shark-toothed lizard') was first known only from its enormous teeth. When these teeth were first described in 1927, they were thought to come from a giant species of *Megalosaurus*. In 1931, however, palaeontologists thought that they were different enough to be given their own name—after the great white shark, whose teeth this dinosaur's resembled.

When parts of this dinosaur's skeleton were finally discovered in northern Africa, they revealed a predator as big as *Tyrannosaurus rex*. Sadly, these fossils, kept in a museum in Munich, Germany, were destroyed by a bomb during World War II. But many decades later, in the summer of 1995, a team of palaeontologists led by Paul Sereno found the most complete fossils yet of *Carcharodontosaurus*. These included most of the skull—including a braincase—as well as some other parts of the skeleton. This showed that *Carcharodontosaurus* was as big as the biggest *Tyrannosaurus!*

CARCHARODONTOSAURUS TEETH SEEM TO BE RELATIVELY COMMON FOSSILS IN NORTHERN AFRICA.

12m

COMPARISON IS WITH A 1.2M TALL CHILD

TIME PERIOD:

252 | 201 | 145 | 66

TRIASSIC | JURASSIC | CRETACEOUS

ABOUT 99–94 MILLION YEARS AGO

CARNOTAURUS

KAHR-no-TORE-us

LOCATION:

Chubut Province, Argentina

WHAT WE KNOW:

YEAR NAMED: 1985

DIET: CARNIVORE
Other dinosaurs

SIZE: Almost 6.5m long, 2m high at the hips

WEIGHT: 1,400–2,000kg

Carnotaurus ('meat-eating bull') was one of the most bizarre meat-eating dinosaurs ever found. Its skull was short, with armour on the top and a pair of blunt horns over its eyes. The neck and shoulder blades were well developed, but the arms were incredibly short, with forearms so shrunken they were practically just wrists! Not even *Tyrannosaurus rex* had such small arms.

With its small skull, *Carnotaurus* might not have been able to attack big plant-eaters, but it was probably fast and could have easily chased down smaller, more agile prey.

The horns of *Carnotaurus* look something like those of a bull—and like a bull, it may have used them in contests with others of its own species. In this way, two *Carnotaurus* could test each other's strength without either of them seriously injuring the other.

FUN FACT!

IN MICHAEL CRICHTON'S NOVEL *THE LOST WORLD: JURASSIC PARK II*, THE GENETICALLY RE-CREATED *CARNOTAURUS* HAD THE POWER OF CHAMELEON-LIKE CAMOUFLAGE. HOWEVER, IT IS EXTREMELY UNLIKELY THAT ANY DINOSAUR REALLY HAD THIS ABILITY.

THE FIRST, AND SO FAR ONLY, DISCOVERED SPECIMEN OF CARNOTAURUS WAS FOUND WITH IMPRESSIONS OF SKIN FROM ALL OVER THE BODY.

COMPARISON IS WITH A 1.2M TALL CHILD

TIME PERIOD:

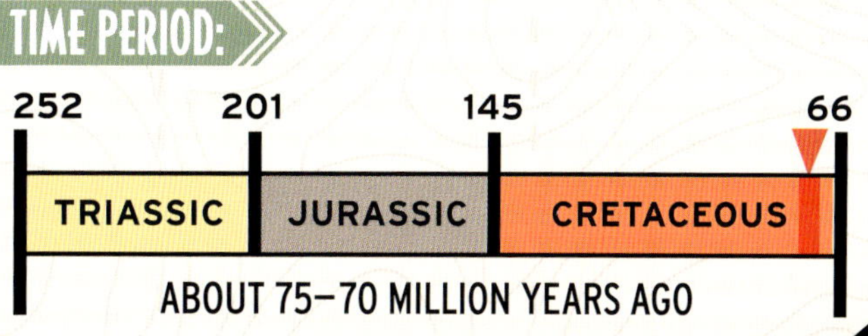

ABOUT 75–70 MILLION YEARS AGO

CAUDIPTERYX

kaw-DIP-ter-iks

LOCATION:

Liaoning Province, China

WHAT WE KNOW:

YEAR NAMED: 1998

DIET: OMNIVORE
Possibly plants, small reptiles and mammals, eggs

SIZE: About 61cm long, almost 50cm high at the hips

WEIGHT: 6–11kg

SOME *CAUDIPTERYX* FOSSILS HAVE BEEN FOUND WITH STOMACH STONES, WHICH WOULD HAVE HELPED GRIND UP THEIR FOOD.

FUN FACT!

ONE OF THE NEWEST DINOSAUR MUSEUMS IN THE WORLD IS IN CHINA, NEXT TO THE SITE WHERE *CAUDIPTERYX* AND OTHER FEATHERED DINOSAUR FOSSILS WERE FOUND.

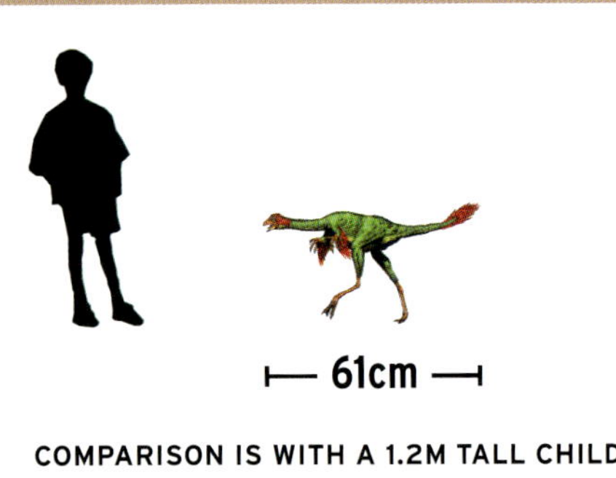

COMPARISON IS WITH A 1.2M TALL CHILD

Caudipteryx ('tail feathers') was one of the most amazing dinosaur discoveries of the 20th century. It showed a dinosaur that was not a bird but had true feathers on its arms and tail.

Some scientists thought *Caudipteryx* was no more than some kind of primitive flightless bird, but when the skeleton of this little creature was studied in detail, it turned out to be an oviraptorosaur. Oviraptorosaurs were a type of meat-eating dinosaur common in the Late Cretaceous of Asia and North America. *Caudipteryx* was the oldest of the oviraptorosaurs and one of the most primitive.

The arms of *Caudipteryx* were very short, so it certainly could not fly. Then why did it have feathers? Palaeontologists suggest a number of possibilities. It might be that they were used for signalling other *Caudipteryx*, as a peacock does. They might have been used to cover *Caudipteryx's* eggs while it brooded its nest. Or possibly the ancestors of *Caudipteryx* really did fly but later become grounded (as happened with ostriches, kiwis and chickens). We may never know for sure.

TIME PERIOD:

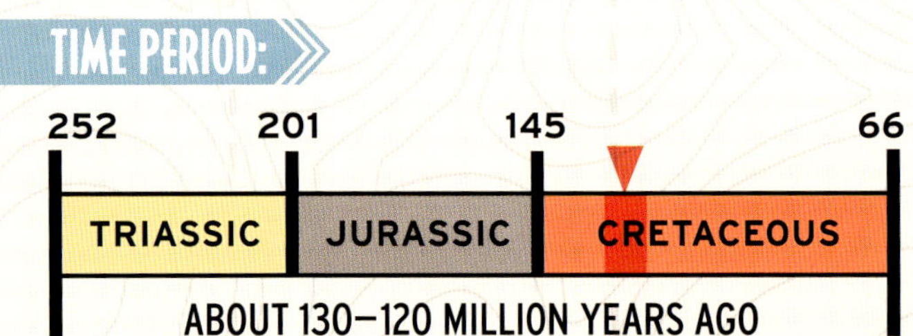

CENTROSAURUS

SEN-tro-SOAR-us

LOCATION:

Alberta, Canada

WHAT WE KNOW:

YEAR NAMED: 1904

DIET: **HERBIVORE**
Conifers, cycads, ginkgos, flowering plants

SIZE: 6m long, 2m high at the hips

WEIGHT: 3,000kg

In the 1800s, *Centrosaurus* ('spur lizard') was discovered in what is now called Dinosaur Provincial Park, in Alberta, Canada. This is one of the largest dinosaur graveyards in the world. In the 1980s, palaeontologists discovered the '*Centrosaurus* Bonebed' within the park. The bonebed contains the skeletons of thousands of *Centrosaurus* that perished while crossing a river during a flood. This allows scientists a rare chance to see how *Centrosaurus* changed as it grew old.

Scientists had argued for years over whether *Centrosaurus* was the same animal as *Monoclonius*. The confusion resulted from the fact that horned dinosaurs' heads changed a lot as the animals grew older. Juveniles did not have the bumps, hooks, spikes, and knobs found on the skulls of adults. The dinosaur once known as *Monoclonius* is now regarded as a juvenile form of *Centrosaurus* and other horned dinosaurs.

FUN FACT!

ONE OF THE MOST COMMON INJURIES IN *CENTROSAURUS* SKELETONS IS A BROKEN TAIL. APPARENTLY, IT WAS QUITE COMMON FOR THEM TO GET STEPPED ON!

DINOSAUR PROVINCIAL PARK IS A WORLD HERITAGE PRESERVE. THIS MEANS THAT THE UNITED NATIONS REGARDS THIS PARK AS A TREASURE FOR THE WHOLE WORLD.

6m

COMPARISON IS WITH A 1.2M TALL CHILD

TIME PERIOD:

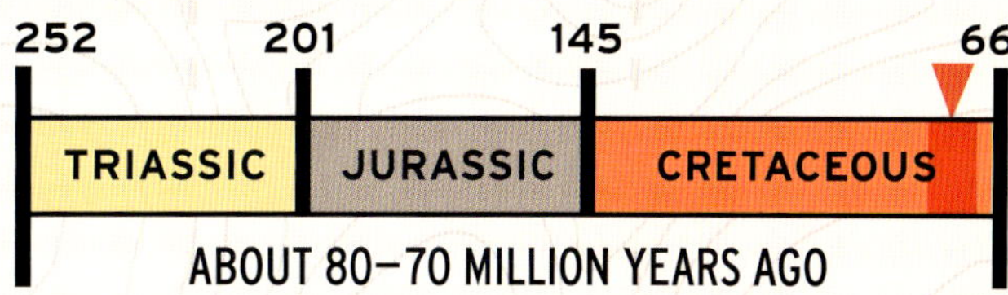

CERATOSAURUS

se-RAT-oh-SOAR-us

LOCATION:

Colorado, Utah, Wyoming, USA

WHAT WE KNOW:

YEAR NAMED: 1884

DIET: CARNIVORE
Other dinosaurs (sauropods, stegosaurs, ornithopods, smaller theropods)

SIZE: 7.2m long, over 1.9m high at the hips

WEIGHT: 900–1,100kg

FUN FACT!

THE HORNS ON THE NOSE AND IN FRONT OF THE EYES OF *CERATOSAURUS* GOT BIGGER AS THE DINOSAUR GOT OLDER. THE ORIGINAL SPECIMEN IS AT THE SMITHSONIAN.

7.2m

COMPARISON IS WITH A 1.2M TALL CHILD

Ceratosaurus ('horned lizard') was one of the first meat-eating dinosaurs known from a nearly complete skeleton. The first *Ceratosaurus* was found in 1883 in the Garden Park Quarry of Canyon City, Colorado. This area has produced many of the most important Jurassic fossils known. Although some parts of the arms and legs were missing, the rest of the skeleton was almost complete. Before this discovery, no skeleton of a large meat-eating dinosaur had been found that was more than half complete. These bones gave palaeontologists many of their first insights into predatory dinosaurs.

Ceratosaurus was unusual for a meat-eater—it had a horn on its nose. The horn was very thin side-to-side (unlike the horns of the plant-eaters like *Centrosaurus* and *Triceratops,* which were cone-shaped). This horn, and the smaller horns just in front of its eyes, were very delicate and probably used only for signaling to other *Ceratosaurus.* The huge teeth and powerful jaws were probably *Centrosaurus's* main weapons, since its arms and claws were small.

ALTHOUGH IT WAS SMALLER OVERALL THAN *ALLOSAURUS*, *CERATOSAURUS* HAD BIGGER TEETH THAN ITS RIVAL.

TIME PERIOD:

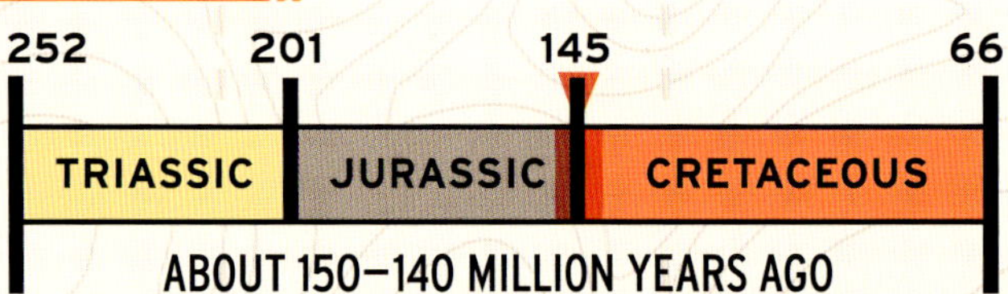

COELOPHYSIS

SEEL-oh-FIE-sis

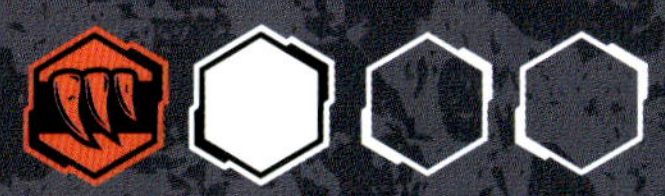

LOCATION:

New Mexico, Arizona, USA

WHAT WE KNOW:

YEAR NAMED: 1889

DIET: CARNIVORE
Small reptiles and fish

SIZE: 3m long, 60cm high at the hips

WEIGHT: 25kg

FRIENDS: None

ENEMIES: *Postosuchus* (a giant predatory crocodile relative)

Coelophysis ('hollow form') was one of the first meat-eating dinosaurs. When *Coelophysis* lived, dinosaurs had just evolved, and they did not yet dominate the land. Instead, giant relatives of crocodilians were the top predators, and armoured crocodile relatives and ox-sized protomammals—primitive synapsids related to the ancestors of mammals—were the big plant-eaters. *Coelophysis* was a minor predator in its environment, but it was very successful. Unlike their crocodilian relatives, *Coelophysis* and other early dinosaurs were fast-running, agile hunters.

In 1947, hundreds of *Coelophysis* skeletons were found buried together at Ghost Ranch, New Mexico. This spectacular discovery included old individuals, babies, and all ages in between. Except for a few other reptiles, the only skeletons in this quarry were from *Coelophysis*. This suggests that these early dinosaurs would group together, at least occasionally.

FUN FACT!

COELOPHYSIS IS KNOWN FROM MORE SKELETONS THAN ANY OTHER MEAT-EATING DINOSAUR OF THE MESOZOIC.

COELOPHYSIS IS THE STATE FOSSIL OF NEW MEXICO.

COMPARISON IS WITH A 1.2M TALL CHILD

TIME PERIOD:

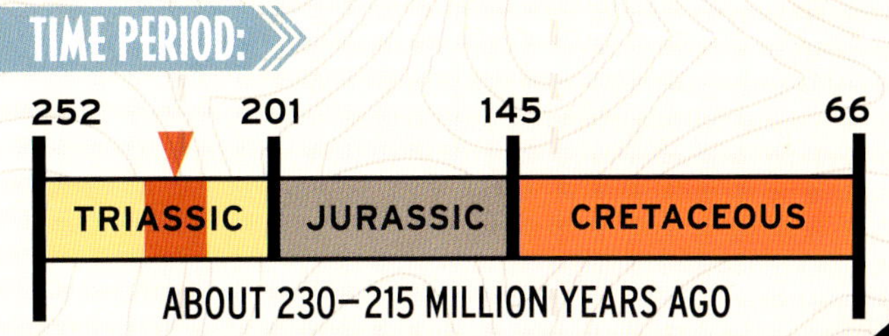

ABOUT 230–215 MILLION YEARS AGO

COMPSOGNATHUS

komp-SOG-na-thus (KOMP-so-NAH-thus)

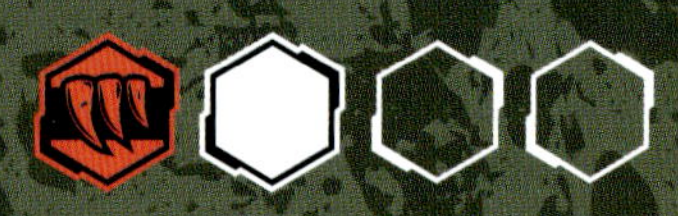

LOCATION:

France;
Germany

WHAT WE KNOW:

YEAR NAMED: 1859

DIET: CARNIVORE
Small reptiles and mammals, possibly insects

SIZE: 1.1m long, 26cm high at the hips

WEIGHT: 3.5kg

FRIENDS: None

ENEMIES: Bigger theropods

FUN FACT!

COMPSOGNATHUS WAS THE FIRST DINOSAUR KNOWN FROM A NEARLY COMPLETE FOSSIL.

Compsognathus ('delicate jaw') was once considered the smallest known dinosaur. The first discovered fossil of *Compsognathus* was less than 70cm long; however, this specimen was probably not fully grown. Even so, adult *Compsognathus* probably weighed only about 3.5kg. Although scientists now regard birds as dinosaurs (and therefore, there are many living dinosaurs smaller than *Compsognathus),* this little meat-eater from the Jurassic Period of Europe is still one of the smallest dinosaurs known from the Mesozoic Era, the Age of Dinosaurs.

Inside the belly of the original *Compsognathus* specimen is the skeleton of a fast-running lizard. This shows that *Compsognathus* was a meat-eater like its bigger relatives (such as *Tyrannosaurus* and *Giganotosaurus),* but it hunted much smaller prey. It lived on the same tropical islands as *Archaeopteryx,* and perhaps it would even eat its smaller flying relative.

COMPARISON IS WITH A 1.2M TALL CHILD

TIME PERIOD:

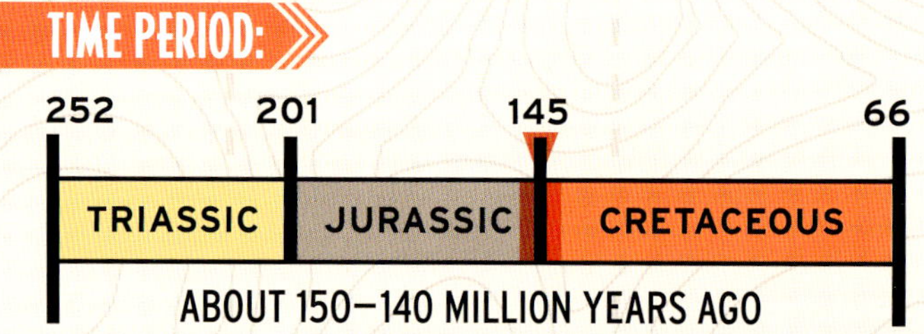

ABOUT 150–140 MILLION YEARS AGO

Compsognathus had short arms that were probably not very useful in catching prey, but could have been handy for holding on to victims it snatched up in its jaws. For many years, it was thought that *Compsognathus* had only two fingers on each hand (as in *Tyrannosaurus* and other tyrant dinosaurs). However, it now seems that *Compsognathus* had three fingers on each hand like most meat-eaters.

ONLY TWO SKELETONS OF *COMPSOGNATHUS* ARE PRESENTLY KNOWN: ONE FROM GERMANY AND A SLIGHTLY LARGER ONE FROM FRANCE.

FEATHERY FACTS!

Compsognathus seems to have been a close relative of the Chinese _Sinosauropteryx_ (pictured below), and like that Asian dinosaur it probably had a covering of 'protofeathers'. Unfortunately, neither protofeathers nor scales were preserved in the known fossils of _Compsognathus_.

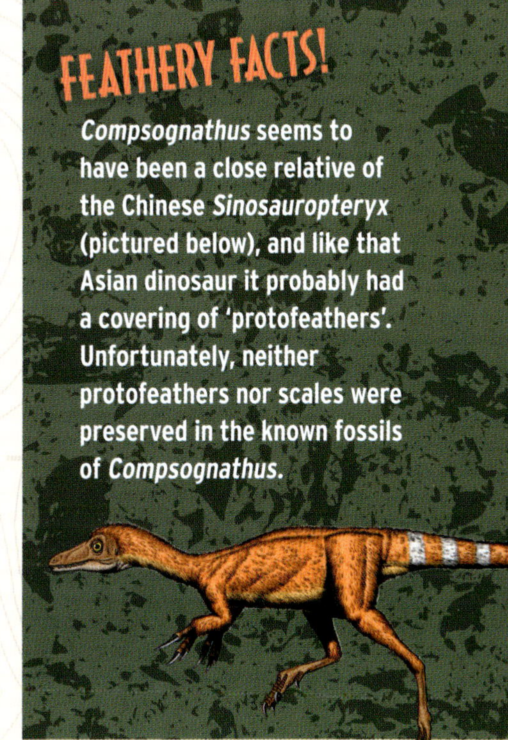

CONFUCIUSORNIS

kon-FYOO-shis-OR-nis

LOCATION:

Liaoning Province, China

WHAT WE KNOW:

YEAR NAMED: 1995

DIET: OMNIVORE
Possibly insects and plants

SIZE: 20cm long, 10cm tall, 36cm wingspan

WEIGHT: 400g

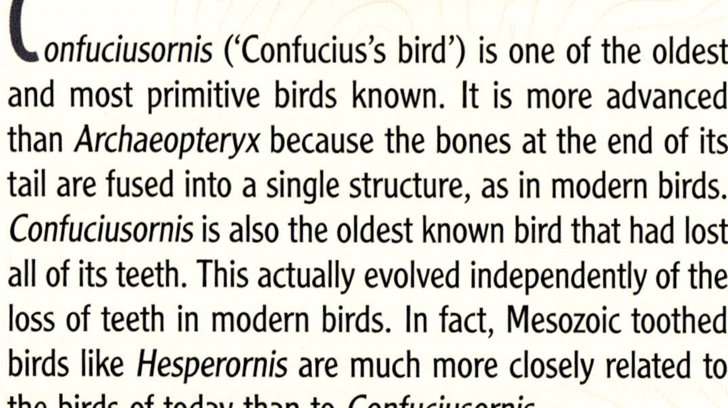

Confuciusornis ('Confucius's bird') is one of the oldest and most primitive birds known. It is more advanced than *Archaeopteryx* because the bones at the end of its tail are fused into a single structure, as in modern birds. *Confuciusornis* is also the oldest known bird that had lost all of its teeth. This actually evolved independently of the loss of teeth in modern birds. In fact, Mesozoic toothed birds like *Hesperornis* are much more closely related to the birds of today than to *Confuciusornis*.

Confuciusornis comes from the spectacular Yixian Formation of China, so the feathers in most specimens are very well preserved. From this we see that some *Confuciusornis* had two long tail feathers, while most did not. Perhaps the ones with the long tail feathers were males, and the ones without were females.

Confuciusornis is known from hundreds of skeletons. Perhaps great flocks of *Confuciusornis* flew across the skies of Early Cretaceous China.

FUN FACT!

CONFUCIUSORNIS **IS KNOWN FROM SO MANY FOSSILS THAT IT MAY BE THE MOST COMMON MESOZOIC DINOSAUR EVER FOUND.**

PEOPLE HAVE OFTEN TRIED TO SELL FAKE *CONFUCIUSORNIS* SKELETONS. THEY SOMETIMES GIVE THEM EXTRA LEG BONES OR LEAVE BONES OUT!

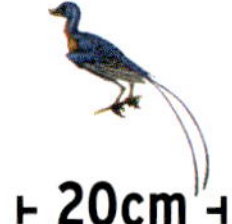

COMPARISON IS WITH A 1.2M TALL CHILD

TIME PERIOD:

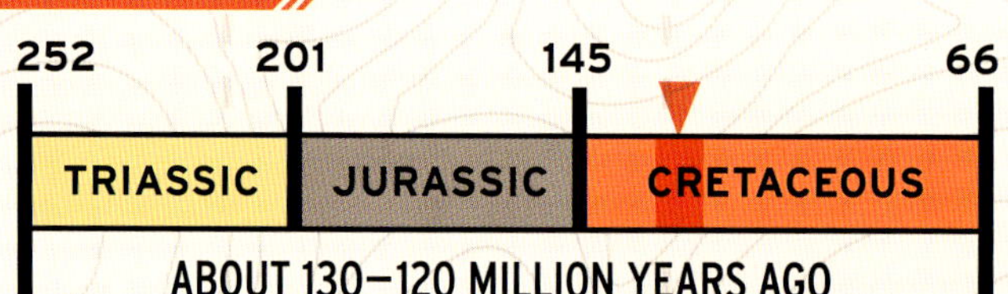

ABOUT 130–120 MILLION YEARS AGO

CORYTHOSAURUS

ko-RITH-oh-SOAR-us

LOCATION:

Alberta, Canada

WHAT WE KNOW:

YEAR NAMED: 1914

DIET: HERBIVORE
Conifers, cycads, ginkgos, angiosperms

SIZE: 10m long, 2m high at the hips

WEIGHT: 3,000–5,000kg

Corythosaurus ('Corinthian helmet lizard') is one of the crested duckbill dinosaurs. At one time, over six species were named based on slight differences in the crest on the skull. But in 1975, palaeontologist Peter Dodson showed that these changes are due to sexual dimorphism and growth allometry. In other words, they were all the same species, and the differences in the skulls and crests were normal among a large population of juveniles and adults of both sexes.

The famous crest of *Corythosaurus* is formed from the upper lip bone and the nasal bone. These two bones have grown back and up over the skull, taking the nasal passage with them. The result is a folded nasal passage comparable to a woodwind instrument, such as a clarinet. Each species of crested duckbill dinosaur would have made its own unique sound, like different instruments in an orchestra. The crest also housed the enlarged olfactory lobes of the brain, increasing the duckbill's sense of smell. In some species, the olfactory lobes are actually bent toward the hollow crest in order to be closer to the nasal chambers!

THE MOST BEAUTIFUL AND COMPLETE *CORYTHOSAURUS* SKELETON IS ON DISPLAY AT THE AMERICAN MUSEUM OF NATURAL HISTORY IN NEW YORK CITY.

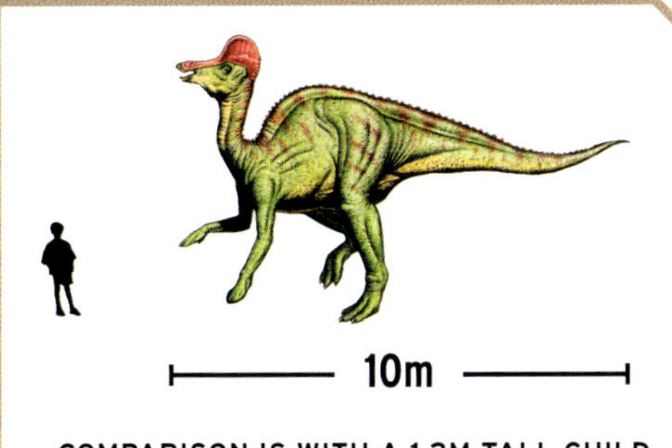

COMPARISON IS WITH A 1.2M TALL CHILD

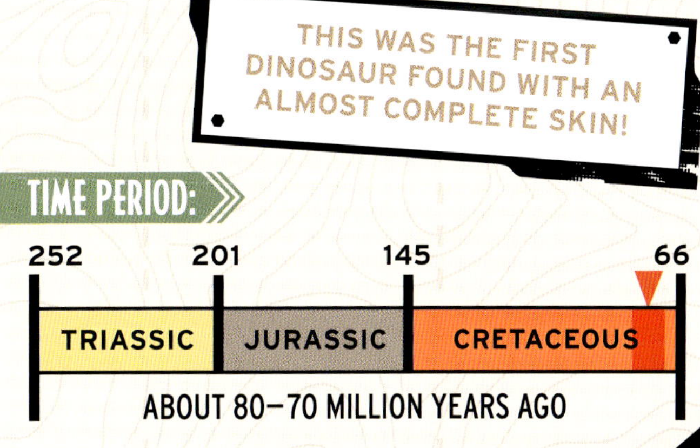

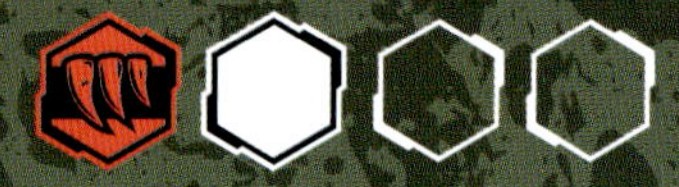

LOCATION:
Antarctica

WHAT WE KNOW:

YEAR NAMED: 1994

DIET: CARNIVORE
Other dinosaurs

SIZE: 6m long, perhaps 1.5m high at the hips

WEIGHT: 500kg

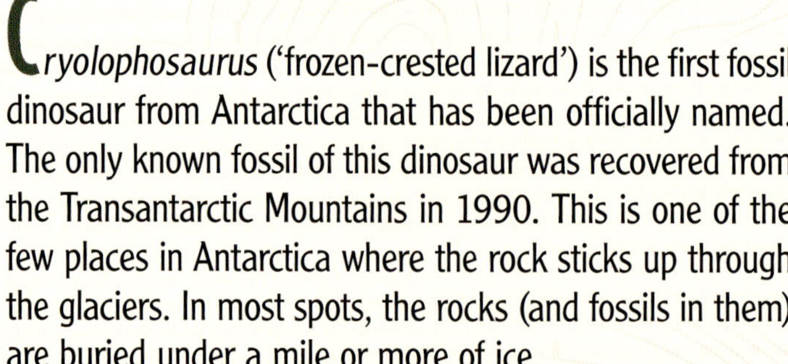

Cryolophosaurus ('frozen-crested lizard') is the first fossil dinosaur from Antarctica that has been officially named. The only known fossil of this dinosaur was recovered from the Transantarctic Mountains in 1990. This is one of the few places in Antarctica where the rock sticks up through the glaciers. In most spots, the rocks (and fossils in them) are buried under a mile or more of ice.

Although a frozen land now, Antarctica was not always covered in ice. During the Age of Dinosaurs, the world was warmer in general, and Antarctica was further north than it is today. All sorts of animals and plants once flourished there. It was only after the Age of Dinosaurs that Antarctica shifted over the South Pole and became buried in ice.

Cryolophosaurus was a meat-eating dinosaur. Its most distinctive feature is its forward-facing crest. The remains of a prosauropod dinosaur named *Glacialisaurus* were found with the skeleton of *Cryolophosaurus*, so it is likely that prosauropods were the prey of choice.

FUN FACT!

ALTHOUGH *CRYOLOPHOSAURUS* IS THE FIRST NAMED MESOZOIC DINOSAUR FROM ANTARCTICA, PENGUINS ARE THE BEST-KNOWN DINOSAURS FROM THE FROZEN LAND. (REMEMBER: BIRDS ARE A KIND OF DINOSAUR, AND PENGUINS ARE A KIND OF BIRD!)

6m

COMPARISON IS WITH A 1.2M TALL CHILD

OTHER DINOSAURS FROM ANTARCTICA INCLUDE ANKYLOSAURS *ANTARCTOPELTA* AND THE ORNITHOPOD *TRINISAURA*, BOTH FROM THE CRETACEOUS PERIOD.

TIME PERIOD:

252 | 201 | 145 | 66

TRIASSIC | JURASSIC | CRETACEOUS

ABOUT 180–170 MILLION YEARS AGO

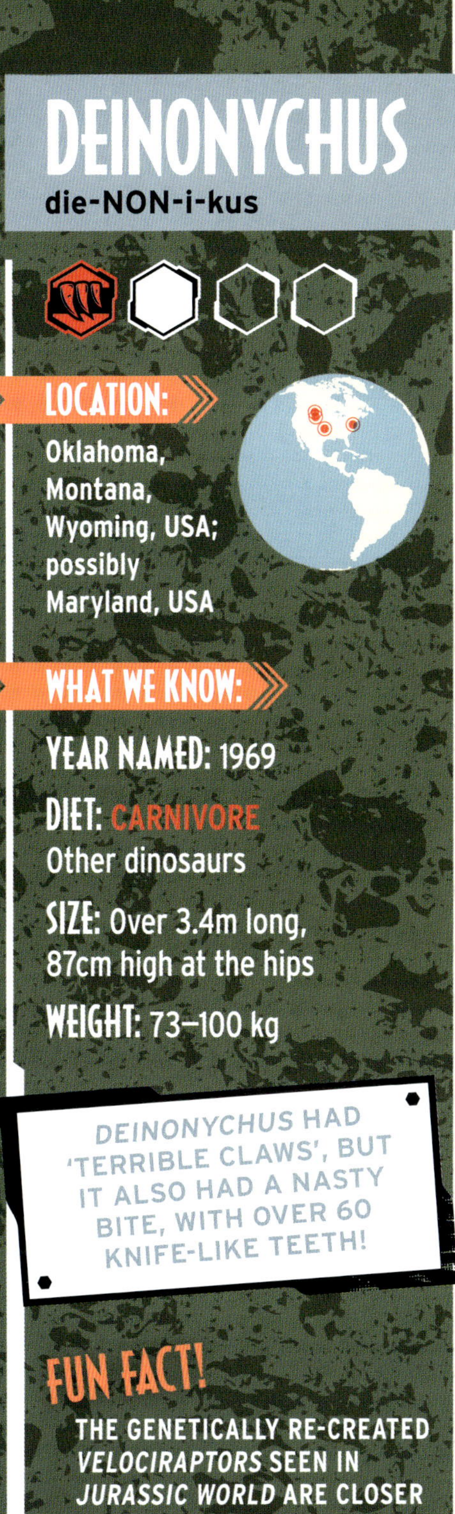

Deinonychus ('terrible claw') is one of the most important dinosaurs ever found because it changed the way palaeontologists thought about dinosaurs. For most of the 20th century, dinosaurs were generally thought of as being strange evolutionary 'dead ends', with no living descendants, mostly slow and sluggish. Then dinosaur palaeontogist Dr John Ostrom discovered *Deinonychus* in 1964.

Dr Ostrom believed that this dinosaur was an agile, swift predator, more like a warm-blooded mammal or bird than a cold-blooded crocodile. His study of *Deinonychus*—and of the early bird *Archaeopteryx*—led him to realise that birds were in fact the descendants of dinosaurs, and that raptor dinosaurs such as *Deinonychus* and *Velociraptor* were among the closest relatives of birds.

Deinonychus was the first of the raptors (technically called 'dromaeosaurs') to be known from a nearly complete skeleton. *Velociraptor* had been discovered forty years earlier but was known only from a skull and a few bones of its hands and feet. The skeletons of *Deinonychus* were the first to show the now infamous sickle-shaped retractable foot claw, used for ripping open the guts of its prey.

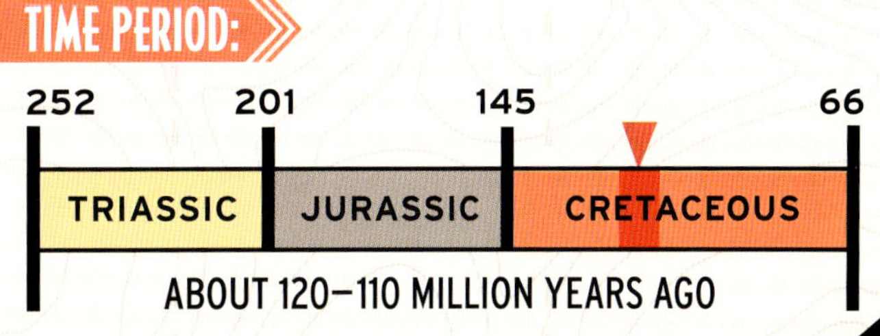

DILOPHOSAURUS

die-LOF-oh-SOAR-us

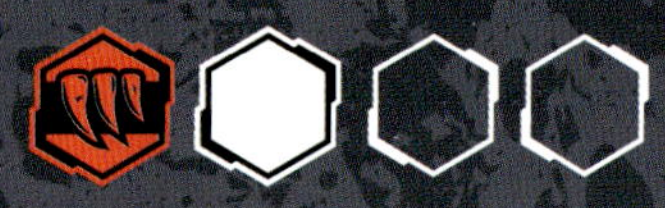

LOCATION:

Arizona, USA

WHAT WE KNOW:

YEAR NAMED: 1970

DIET: CARNIVORE
Prosauropods, primitive bird-hipped dinosaurs

SIZE: Over 6.8m long, 1.5m high at the hips

WEIGHT: 400kg

WHEN THE FIRST SKELETON OF THIS DINOSAUR WAS FOUND (IN 1942), IT WAS THOUGHT TO BE FROM A NEW SPECIES OF *MEGALOSAURUS*. ONLY LATER IN THE LAB DID PALAEONTOLOGIST SAM WELLES DISCOVER THE PAIR OF CRESTS ON ITS HEAD.

Dilophosaurus ('double-crested lizard') was one of the first large meat-eating dinosaurs. It was a close relative of the smaller dinosaur *Coelophysis*. Little *Coelophysis* lived in the Late Triassic, when *Rauisuchus* and other reptiles related to the ancestors of crocodilians were the top predators. At the end of the Triassic, however, there was a series of great extinctions, and the giant crocodile relatives became extinct. Dinosaurs then became the top meat-eaters.

In general, *Dilophosaurus* looks like a shorter-necked, more heavily built version of *Coelophysis*. Like its little relative, *Dilophosaurus* has a characteristic 'kink' in the front of its snout. This probably helped hold on to struggling victims. One dramatic difference (other than size) between the two is the pair of tall crescent-shaped crests along the top of *Dilophosaurus's* skull. These were very thin and probably used only for display.

Footprints that match the feet of *Dilophosaurus* are found in many parts of the world, dating from Early Jurassic. Since the continents of the Earth were still mostly attached as the supercontinent of Pangaea at this time (see map on page 151), it is possible that the double-crested hunter lived in most parts of the world.

FUN FACT!

THE STATE FOSSIL OF CONNECTICUT IS A DINOSAUR FOOTPRINT, VERY LIKELY THE FOOTPRINT OF *DILOPHOSAURUS* OR A CLOSE RELATIVE.

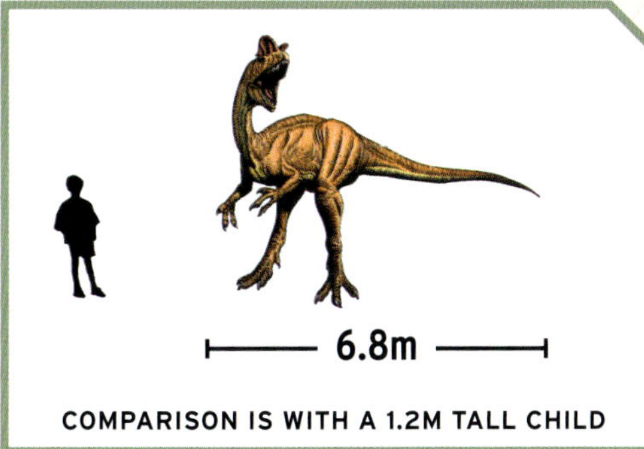
6.8m
COMPARISON IS WITH A 1.2M TALL CHILD

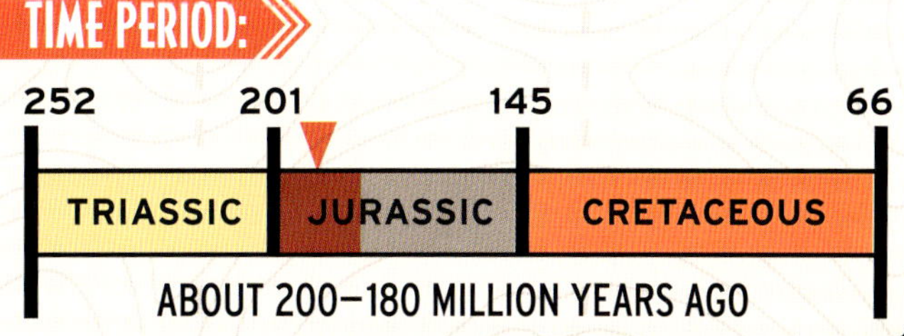
TIME PERIOD:
252
201
145
66
TRIASSIC
JURASSIC
CRETACEOUS
ABOUT 200–180 MILLION YEARS AGO

DRYOSAURUS

DRIE-oh-SOAR-us

LOCATION:

Colorado, Utah, Wyoming, USA

WHAT WE KNOW:

YEAR NAMED: 1894

DIET: HERBIVORE
Conifers, cycads, ginkgos

SIZE: Just under 3m long, 1.7m high at the hips

WEIGHT: 91kg

FRIENDS: *Othnielosaurus, Camptosaurus, Stegosaurus*

ENEMIES: *Coelurus, Ornitholestes, Allosaurus*

FUN FACT!

A CLOSE RELATIVE TO THIS DINOSAUR, NAMED *DYSALOTOSAURUS*, LIVED IN AFRICA AT THE SAME TIME.

COMPARISON IS WITH A 1.2M TALL CHILD

Dryosaurus ('oak-tree lizard') literally lived in the shadows of most Late Jurassic plants. It was a small to medium-sized dinosaur and was very lightly built (as compared to its closest relative, the bulkier *Camptosaurus*). *Dryosaurus* was one of the ornithopods, or beaked dinosaurs. Its pelvis is small compared to the rest of the body. The arms are very short and the long legs not powerfully built. The skull has a short face and relatively big eyes.

A dinosaur like *Dryosaurus* had to rely on running from predators (rather than standing and fighting), so it had to grow as fast as possible. The longer its legs, the faster it would run. Not all dinosaurs grew as fast as *Dryosaurus*. Modern lizards, for example, grow in spurts, depending on the season. But *Dryosaurus's* bones grew fast at all times, which was a great benefit to its survival.

TIME PERIOD:

252	201	145	66
TRIASSIC	JURASSIC	CRETACEOUS	

ABOUT 150–140 MILLION YEARS AGO

DRYPTOSAURUS

DRIP-toe-SOAR-us

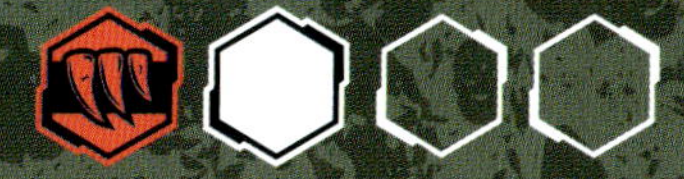

LOCATION:

New Jersey, USA

WHAT WE KNOW:

YEAR NAMED: 1866

DIET: CARNIVORE *Hadrosaurus*

SIZE: Perhaps 6.5m long, 1.8m high at the hips

WEIGHT: 1,200kg

FRIENDS: None

ENEMIES: None

Dryptosaurus ('tearing lizard') has an important place in the history of dinosaur science. Before this species was discovered in 1866, palaeontologists had never found the arms and legs of the same species of a meat-eating dinosaur. Because of this, they thought that meat-eaters were four-legged hunters, like giant lizards or bears. However, when *Dryptosaurus* was found, scientists saw that meat-eating dinosaurs had arms that were much shorter than their legs, and realised they had to be bipedal, or two-footed.

Dryptosaurus was named for its enormous 21cm claw. Its discoverer, Edward Drinker Cope, thought that this claw came from the foot, but it was later realised that this was actually a hand claw. Unfortunately, not much of the skeleton of *Dryptosaurus* was ever found. Palaeontologists must guess at what it may have looked like.

FUN FACT!

A FAMOUS PAINTING BY ARTIST CHARLES R. KNIGHT SHOWS TWO *DRYPTOSAURUS* FIGHTING, WITH ONE OF THEM LEAPING HIGH IN THE AIR TO POUNCE ON THE OTHER. THIS IS AN EXCITING IMAGE BUT AN UNLIKELY SCENARIO FOR ANIMALS OF THEIR SIZE!

DRYPTOSAURUS WAS FIRST NAMED LAELAPS. IT WAS THEN DISCOVERED THAT THE NAME HAD ALREADY BEEN USED–FOR A TYPE OF MITE!

COMPARISON IS WITH A 1.2M TALL CHILD

TIME PERIOD:

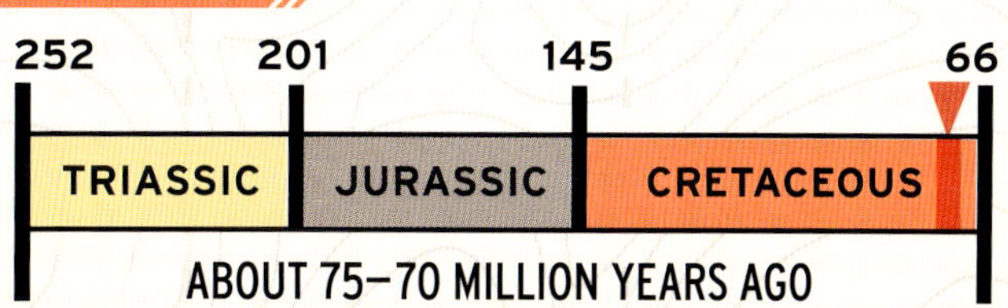

ABOUT 75–70 MILLION YEARS AGO

EDMONTONIA

ED-mon-TOE-nee-uh

LOCATION:

Montana,
South Dakota,
Wyoming,
possibly Alaska,
USA; Alberta, Canada

WHAT WE KNOW:

YEAR NAMED: 1928

DIET: HERBIVORE
Conifers, cycads, ginkgos

SIZE: Just under 7m long, 2m high at the hips

WEIGHT: 3,000kg

THE BEST FULL-SCALE RESTORATION IS ON DISPLAY AT THE ROYAL TYRRELL MUSEUM IN DRUMHELLER, ALBERTA, CANADA.

7m

COMPARISON IS WITH A 1.2M TALL CHILD

Edmontonia ('lizard from Edmonton [Canada]') is a nodosaur, a kind of ankylosaur without a tail club. It had two large spikes on each shoulder that pointed out to the side. These spikes were a great defence against predators because they were at the same level as the knee and calf muscles of a larger theropod, or meat-eating dinosaur. If attacked, this slow-moving tank would throw its weight behind these spikes and drive them into a predator's legs. This would immediately disable the attacker and allow *Edmontonia* to walk away.

Although the skull of *Edmontonia* was long and shallow, it had room for four sinus cavities. This meant the skull was lighter, and probably improved the dinosaur's sense of smell. *Edmontonia's* teeth were amazingly small for such a large animal. One tooth was only 1cm long and barely 5mm wide—far too small for eating most plants. Did *Edmontonia* also eat ants and insects, like the modern anteater? Or were its teeth disappearing over time because its beak did all the work? These are mysteries that dinosaur detectives have yet to solve!

EDMONTONIA HAD FLEXIBLE BODY ARMOUR.

TIME PERIOD:

252 | 201 | 145 | 66

TRIASSIC | JURASSIC | CRETACEOUS

ABOUT 75–70 MILLION YEARS AGO

EDMONTOSAURUS

ED-mon-toe-SOAR-us

LOCATION:

Alaska, Montana, South Dakota, Wyoming, USA; Canada

WHAT WE KNOW:

YEAR NAMED: 1917

DIET: **HERBIVORE**
Plants

SIZE: 10m long, 2.5m high at the hips

WEIGHT: 5,000–7,000kg

FRIENDS: *Triceratops*

ENEMIES: *Tyrannosaurus, Acheroraptor*

FUN FACT!

FOR MANY DECADES, THE ONLY COMPLETE 'DINOSAUR MUMMIES' WERE *EDMONTOSAURUS* AND *CORYTHOSAURUS*, BOTH ON DISPLAY AT THE AMERICAN MUSEUM OF NATURAL HISTORY IN NEW YORK CITY.

10m

COMPARISON IS WITH A 1.2M TALL CHILD

Edmontosaurus ('Edmonton lizard') was the largest, and last, of the non-crested duckbill dinosaurs. Its name refers to the city of Edmonton, Canada. *Edmontosaurus* is part of the Hadrosauridae, or duckbill family of dinosaurs, who are known for their amazing teeth—or as palaeontologists call it, their 'dental battery'. On each side of *Edmontosaurus's* jaw are three rows of sixty or more perfectly interlocking teeth—that's 720 per mouth, compared to thirty-two in an adult human! Not only did *Edmontosaurus* have a lot of teeth, but when one fell out, another from inside its jaw would take its place! Teeth like these are called 'evergrowing'.

Edmontosaurus ate plants and had to be on constant alert for predators such as *Tyrannosaurus* and *Acheroraptor. Edmontosaurus* could not outrun any of the meat-eaters and had to rely on out-maneuvering them—like a crafty football player—or travelling in large herds, where there was safety in numbers.

THERE WERE THREE SPECIES OF *EDMONTOSAURUS*. THE LAST ONE TO APPEAR IS CONSIDERED BY SOME TO BE ITS OWN GENUS–*ANATOTITAN*.

TIME PERIOD:

252	201	145	66
TRIASSIC	JURASSIC	CRETACEOUS	

ABOUT 77–66 MILLION YEARS AGO

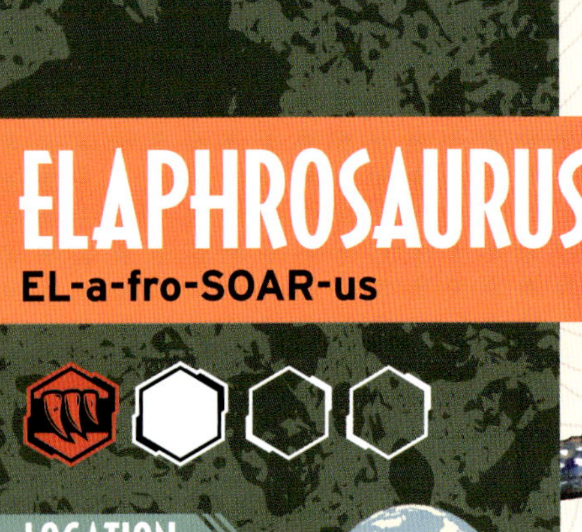

ELAPHROSAURUS

EL-a-fro-SOAR-us

LOCATION:

Tanzania; possibly western USA

WHAT WE KNOW:

YEAR NAMED: 1920

DIET: CARNIVORE
Small reptiles, including smaller dinosaurs

SIZE: Almost 6.2m long, 1.5m high at the hips

WEIGHT: About 210kg

Elaphrosaurus* ('fleet lizard') was a meat-eating dinosaur with a long neck and tail and very long hind legs. Unfortunately, we don't know what its head looked like because the skull has never been found.

What scientists know of *Elaphrosaurus* comes from a nearly complete skeleton recovered from the Tendaguru Beds of Tanzania. These beds contain the best Late Jurassic Epoch dinosaur fossils in Africa. They are famous for the many skeletons of giant long-necked sauropods, plated stegosaurs, and beaked ornithopods that have been found there.

Unfortunately, palaeontologists digging at Tendaguru have found very few fossils of theropods, or meat-eating dinosaurs. They have found teeth and bones and other bits, but the only nearly complete skeleton of a theropod found there was *Elaphrosaurus.*

Bones that might be from *Elaphrosaurus* (or a very closely related dinosaur) were found in the Morrison Formation, a famous series of rocks in western North America from the same time period as the Tendaguru Beds.

FUN FACT!

BASED ON THE PROPORTIONS OF ITS VERY LONG LEGS, PALAEONTOLOGISTS THINK THAT *ELAPHROSAURUS* MAY HAVE BEEN THE FASTEST DINOSAUR OF THE JURASSIC PERIOD.

THE ONLY KNOWN SKELETON OF *ELAPHROSAURUS* ON DISPLAY IS MOUNTED WITH A SKULL BASED ON THAT OF A *VELOCIRAPTOR.*

6.2m

COMPARISON IS WITH A 1.2M TALL CHILD

TIME PERIOD:

252 | 201 | 145 | 66

TRIASSIC | JURASSIC | CRETACEOUS

ABOUT 150–140 MILLION YEARS AGO

EORAPTOR

EE-oh-RAP-tor

LOCATION:

Valle de la Luna (Valley of the Moon), Chile; Argentina

WHAT WE KNOW:

YEAR NAMED: 1993

DIET: OMNIVORE
Small reptiles and mammals, plants

SIZE: 1m long, 39cm high at the hips

WEIGHT: 4–10kg

FUN FACT!

WHEN THE THIGHBONE OF *EORAPTOR* WAS FIRST FOUND, PALAEONTOLOGISTS AT FIRST THOUGHT IT WAS A LITTLE CROCODILE RELATIVE. THEY REALISED THAT IT WAS A DINOSAUR WHEN THE REST OF THE SKELETON WAS DUG UP.

Eoraptor ('dawn hunter') is the most primitive known dinosaur, and for palaeontologists it serves as a model for what the very first dinosaur probably looked like.

Before *Eoraptor* was found, scientists looked at the oldest and most primitive members of each of the major groups of dinosaurs. They saw that most of these were only about 1m long, and that they walked on their back legs. Then, in 1991, Ricardo Martinez found the skeleton of *Eoraptor* in Argentina. It matched what palaeontologists had expected to find in a common ancestor. It was only 1m long, and it walked on its back legs.

Was Eoraptor the ancestor of all dinosaurs?

Unfortunately, no. It lived too late in time. Other, more advanced dinosaurs were found in the same Late Triassic rocks where *Eoraptor* was found. But palaeontologists haven't given up the search for that very first dinosaur. They are now searching for new fossils in even older rocks.

EORAPTOR WAS FOUND IN VALLE DE LA LUNA, SAN PEDRO DE ATACAMA, CHILE.

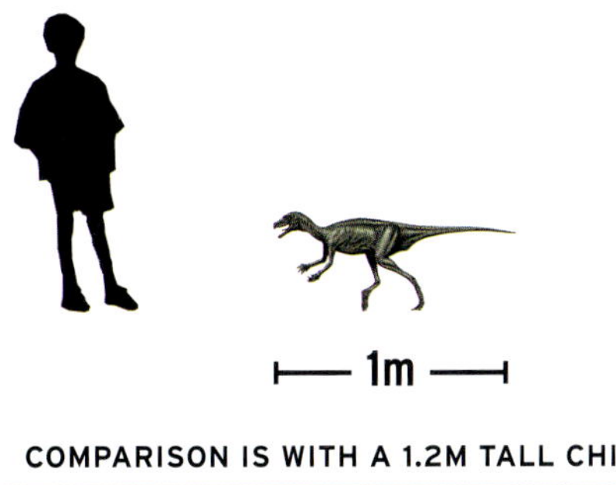

COMPARISON IS WITH A 1.2M TALL CHILD

TIME PERIOD:

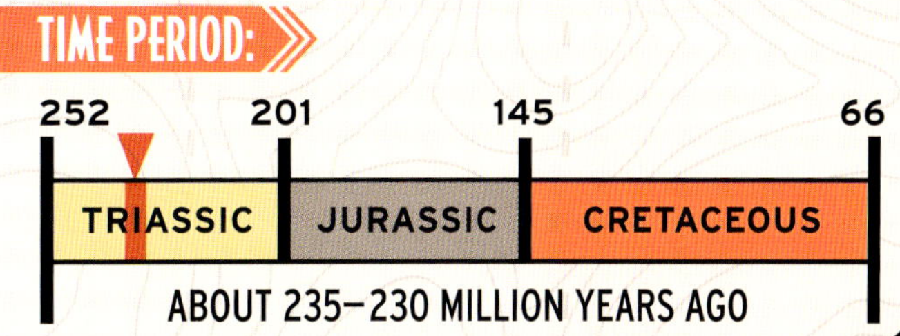

ABOUT 235–230 MILLION YEARS AGO

GALLIMIMUS

GAL-ee-MIME-us

LOCATION:

Mongolia

WHAT WE KNOW:

YEAR NAMED: 1972

DIET: **OMNIVORE**
Possibly small mammals and reptiles, plants, insects

SIZE: 6m long, 1.9m high at the hips

WEIGHT: 200–400kg

GALLIMIMUS WAS NOT THE LARGEST OF ALL THE OSTRICH DINOSAURS. *DEINOCHEIRUS* FROM MONGOLIA WAS NEARLY AS BIG AS *T. REX*.

FUN FACT!

PALAEONTOLOGISTS HAVE NOT FOUND SKELETONS OF DIFFERENT *GALLIMIMUS* TOGETHER, BUT THERE WAS A DISCOVERY THAT AN EARLIER RELATED MONGOLIAN DINOSAUR DID LIVE IN FLOCKS.

Gallimimus ('chicken mimic') is one of the largest of the ornithomimosaurs (or 'bird mimics'). Ornithomimosaurs are often called 'ostrich dinosaurs' because they are shaped very similar to modern flightless birds.

Ostrich dinosaurs were compact, with long arms and legs. The arms ended in long hands with hook-like fingers all curling in the same direction. Their feet were long, narrow, and compact, and had a special shock-absorbing shape that let them run very fast. In fact, ostrich dinosaurs were probably the fastest dinosaurs of the Cretaceous Period. This would have been useful, since both raptors and tyrant dinosaurs hunted in the places where *Gallimimus* and its relatives lived!

Although *Pelecanimimus* and other early ostrich dinosaurs had teeth in their jaws, *Gallimimus* and its relatives were totally toothless. Their beaked heads had large eyes and were at the end of long, slender necks.

Some palaeontologists think that ostrich dinosaurs ate only meat, although without good grasping hands or strong jaws they could kill only smaller animals. Others think that they were plant-eaters. Many suspect that like the modern ostrich, they ate small animals and plants.

COMPARISON IS WITH A 1.2M TALL CHILD

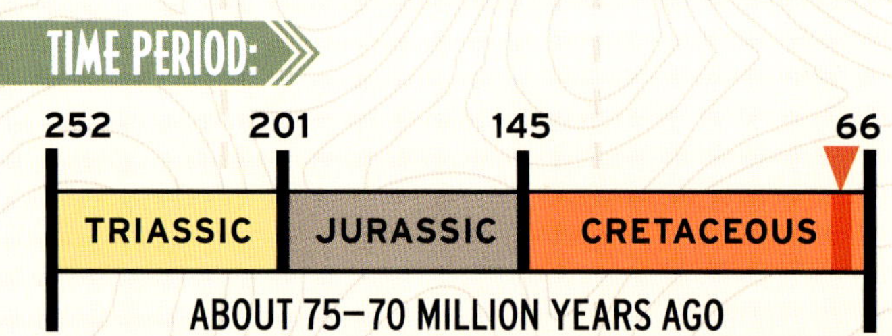

gahr-GOI-lee-o-SOAR-us

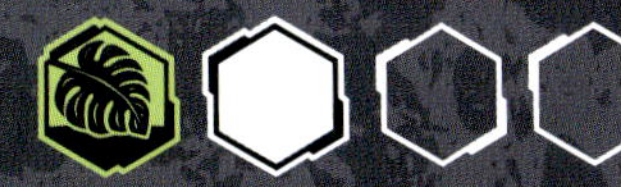

LOCATION:

Wyoming, USA

WHAT WE KNOW:

YEAR NAMED: 1998

DIET: **HERBIVORE**
Conifers, cycads, ginkgos

SIZE: 3m long, 1m high at the hips

WEIGHT: 1,000kg

FRIENDS: *Stegosaurus, Othnielosaurus, Mymoorapelta*

ENEMIES: *Ornitholestes, Torvosaurus*

Gargoyleosaurus ('gargoyle lizard') is one of the rarest of the armoured dinosaurs. It is from the Jurassic Period, not the Cretaceous like most ankylosaurs. It has many primitive features. For example, in most ankylosaurs, the upper part of the beak has no teeth. The more teeth present in the beak, the more primitive the dinosaur. *Gargoyleosaurus* has seven teeth, more than in any other ankylosaur. Most ankylosaurs also have a set of large, folded nasal air passages. In *Gargoyleosaurus,* the small nasal air passage is straight. The most highly armoured ankylosaurs have solid plates of bone (armour) on the outside of the body. In *Gargoyleosaurus,* they are hollow.

Ankylosaurs and stegosaurs are classified together in a larger group called the Thyreophora, or 'armoured dinosaurs'. They share the common feature known as 'dermal armour', or armour that grows out of the skin.

FUN FACT!

GARGOYLEOSAURUS **LIVED IN WHAT IS NOW THE MORRISON FORMATION, A FAMOUS SET OF ROCKS IN THE WESTERN USA MADE OF SEDIMENT DEPOSITED DURING THE LATE JURASSIC PERIOD**

THE FIRST *GARGOYLEOSAURUS* SKULL AND SKELETON ON DISPLAY ARE IN THE DENVER MUSEUM OF NATURAL HISTORY.

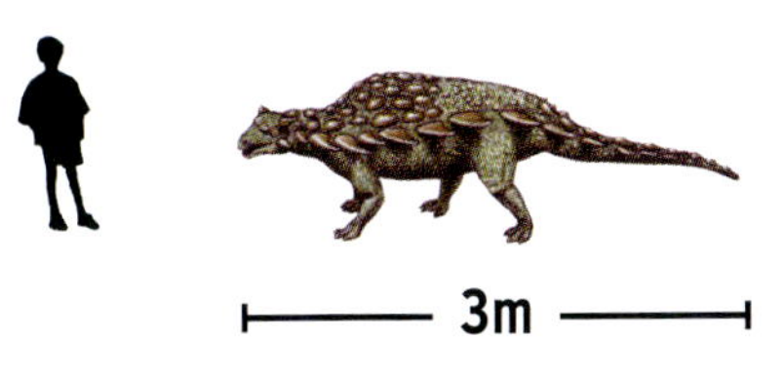

COMPARISON IS WITH A 1.2M TALL CHILD

TIME PERIOD:

252	201	145	66
TRIASSIC	JURASSIC	CRETACEOUS	

ABOUT 154–150 MILLION YEARS AGO

GASPARINISAURA

gas-pah-REEN-ee-SOAR-a

LOCATION:

Patagonia, Argentina

WHAT WE KNOW:

YEAR NAMED: 1996

DIET: **HERBIVORE**
Conifers, cycads, ginkgos, possibly early weed-like flowering plants

SIZE: 80cm long, 30cm high at the hips

WEIGHT: 15–30kg

Gasparinisaura ('[Dr Zulma B.] Gasparini's lizard') is one of the rare ornithopods, or beaked dinosaurs, from the middle of the Cretaceous Period. Remains of dinosaurs from this time span are so extremely rare, all the specimens in the world would fit in one small exhibit hall!

Gasparinisaura is also one of those rare small dinosaurs that had a primitive body design. The features of its skeleton place it with the dryosaurs, from the Jurassic Period, but *Gasparinisaura* lived well into the Cretaceous Period—a time when the hadrosaurs, the most evolved of the ornithopods, had already appeared. Many features of the skull are primitive: for example, the teeth with low crowns (not much showing above the gum line) and the shortened face (later ornithopods have a long muzzle). Normally, the skull evolves faster than the body bones. But in *Gasparinisaura,* the reverse has occurred. The hip bone is more like that of the later hadrosaurs. This indicates a dinosaur with a well-developed hip musculature.

FUN FACT!

ORNITHOPODS ARE VERY COMMON IN NORTH AMERICA, BUT THEY ARE EXTREMELY RARE IN SOUTH AMERICA, WHERE THE SAUROPODS WERE THE MAIN HERBIVORES.

THE SCIENTISTS WHO ARE STUDYING THE VERY SMALL *GASPARINISAURA* ARE THE SAME SCIENTISTS AT WORK ON THE VERY LARGE *GIGANOTOSAURUS*.

⊢ 80cm ⊣

COMPARISON IS WITH A 1.2M TALL CHILD

TIME PERIOD:

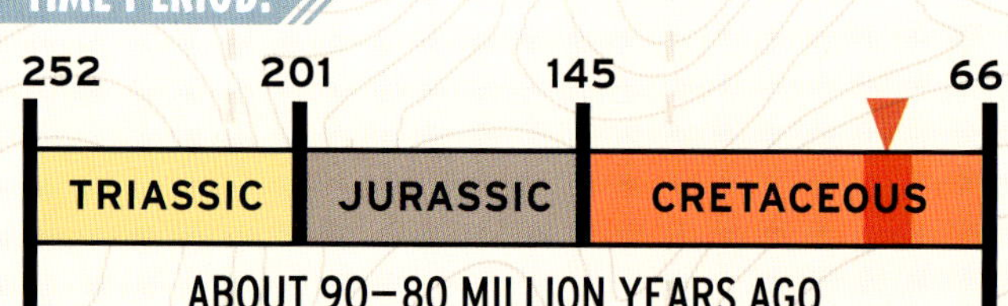

ABOUT 90–80 MILLION YEARS AGO

GASTONIA

gas-TOE-nee-ah

LOCATION:

Utah, USA

WHAT WE KNOW:

YEAR NAMED: 1998

DIET: HERBIVORE
Conifers, cycads, ginkgos

SIZE: 6m long, almost 2m high at the hips

WEIGHT: 1,500–1,900kg

FRIENDS: Other small ankylosaurs

ENEMIES: *Utahraptor*

Gastonia ('[Robert] Gaston's lizard') is a small, armoured dinosaur with large, curved spikes projecting out of its back and along both sides of its body. The tail has sideways-aiming spikes along the sides. *Gastonia* was one of the most highly ornamented of all the ankylosaurs, or tank dinosaurs. Although it has an armoured shield over the pelvis like the polacanthid ankylosaurs of Europe, it also has spiked armour, more like the nodosaurid ankylosaurs of North America.

Gastonia shares one major feature with most other later ankylosaurs. It has very short, powerful legs. This means that *Gastonia* could not outrun a predator but would stand and fight (which explains the fancy armour). Since *Gastonia* had spikes from the shoulder to the tip of the tail, plus a large shield of bone over the hips, there was no good place for a meat-eater to take a bite!

FUN FACT!

THE ORIGINAL SPECIMEN IS IN THE COLLECTIONS AT THE COLLEGE OF EASTERN UTAH IN PRICE, UTAH.

THE SPECIES NAME (*GASTONIA BURGEI*) HONOURS DON BURGE, A DINOSAUR HUNTER FROM UTAH.

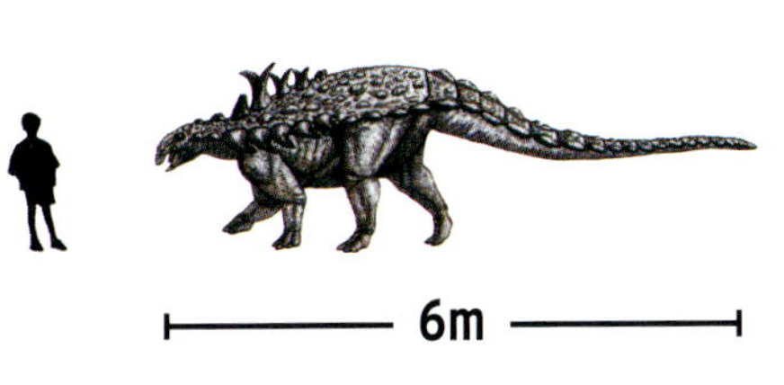

COMPARISON IS WITH A 1.2M TALL CHILD

TIME PERIOD:

252 | 201 | 145 | 66

TRIASSIC | JURASSIC | CRETACEOUS

ABOUT 130–120 MILLION YEARS AGO

GIGANOTOSAURUS

jig-a-NO-to-SOAR-us

LOCATION:

Argentina

WHAT WE KNOW:

YEAR NAMED: 1995

DIET: CARNIVORE
Titanosaurs and other sauropods

SIZE: Almost 13m long, 3.9m high at the hips

WEIGHT: About 8,000kg

FUN FACT!

A CAST OF THE SKELETON OF *GIGANOTOSAURUS* IS ON DISPLAY AT THE ACADEMY OF NATURAL SCIENCES IN PHILADELPHIA.

COMPARISON IS WITH A 1.2M TALL CHILD

TIME PERIOD:

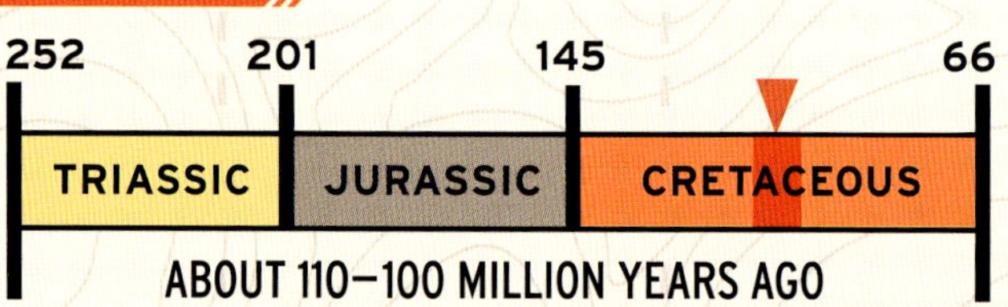

ABOUT 110–100 MILLION YEARS AGO

GIGA-NOT-O-SAURUS

Giganotosaurus might be the dinosaur whose name is most often misspelled and/or mispronounced. People often call it *Gigantosaurus* (with only one 'o') instead of the proper *Giganotosaurus*, with two.

THIS DINOSAUR IS NOT TO BE CONFUSED WITH THE *GIGANTOSAURUS*, A BRITISH LONG-NECKED SAUROPOD DINOSAUR NAMED BACK IN 1869.

Giganotosaurus ('giant southern lizard') is one of the largest known meat-eating dinosaurs ever. For many years *Tyrannosaurus* held that record (although bits and pieces of *Carcharodontosaurus* and *Spinosaurus* showed that they were as large as any individual *T. rex*). Then, in 1995, palaeontologists Rodolfo Coria and Leonardo Salgado reported the discovery of a new meat-eater at least as large as the biggest *T. rex*.

They named this dinosaur *Giganotosaurus*. The skull alone was 1.8m long! What's more, a lower jawbone was later found from an individual even bigger than the first one—with a skull perhaps 2m long. Clearly, *Giganotosaurus* was a gigantic dinosaur.

When *Giganotosaurus* was alive, the most common plant-eaters in South America were the titanosaur sauropods. While a single *Giganotosaurus* could kill a young titanosaur, it would take many *Giganotosaurus* to bring down a giant adult. At present, there is no evidence that *Giganotosaurus* hunted in groups, but a recent discovery from slightly younger rocks shows that the as-yet-unnamed descendant of *Giganotosaurus* may have lived in packs.

GORGOSAURUS

GOR-go-SOAR-us

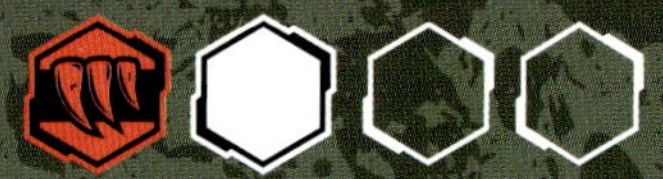

LOCATION:

Alberta, Canada

WHAT WE KNOW:

YEAR NAMED: 1914

DIET: CARNIVORE
Centrosaurus, Corythosaurus, Edmontonia, Euoplocephalus, Lambeosaurus, Styracosaurus

SIZE: Over 8.6m long, 2.8m high at the hips

WEIGHT: 2,500kg

FRIENDS: None

ENEMIES: *Daspletosaurus*

FUN FACT!

GORGOSAURUS WAS ONCE CONSIDERED A SPECIES OF *ALBERTOSAURUS*, WHICH IS REALLY A DIFFERENT (BUT CLOSELY RELATED) TYRANT DINOSAUR FROM LATER IN THE CRETACEOUS.

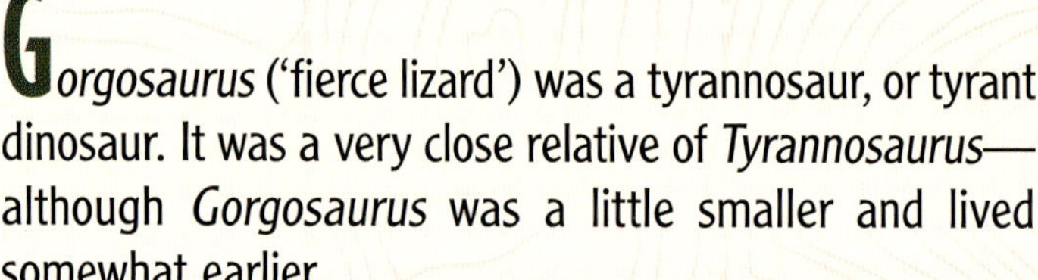

Gorgosaurus ('fierce lizard') was a tyrannosaur, or tyrant dinosaur. It was a very close relative of *Tyrannosaurus*—although *Gorgosaurus* was a little smaller and lived somewhat earlier.

The tyrant dinosaurs were very specialised meat-eaters. Their arms were extremely short, and they had only two fingers (the thumb and the index finger). The arms of *Gorgosaurus*—like those of *Tyrannosaurus*—were so short they couldn't even reach its mouth!

Tyrant dinosaurs' legs were long and slender, and their narrow, compact feet had a special shock-absorbing shape. A young *Gorgosaurus* was probably as fast as an ostrich dinosaur, and even an adult was probably faster than any of the duckbills and horned dinosaurs it hunted. Although its arms would be useless in catching prey, it could use its powerful jaws, filled with many strong teeth, to grab its victims. Tyrant dinosaurs' teeth, unlike those of most theropods, or meat-eating dinosaurs, were not shaped like blades. Instead, they were thick and round

COMPARISON IS WITH A 1.2M TALL CHILD

TIME PERIOD:

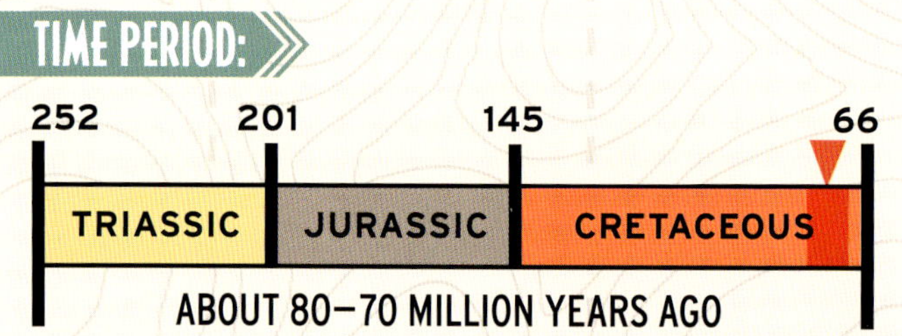

ALMOST EVERY DINOSAUR LABELED *'ALBERTOSAURUS'* IN A MUSEUM IS REALLY A *GORGOSAURUS*!

in cross-section. This meant that the teeth could be used to hold and grip tighter, and maybe even to crush bone.

When tyrant dinosaurs were around, they were the largest predators in their environment. The only meat-eater a *Gorgosaurus* had to fear was another *Gorgosaurus,* or the even larger tyrant dinosaur *Daspletosaurus,* which lived at the same time. Of course, *Gorgosaurus* would have to be careful when attacking a *Centrosaurus* or other horned dinosaur. Although these ceratopsians ate plants, they could still defend themselves with their deadly horns.

TYRANT DINOSAURS

There is some debate about whether tyrannosaurs, like *Gorgosaurus* or *Tyrannosaurus* (pictured below), killed their food as hunters or fed off carcasses as scavengers. However, both may be true! Tyrannosaurs, like many large meat eaters today, probably fed opportunistically, scavenging when they could and hunting when they had to.

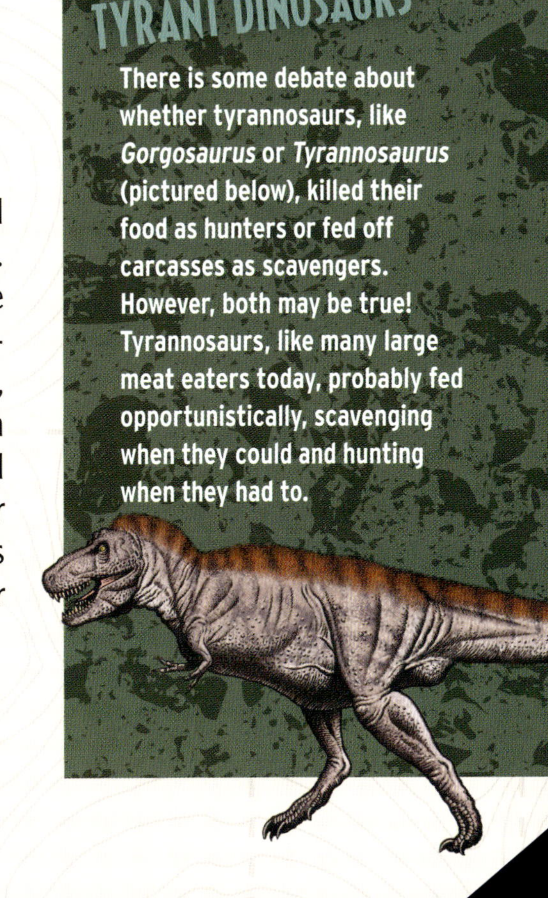

GRYPOSAURUS

GRIP-oh-SOAR-us

LOCATION:

Montana, Utah, USA; Canada

WHAT WE KNOW:

YEAR NAMED: 1914

DIET: HERBIVORE
Flowering plants like magnolias and cycads

SIZE: 8.4m long, 2.1m high at the hips

WEIGHT: 3,500kg

FUN FACT!

GRYPOSAURUS **HAD OVER 300 TEETH TO SLICE UP PLANT MATERIAL. INSIDE ITS JAW BONE, THERE WERE MANY REPLACEMENT TEETH WAITING, MEANING THIS DINOSAUR MAY HAVE CARRIED MORE THAN 800 TEETH!**

Gryposaurus ('hook-nosed lizard') is a duckbill dinosaur known from several complete skeletons and skulls. Nevertheless, its relationship with other duckbills is shrouded in mystery. In the 1850s, a partial duckbill was discovered in New Jersey. It was named *Hadrosaurus.* In 1910, another, more complete duckbill was found in New Mexico. It was named *Kritosaurus.* Although *Hadrosaurus* lacked a skull, the body looked just like *Kritosaurus.* Then in 1914, the first complete duckbill was found in Alberta, Canada. It had an excellent skull and was named *Gryposaurus.*

Some scientists considered *Gryposaurus* and *Kritosaurus* to be the same creature. Priority went to the name *Kritosaurus* because it was named first.

Enter Jack Horner in the early 1990s. Horner believed that only *Gryposaurus* was complete enough to have a valid name, and he confined the name *Kritosaurus* to the skeleton in New Mexico.

EVIDENCE SUGGESTS HADROSAURS NESTED IN COLONIES AND MAY HAVE TAKEN CARE OF THEIR YOUNG.

COMPARISON IS WITH A 1.2M TALL CHILD

TIME PERIOD:

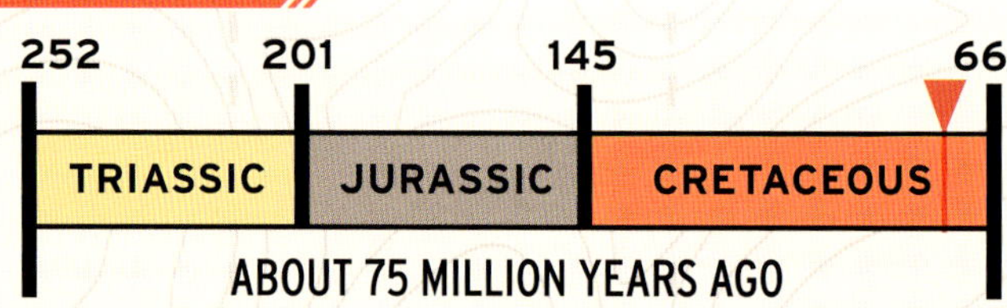

ABOUT 75 MILLION YEARS AGO

HADROSAURUS

HAD-ro-SOAR-us

LOCATION:

New Jersey, USA

WHAT WE KNOW:

YEAR NAMED: 1854

DIET: HERBIVORE
Flowering plants, conifers, cycads, ginkgos

SIZE: 8m long, about 2m high at the hips

WEIGHT: 3,000kg

FRIENDS: Other duckbills and ceratopsians, or horned dinosaurs

ENEMIES: Theropods, or meat-eaters, of any size

FUN FACT!

SCIENTISTS FIRST THOUGHT THAT *HADROSAURUS* LEANED ON ITS TAIL LIKE A KANGAROO!

COMPARISON IS WITH A 1.2M TALL CHILD

Hadrosaurus ('sturdy lizard') was—in the 1860s—the first dinosaur skeleton to be exhibited in North America. Its skeleton proved the theory that some dinosaurs walked on two legs, and not on all fours, as scientists of the time had thought. This dinosaur is poorly known because, to date, no skull has ever been found for it and no new skeletons have been found.

As there is no skull for reference, illustrators must base their drawings on the latest information from the study of hadrosaurs. At one time, scientists believed they had found the skull of *Hadrosaurus,* but it turned out to be the skull of another duckbill dinosaur, its closest relative, called *Gryposaurus.*

THE ONLY *HADROSAURUS* SPECIMEN ON EXHIBIT IN THE WORLD IS AT THE ACADEMY OF NATURAL SCIENCES IN PHILADELPHIA.

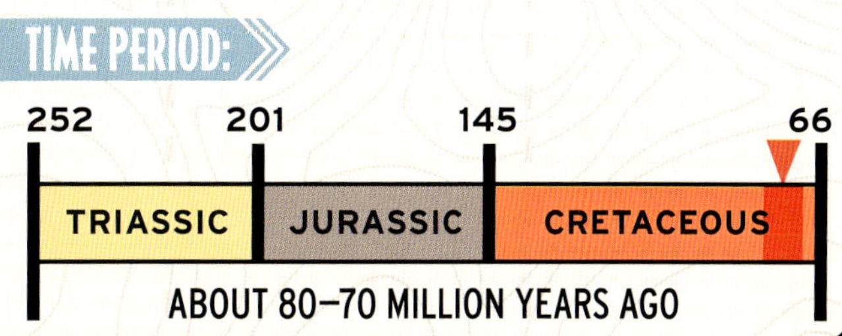

HERRERASAURUS

he-RARE-a-SOAR-us

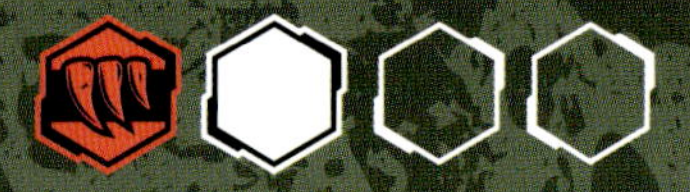

LOCATION:

Argentina

WHAT WE KNOW:

YEAR NAMED: 1963

DIET: CARNIVORE
Eoraptor and prosauropods, and primitive bird-hipped dinosaurs

SIZE: Almost 3.9m long, 1.1m high at the hips

WEIGHT: 210kg

FRIENDS: None

ENEMIES: *Saurosuchus* (a giant crocodile relative)

FUN FACT!

BEFORE THE FIRST SKULL WAS DISCOVERED IN 1988, *HERRERASAURUS* WAS THOUGHT TO BE A PROSAUROPOD, AN EARLY FORM OF THE GIANT LONG-NECKED PLANT-EATERS, LIKE *PLATEOSAURUS*.

3.9m

COMPARISON IS WITH A 1.2M TALL CHILD

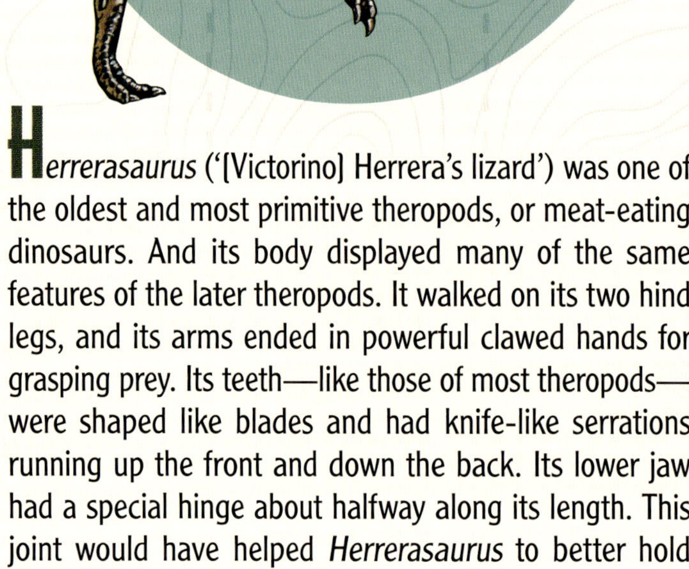

Herrerasaurus ('[Victorino] Herrera's lizard') was one of the oldest and most primitive theropods, or meat-eating dinosaurs. And its body displayed many of the same features of the later theropods. It walked on its two hind legs, and its arms ended in powerful clawed hands for grasping prey. Its teeth—like those of most theropods—were shaped like blades and had knife-like serrations running up the front and down the back. Its lower jaw had a special hinge about halfway along its length. This joint would have helped *Herrerasaurus* to better hold on to struggling victims. Many later theropods also had this hinge.

Although *Herrerasaurus* shared the basic body design of future rulers of the Earth (like *Allosaurus, Giganotosaurus,* and *Tyrannosaurus),* it lived at a time when dinosaurs were not the most powerful predators. *Herrerasaurus* would have had to run away from the much larger *Saurosuchus,* a giant land-dwelling crocodile relative, which was the largest meat-eater in Argentina during the beginning of the Age of Dinosaurs.

ONE OF THE MOST COMPLETE MOUNTED SKELETONS OF *HERRERASAURUS* CAN BE SEEN AT THE FIELD MUSEUM OF NATURAL HISTORY IN CHICAGO.

TIME PERIOD:

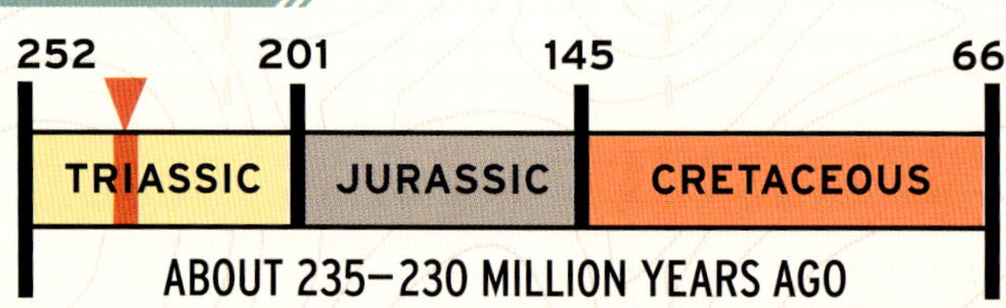

HESPERORNIS

HES-pe-ROAR-nis

LOCATION:

Kansas, USA; Canada

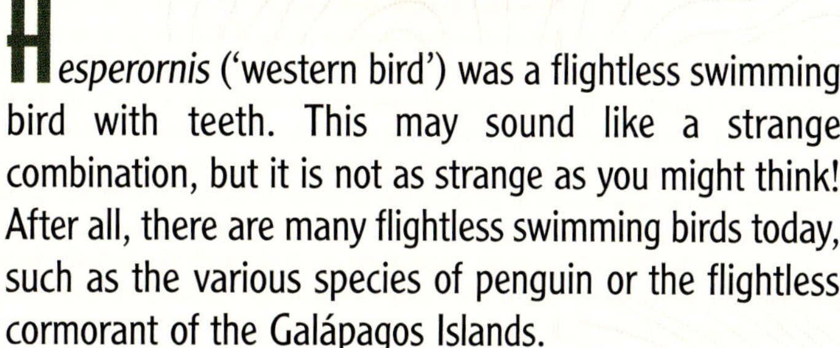

WHAT WE KNOW:

YEAR NAMED: 1872

DIET: CARNIVORE
Fish, squid

SIZE: About 1.5m long

WEIGHT: About 60kg

Hesperornis ('western bird') was a flightless swimming bird with teeth. This may sound like a strange combination, but it is not as strange as you might think! After all, there are many flightless swimming birds today, such as the various species of penguin or the flightless cormorant of the Galápagos Islands.

Birds and raptors are closely related to each other, and both types of dinosaurs diverged from a common ancestor during the Jurassic. Birds evolved the ability to fly, and most birds of the Cretaceous were fliers. The ancestors of *Hesperornis,* however, became swimmers that chased fish. As time went by, the wings of this group of birds became shorter and shorter, until nothing remained of each wing but a simple spike. *Hesperornis* swam by using its feet to push itself quickly through the water, chasing after fish and squid. Its legs were so far back on its body that it probably had problems moving on land. However, like modern penguins, *Hesperornis* almost certainly came up onto land to lay its eggs.

FUN FACT!

DURING THE LATE CRETACEOUS, MOST OF THE MIDDLE OF NORTH AMERICA WAS COVERED BY A SHALLOW TROPICAL SEA. YOU COULD HAVE TAKEN A BOAT AND SAILED FROM THE GULF OF MEXICO TO THE ARCTIC OCEAN OVER LANDS THAT ARE NOW PRAIRIES!

BECAUSE BIRDS ARE NOW CLASSIFIED AS A KIND OF DINOSAUR, *HESPERORNIS* IS TECHNICALLY A SWIMMING DINOSAUR.

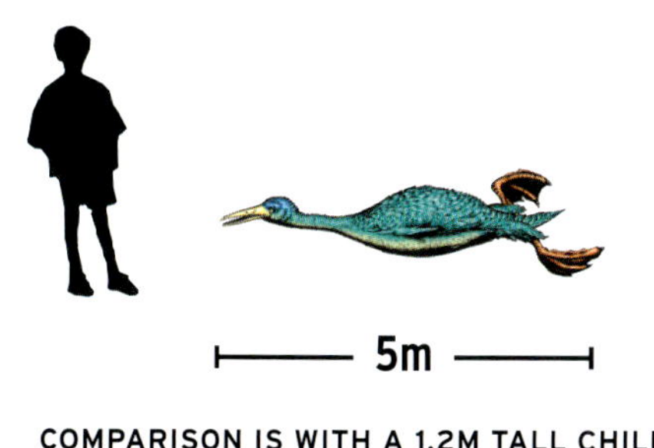

COMPARISON IS WITH A 1.2M TALL CHILD

TIME PERIOD:

252 | 201 | 145 | 66

TRIASSIC | JURASSIC | CRETACEOUS

ABOUT 85–80 MILLION YEARS AGO

HETERODONTOSAURUS

HET-eh-ro-DON-toe-SOAR-us

LOCATION:

Cape Province, South Africa

WHAT WE KNOW:

YEAR NAMED: 1962

DIET: OMNIVORE
Conifers, cycads, ginkgos, possibly insects

SIZE: Just over 1m long, less than 50cm high at the hips

WEIGHT: 45kg

FRIENDS: Other early ornithopods

ENEMIES: Juvenile theropods, crocodiles

Heterodontosaurus ('different-tooth lizard') was a small, fast dinosaur with strong, grasping hands, long arms and a powerful bite. These features are, for the most part, unnecessary in a plant-eater. It does not take speed, agility, and dexterity to overpower a leaf! *Heterodontosaurus's* most notable feature, however, is the set of 'fangs' at the front of its mouth. It is quite unusual for a plant-eating dinosaur to have teeth like this, which you'd normally expect in a meat-eater.

We know of only one other Early Jurassic group of dinosaurs—the prosauropods—where some of its members had teeth structurally intermediate between those of meat-eaters and of plant-eaters. The same may be true here. *Heterodontosaurus* and prosauropods both might be examples of the transition from meat-eater to plant-eater.

ITS CLOSE RELATIVE, *TIANYULONG*, WAS THE FIRST BIRD-HIPPED DINOSAUR FOUND WITH BODY FUZZ.

FUN FACT!

THIS SMALL DINOSAUR COULD HAVE OUTRUN A TEN-YEAR-OLD HUMAN.

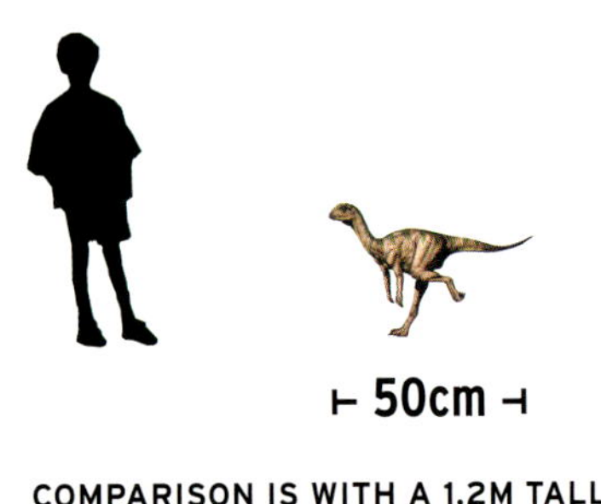

COMPARISON IS WITH A 1.2M TALL CHILD

TIME PERIOD:

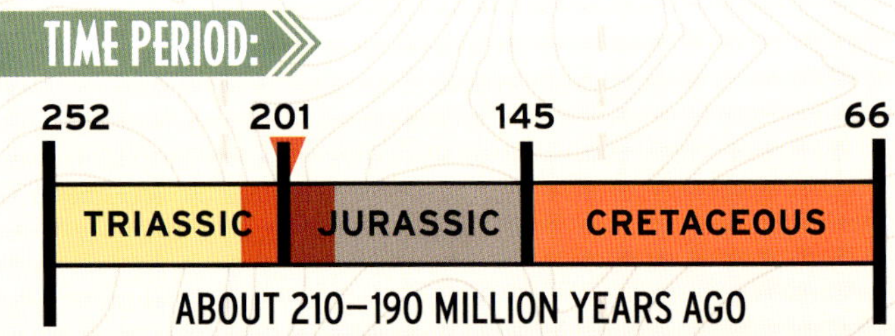

ABOUT 210–190 MILLION YEARS AGO

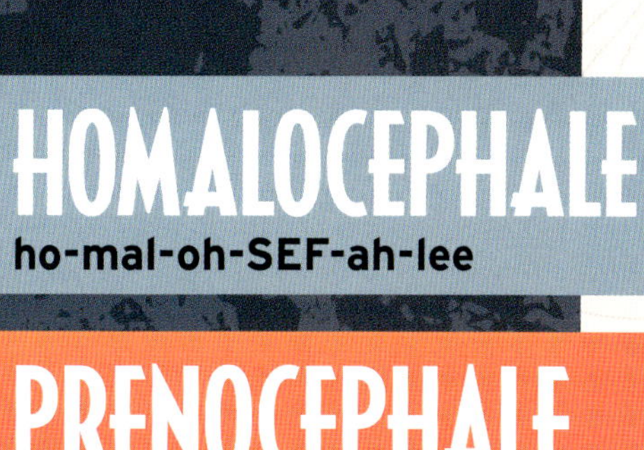

HOMALOCEPHALE

ho-mal-oh-SEF-ah-lee

PRENOCEPHALE

PREEN-oh-SEF-ah-lee

LOCATION:

Mongolia

WHAT WE KNOW:

YEAR NAMED: 1974

DIET: HERBIVORE
Plants

SIZE: About 1.5m long, 90cm high at the hips

WEIGHT: 159kg

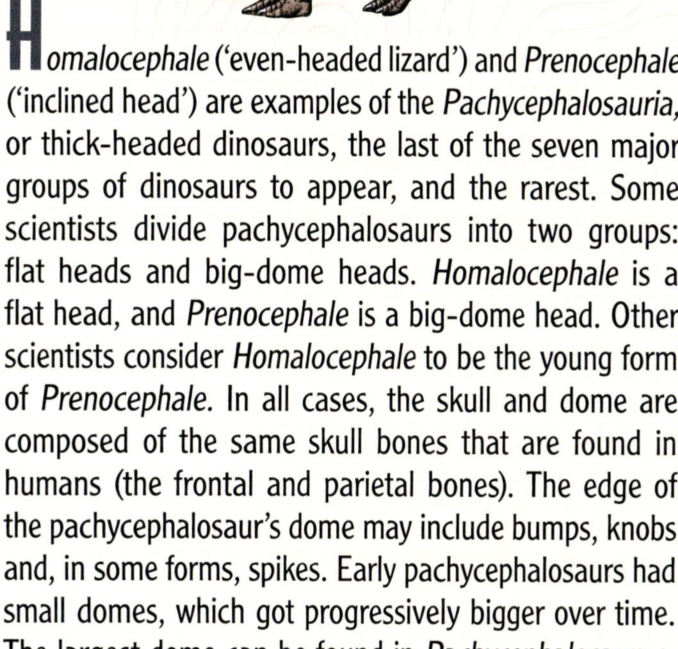

Homalocephale ('even-headed lizard') and *Prenocephale* ('inclined head') are examples of the *Pachycephalosauria,* or thick-headed dinosaurs, the last of the seven major groups of dinosaurs to appear, and the rarest. Some scientists divide pachycephalosaurs into two groups: flat heads and big-dome heads. *Homalocephale* is a flat head, and *Prenocephale* is a big-dome head. Other scientists consider *Homalocephale* to be the young form of *Prenocephale.* In all cases, the skull and dome are composed of the same skull bones that are found in humans (the frontal and parietal bones). The edge of the pachycephalosaur's dome may include bumps, knobs and, in some forms, spikes. Early pachycephalosaurs had small domes, which got progressively bigger over time. The largest dome can be found in *Pachycephalosaurus.*

Both dinosaurs are known from unusually complete skeletons. They were found in Mongolia—in an area supposedly barren of fossils!

FUN FACT!

YOU CAN READ AN ACCOUNT OF THE AMAZING EXPEDITION THAT UNCOVERED THE FOSSILS OF THESE DINOSAURS IN *HUNTING FOR DINOSAURS* BY ZOFIA KIELAN-JAWOROWSKA.

SOME PALAEONTOLOGISTS THINK HOMALOCEPHALE IS JUST A YOUNG *PRENOCEPHALE.*

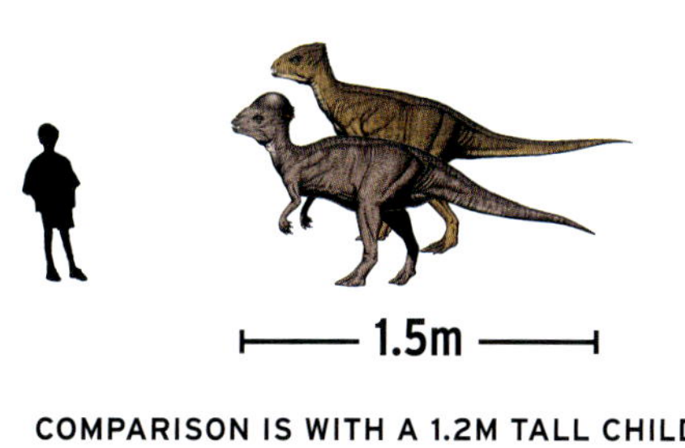

COMPARISON IS WITH A 1.2M TALL CHILD

TIME PERIOD:

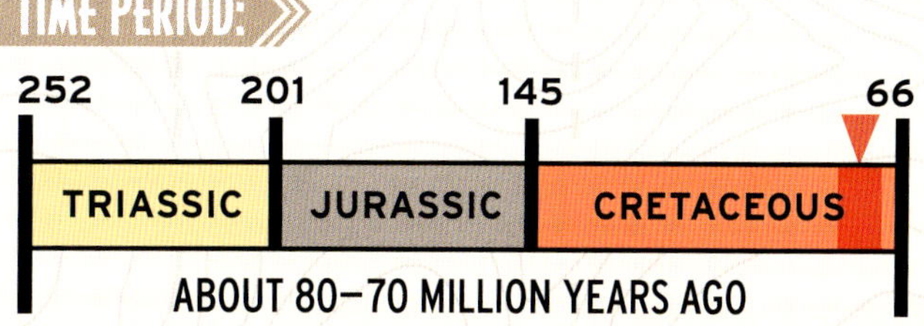

ABOUT 80–70 MILLION YEARS AGO

IGUANODON

ih-GWAHN-oh-don

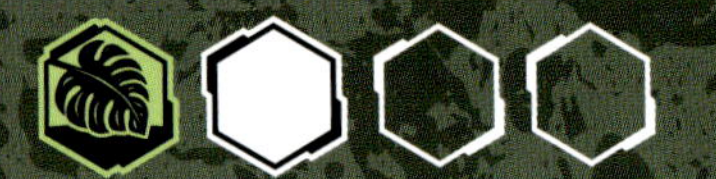

LOCATION:

Western Europe; Belgium; England

WHAT WE KNOW:

YEAR NAMED: 1825

DIET: HERBIVORE
Conifers, cycads, ginkgos

SIZE: About 11m long, 2.7m high at the hips

WEIGHT: 5,000kg

Iguanodon ('iguana tooth') was the first really huge ornithopod, or two-legged plant-eating dinosaur. The arms were longer than an adult human's, and all the bones of the skeleton were thick. This was a very powerful dinosaur that could defend itself quite well. Its massive arms ended in large hands that carried 'thumb spikes'. These were the perfect weapons to put out the eye of an attacking theropod.

Iguanodon is one of the original three members of the group Dinosauria. When Richard Owen coined the word 'dinosaur' in 1842, he defined it to mean 'fearfully great, a lizard'. He based the name on three dinosaurs—*Megalosaurus, Iguanodon* and *Hylaeosaurus.* The story of the discovery and naming of *Iguanodon* has been the subject of several books. No other two-footed plant-eater is as historically famous. One reason for this was a spectacular find in Bernissart, Belgium, in 1878. Workers in a coal mine found over a dozen well-preserved skeletons at a depth of over 300m.

FUN FACT!

THE OWNERS OF THE COAL MINE IN BELGIUM SHUT IT DOWN FOR TWO YEARS SO THAT SCIENTISTS COULD EXCAVATE THE BONES!

MOST *IGUANODON* SKELETONS ARE EXHIBITED IN THE 'OLD STYLE', WITH THE TAIL DRAGGING ON THE GROUND. WE NOW KNOW THAT DINOSAURS DID NOT DRAG THEIR TAILS.

COMPARISON IS WITH A 1.2M TALL CHILD

TIME PERIOD:

252	201	145	66
TRIASSIC	JURASSIC	CRETACEOUS	

ABOUT 135–120 MILLION YEARS AGO

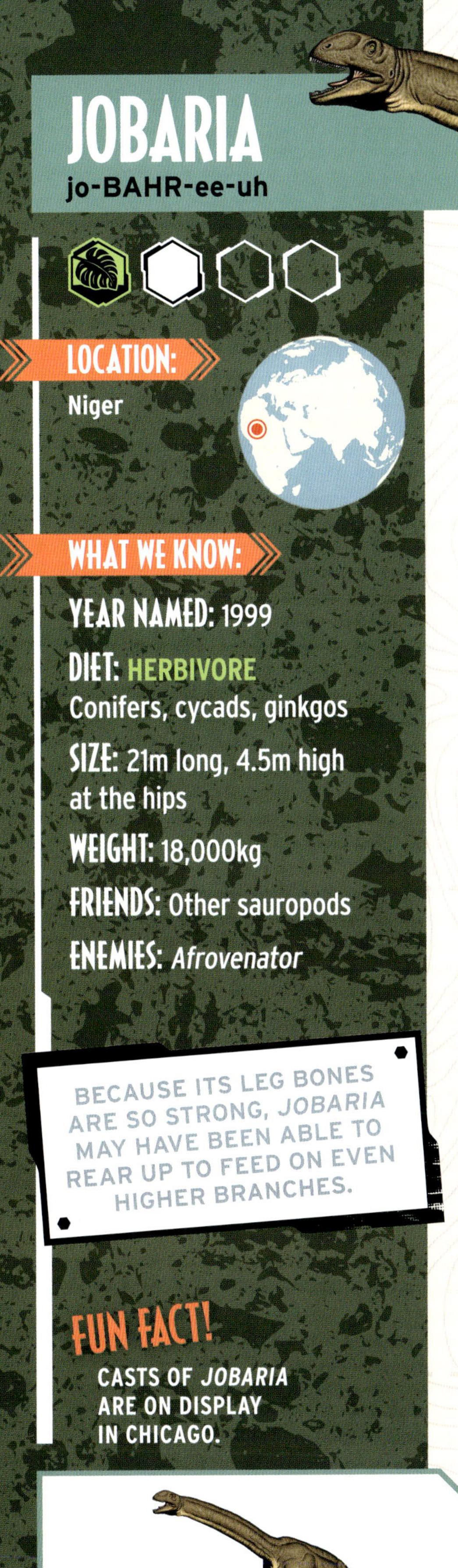

JOBARIA

jo-BAHR-ee-uh

LOCATION:

Niger

WHAT WE KNOW:

YEAR NAMED: 1999

DIET: HERBIVORE
Conifers, cycads, ginkgos

SIZE: 21m long, 4.5m high at the hips

WEIGHT: 18,000kg

FRIENDS: Other sauropods

ENEMIES: *Afrovenator*

BECAUSE ITS LEG BONES ARE SO STRONG, *JOBARIA* MAY HAVE BEEN ABLE TO REAR UP TO FEED ON EVEN HIGHER BRANCHES.

FUN FACT!

CASTS OF *JOBARIA* ARE ON DISPLAY IN CHICAGO.

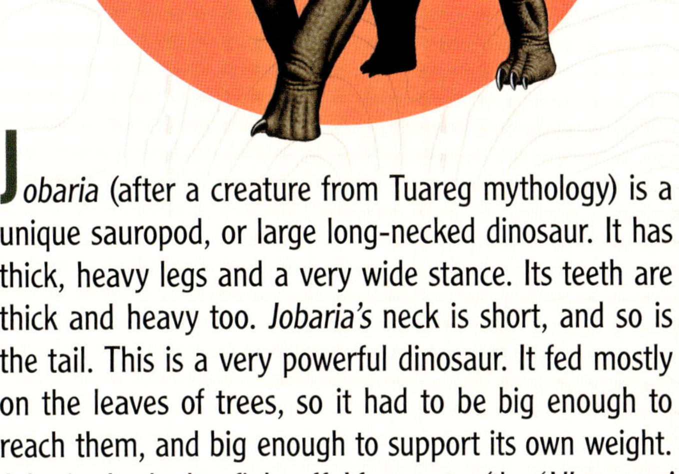

Jobaria (after a creature from Tuareg mythology) is a unique sauropod, or large long-necked dinosaur. It has thick, heavy legs and a very wide stance. Its teeth are thick and heavy too. *Jobaria's* neck is short, and so is the tail. This is a very powerful dinosaur. It fed mostly on the leaves of trees, so it had to be big enough to reach them, and big enough to support its own weight. *Jobaria* also had to fight off *Afrovenator* (the *'Allosaurus'* of this time) with its thumb claw!

Jobaria was found in 1997 but not named until 1999. Skeletons of several other specimens of *Jobaria* were unearthed at the same time, so it took years for the material to be prepared. Without the help of laboratory technicians who prepare the bones, scientists would need decades to describe and prepare new finds by themselves.

Imagine finding a dinosaur in the field. It has over 200 bones, many up to 1.8m long and weighing several hundred pounds. You are working in a desert. The daily temperature is over 37 degrees, and the wind blasts sand in your face, clothes and food. The nearest English-speaking country is over 1,600km away! That's what Paul Sereno and his University of Chicago crew had to deal with while digging in the Sahara Desert for *Jobaria*.

COMPARISON IS WITH A 1.2M TALL CHILD

TIME PERIOD:

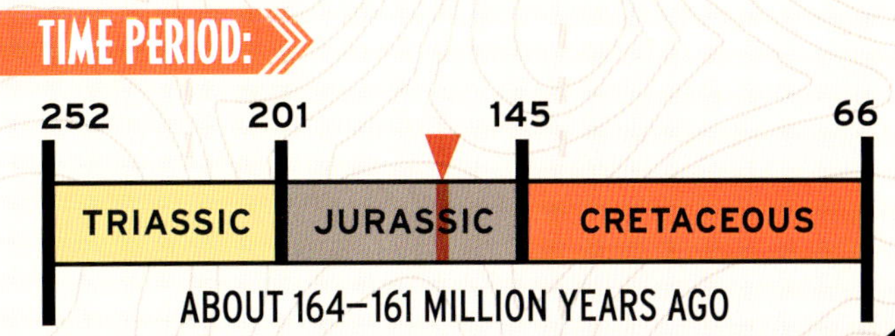

ABOUT 164–161 MILLION YEARS AGO

KENTROSAURUS

KEN-tro-SOAR-us

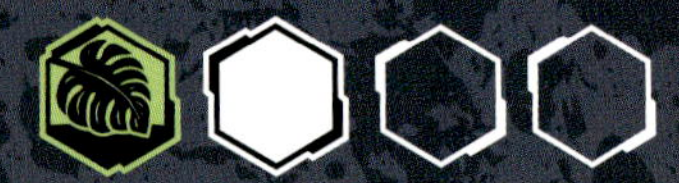

LOCATION:

Tanzania

WHAT WE KNOW:

YEAR NAMED: 1915

DIET: HERBIVORE
Conifers, cycads, ginkgos

SIZE: 5.5m long, 1.5m high at the hips

WEIGHT: 1,000kg

FRIENDS: *Dicraeosaurus, Dryosaurus, Tornieria*

ENEMIES: *Elaphrosaurus, Veterupristisaurus*

Kentrosaurus ('spiked lizard') is well named. A member of the Stegosauria, it has large spikes from the middle of its back down to the base of its tail. When compared to the North American *Stegosaurus, Kentrosaurus* has smaller plates. It appears that spikes evolved first in the *Stegosauria,* then plates developed from the spikes.

The bases of *Kentrosaurus's* tail spikes are large and rounded, showing that they were solidly planted into the skin. This means that the spikes could not be waved independently in the direction of an attacker. There is also another shoulder spike that has been restored at times as facing both forwards and backwards. A backwards-facing spike is more logical, however. With a forward-facing spike, *Kentrosaurus* might have impaled itself in the neck!

THE STEGOSAURS ARE THE SECOND RAREST MAJOR GROUP OF DINOSAURS (THE FIRST ARE THE PACHYCEPHALOSAURS).

FUN FACT!

THE HUMBOLDT MUSEUM IN GERMANY HAS THE ONLY MOUNTED *KENTROSAURUS* SKELETON ON DISPLAY.

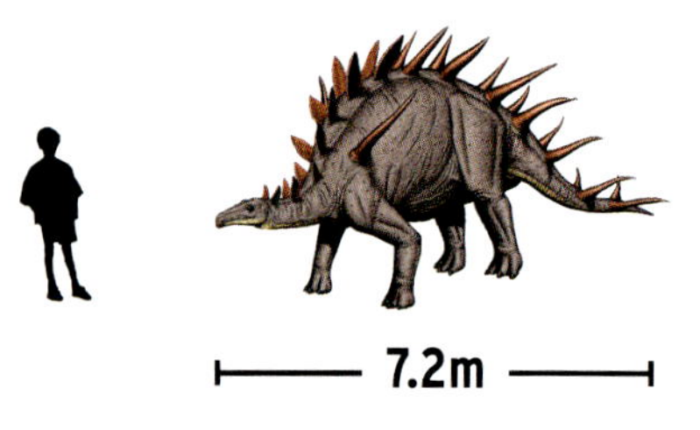

COMPARISON IS WITH A 1.2M TALL CHILD

TIME PERIOD:

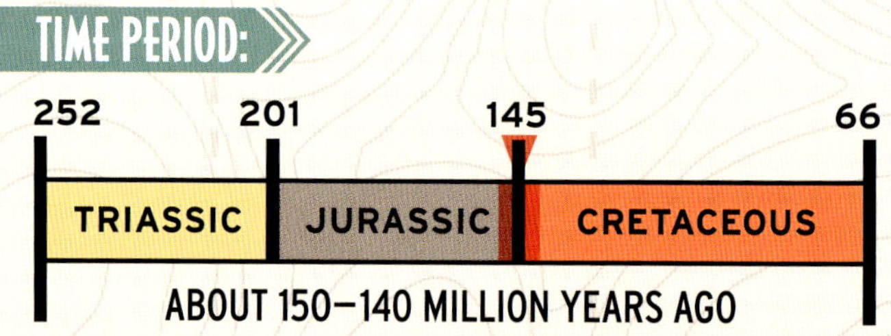

LEPTOCERATOPS

LEP-to-SAIR-ah-tops

LOCATION:

Wyoming, USA; Alberta, Canada

WHAT WE KNOW:

YEAR NAMED: 1914

DIET: HERBIVORE
Ground cover such as cycads and flowering plants

SIZE: 2m long, 75cm high at the hips

WEIGHT: 68kg

FRIENDS: *Edmontosaurus, Thescelosaurus*

ENEMIES: *Troodon,* juvenile tyrannosaurids

FUN FACT!

THE BEST DISPLAY OF *LEPTOCERATOPS* FOSSILS IS AT THE MUSEUM OF NATURE IN OTTAWA, CANADA.

Leptoceratops ('slender horned face') had a head that was relatively large for its stocky body. This may mean that it never grew big, or that we have only found fossils of juveniles. *Leptoceratops* had only one defence, its parrot-like beak. The jaws of horned dinosaurs like *Leptoceratops* were the most powerful for their size of any plant-eater's. They had enough power, for example, to break the arm of any similar-sized theropod.

Leptoceratops is most similar to the earlier *Psittacosaurus* and *Protoceratops.* But *Leptoceratops* lived over 30 million years later, at the very end of the Age of Dinosaurs in North America. There are two possible explanations for this. The first is that *Leptoceratops,* or its ancestors, immigrated across the land bridge between Asia and North America at the end of the Cretaceous, but their fossils have so far been found only in North America. The second is that they were an early group of immigrants that survived only in North America, while their Asian ancestors went extinct.

LEPTOCERATOPS WAS NAMED BY BARNUM BROWN, THE SAME MAN WHO FOUND TYRANNOSAURUS REX.

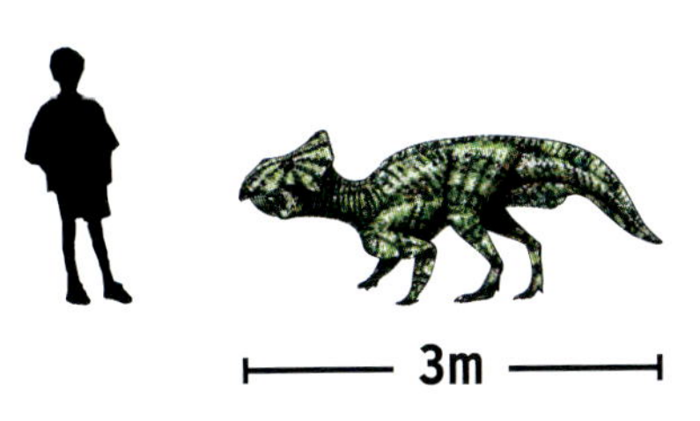

COMPARISON IS WITH A 1.2M TALL CHILD

TIME PERIOD:

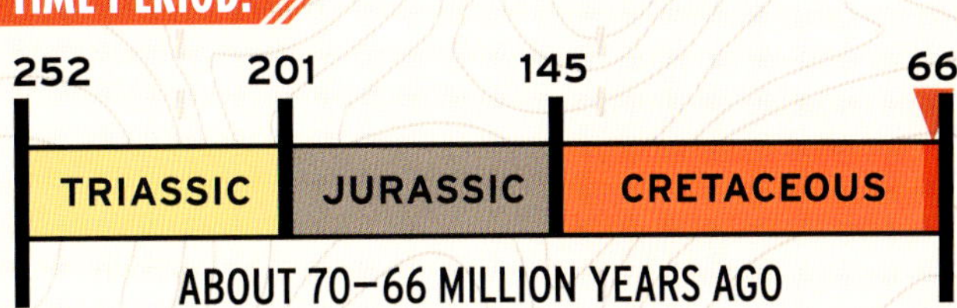

MAJUNGASAURUS

mah-JOONG-gah-SOAR-us

LOCATION:

Madagascar

WHAT WE KNOW:

YEAR NAMED: 1979

DIET: CARNIVORE
Titanosaurs

SIZE: About 8m long, 2.4m high at the hips

WEIGHT: About 1,900kg

FRIENDS: Unknown

ENEMIES: Unknown

FUN FACT!

THE FIRST PIECES OF *MAJUNGASAURUS* FOUND—SOME TEETH AND A JAWBONE—WERE THOUGHT TO BE FROM *MEGALOSAURUS.*

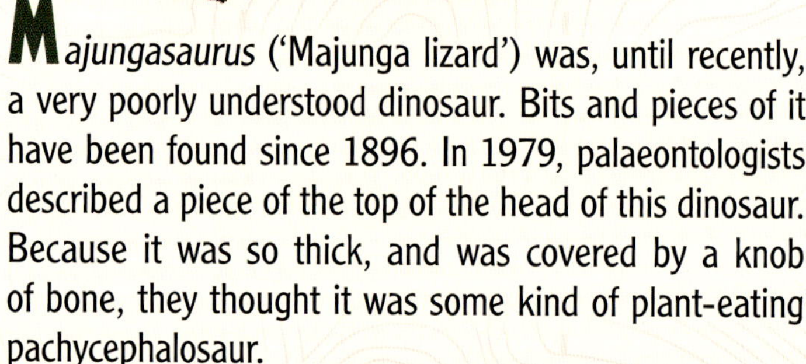

Majungasaurus ('Majunga lizard') was, until recently, a very poorly understood dinosaur. Bits and pieces of it have been found since 1896. In 1979, palaeontologists described a piece of the top of the head of this dinosaur. Because it was so thick, and was covered by a knob of bone, they thought it was some kind of plant-eating pachycephalosaur.

In 1996, an expedition in Madagascar found the first good *Majungasaurus* skull. It turned out that the thick dome and knob belonged not to a plant-eating pachycephalosaur but to a meat-eater! In fact, *Majungasaurus* was a close relative to *Abelisaurus* and *Carnotaurus* (who also had thick skull roofs, although not as thick as that of *Majungasaurus*).

Like *Carnotaurus, Majungasaurus* had a fairly short skull with small teeth. It probably could not kill extremely large animals but could easily hunt down young ones. Also, like most theropods or meat-eating dinosaurs, *Majungasaurus* would almost certainly have scavenged a dinosaur corpse if it found one.

FOR MOST OF THE MESOZOIC, WHAT IS NOW THE ISLAND OF MADAGASCAR WAS CONNECTED TO INDIA.

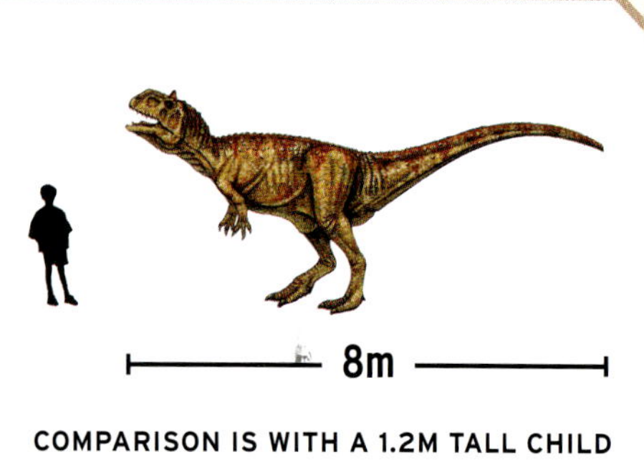

COMPARISON IS WITH A 1.2M TALL CHILD

TIME PERIOD:

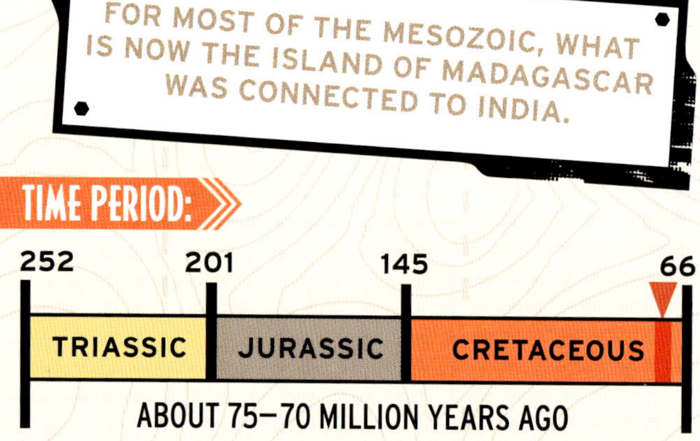

ABOUT 75–70 MILLION YEARS AGO

MAMENCHISAURUS

mah-MEN-chee-SOAR-us

LOCATION:

China

WHAT WE KNOW:

YEAR NAMED: 1954

DIET: HERBIVORE
Conifers, cycads, ginkgos

SIZE: About 24m long, 4.5m high at the hips

WEIGHT: 20,000kg

FRIENDS: *Omeisaurus, Tuojiangosaurus, Chungkingosaurus*

ENEMIES: *Szechuanosaurus, Yangchuanosaurus*

Mamenchisaurus ('lizard from Mamen's Brook') is basically a giant neck attached to a small body. The neck is about 12m long, and the body is about the same length! The purpose of this short, wide body is to act as a stable, heavy base to anchor the neck. At the end of the neck is a short head with thick teeth. Its length allowed *Mamenchisaurus* to eat the leafy parts at the tops of some Jurassic trees. By doing so, it did not have to compete with its own young, who had to eat plants closer to the ground.

Functionally, this dinosaur could be called a 'plant vacuum'. Its super-long neck allowed it to suck up hundreds of kilograms of leaves from treetops. Structurally, the neck represents the pinnacle of animal engineering. The vertebrae have hollow portions where there is little internal stress on the bones. This lightens the bones and makes them stronger. Struts and braces give added strength for load bearing. On top of the neck vertebrae are split spines that form a V-shaped trough. Inside this trough lies a series of ligaments that function like the cables on suspension bridges, holding up the neck.

FUN FACT!

MAMENCHISAURUS HAD 19 NECK BONES, COMPARED TO THE 9 OR 10 NECK BONES OF A TYPICAL DINOSAUR.

THIS DINOSAUR HAD THE LONGEST NECK IN THE HISTORY OF EARTH.

COMPARISON IS WITH A 1.2M TALL CHILD

TIME PERIOD:

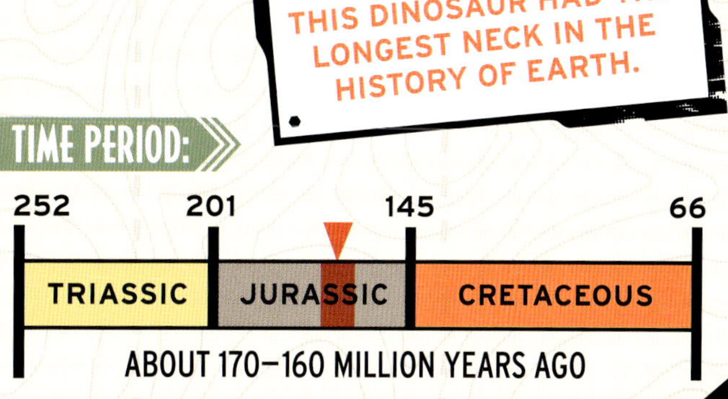

ABOUT 170–160 MILLION YEARS AGO

MASSOSPONDYLUS

mas-oh-SPON-di-lus

LOCATION:

South Africa; Zimbabwe

WHAT WE KNOW:

YEAR NAMED: 1854

DIET: HERBIVORE
Conifers, cycads, ginkgos

SIZE: About 5.7m long, 1.8m high at the hips

WEIGHT: 1,500kg

FRIENDS: *Heterodontosaurus, Lycorhinus*

ENEMIES: *Syntarsus*

Massospondylus ('bulky vertebra') is a long, sleek plant-eating dinosaur with a huge claw on each hand. Theropods during the Early Jurassic had not yet reached 'super size' (like *Allosaurus),* so a claw of this type would make an excellent weapon. Plants take a lot more energy to digest than meat, so *Massospondylus* has a wider pelvis and a larger set of guts in order to process them properly. The neck is longer to get at more food higher up in the trees. Dinosaurs were the first four-legged ground dwellers to be able to feed higher off the ground than sprawling animals. Being able to get at this new food source allowed prosauropods (such as *Massospondylus),* and then sauropods, to become the dominant plant-eaters for the next 50 million years.

For a long time, prosauropods were considered to be the ancestors of true sauropods because they look like smaller versions of the true sauropods. But there are some problems with this theory. Their foot anatomy is different enough from that of true sauropods to suggest that they are just a side branch that died out.

FUN FACT!

MASSOSPONDYLUS COULD BE THE FIRST DINOSAUR TO CLAIM THE NICKNAME 'CLAWS'. THE FIRST MEAT-EATERS TO HAVE A CLAW THAT SIZE DID NOT APPEAR UNTIL TENS OF MILLIONS OF YEARS LATER.

ONLY THE MEAT-EATING THEROPODS HAD BIGGER CLAWS THAN PROSAUROPODS.

5.7m

COMPARISON IS WITH A 1.2M TALL CHILD

TIME PERIOD:

252	201	145	66
TRIASSIC	JURASSIC	CRETACEOUS	

ABOUT 200–183 MILLION YEARS AGO

MEGALOSAURUS

MEG-ah-lo-SOAR-us

LOCATION:
England

WHAT WE KNOW:

YEAR NAMED: 1824

DIET: CARNIVORE
Sauropods, stegosaurs

SIZE: About 7.5m long, 1.9m high at the hips

WEIGHT: 1,100kg

Megalosaurus ('giant lizard') was the first Mesozoic dinosaur to be named. For centuries, fragments of meat-eating dinosaurs had been found, but scientists thought these came from giant human beings (!) or elephants.

Then around 1815, Reverend William Buckland, a scientist at the University of Oxford, came across the remains of a jawbone with teeth, leg bones and other parts of a skeleton. The teeth reminded Buckland of those of the monitor lizards, meat-eating lizards of the modern world. But these teeth and bones came from a reptile far larger than any monitor lizard!

In 1824, this new creature was given the name *Megalosaurus.* Buckland did not call his creature a dinosaur. That word would not be invented until 1842.

No complete *Megalosaurus* skeleton has yet been found. However, we can compare the bones we have found to more complete theropods and see that *Megalosaurus* was a two-legged predator with short but powerful arms. It seems to have been the largest meat-eater on land in Europe during the Middle Jurassic Period.

FUN FACT!

IN THE EARLY DAYS OF PALAEONTOLOGY, ANY MEAT-EATING DINOSAUR FOSSILS WERE CONSIDERED TO COME FROM *MEGALOSAURUS;* HOWEVER, AS MORE AND BETTER SKELETONS WERE FOUND, SCIENTISTS REALISED HOW DIVERSE THE MEAT-EATING DINOSAURS TRULY WERE.

COMPARISON IS WITH A 1.2M TALL CHILD

TIME PERIOD:

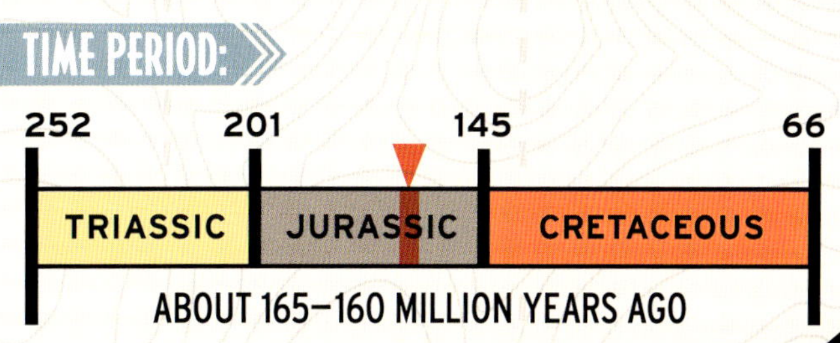

ABOUT 165–160 MILLION YEARS AGO

METRIACANTHOSAURUS

met-ree-ah-KAN-tho-SOAR-us

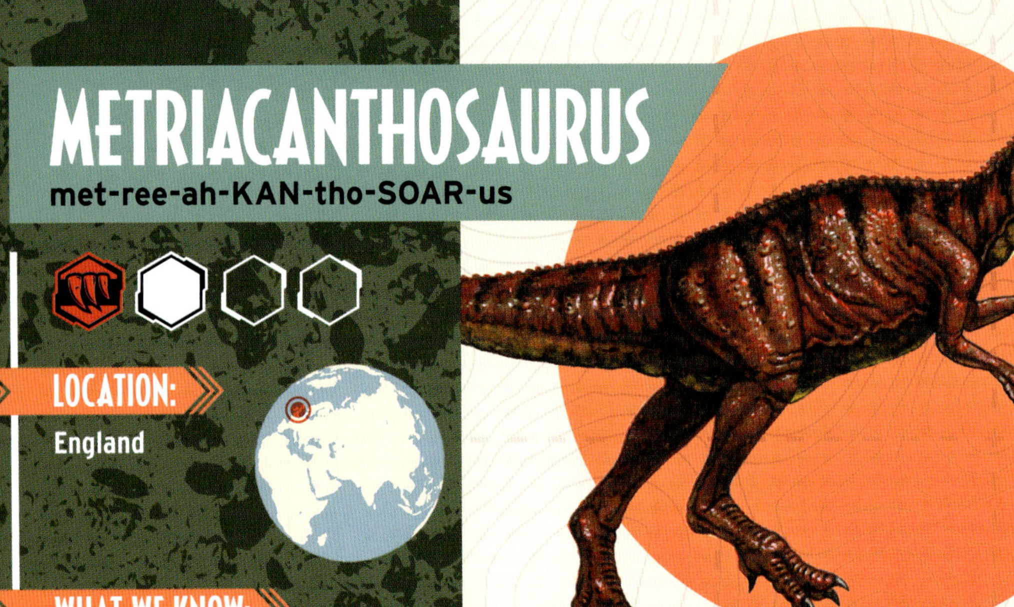

LOCATION:

England

WHAT WE KNOW:

YEAR NAMED: 1964

DIET: CARNIVORE
Sauropods, stegosaurs

SIZE: Perhaps 7m long, almost 1.8m high at the hips

WEIGHT: 1,000kg

FUN FACT!

METRIACANTHOSAURUS GETS ITS NAME FROM ITS BACKBONES, WHICH HAVE SPINES ON TOP THAT ARE TALLER THAN IN MANY MEAT-EATERS (SUCH AS *ALLOSAURUS* OR *TYRANNOSAURUS*) BUT MUCH SMALLER THAN THOSE OF *SPINOSAURUS*.

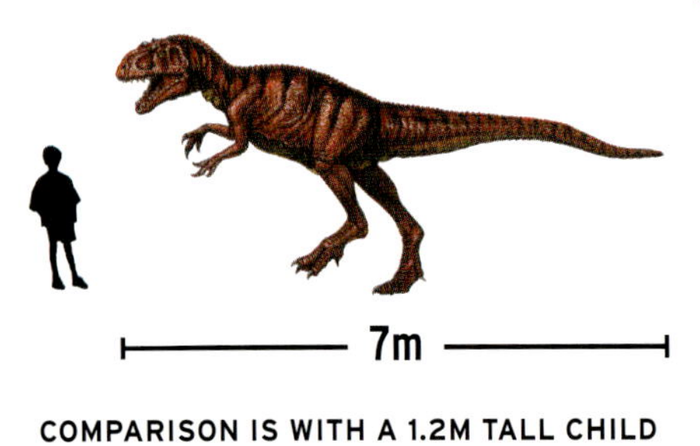

COMPARISON IS WITH A 1.2M TALL CHILD

Metriacanthosaurus ('moderate spine lizard') is one of the many dinosaurs that palaeontologists would like to know more about. In 1923, the great German palaeontologist Friedrich von Huene wrote a scientific paper describing all the theropod (or meat-eating) dinosaur fossils from the Jurassic and Cretaceous Periods of Europe. In his study, he examined a partial skeleton—an incomplete hip, a leg bone and part of the backbone. He named it a new species of *Megalosaurus*. In 1964, however, scientist Alick Walker decided that these bones were too different from those of *Megalosaurus* and named the dinosaur *Metriacanthosaurus*.

Because so little is known about this dinosaur, any pictures of it or speculation on its habits are based on comparisons with meat-eating dinosaurs of which we have more complete skeletons. What is known is that this dinosaur was a theropod distinct from all the others. Perhaps someday more complete remains of this dinosaur will be found.

MANY DINOSAURS ARE KNOWN FROM ONLY ONE VERY INCOMPLETE FOSSIL, LIKE *METRIACANTHOSAURUS*.

TIME PERIOD:

252 | 201 | 145 | 66

TRIASSIC | JURASSIC | CRETACEOUS

ABOUT 160–150 MILLION YEARS AGO

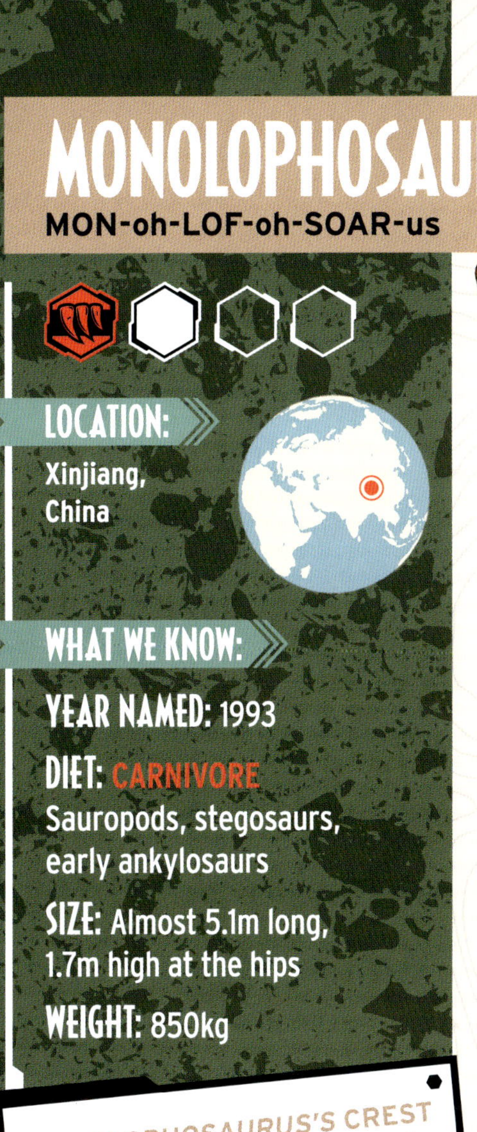

MONOLOPHOSAURUS

MON-oh-LOF-oh-SOAR-us

LOCATION:

Xinjiang, China

WHAT WE KNOW:

YEAR NAMED: 1993

DIET: CARNIVORE
Sauropods, stegosaurs, early ankylosaurs

SIZE: Almost 5.1m long, 1.7m high at the hips

WEIGHT: 850kg

Monolophosaurus* ('single-crested lizard') was the top meat-eating dinosaur in China about the same time that *Megalosaurus* ruled England. In many ways it was a typical medium-sized Jurassic theropod: its skull was about 67cm long; it stood about 1.7m high at the hips; and its jaws were filled with blade-like teeth for slicing through meat.

The most outstanding feature of *Monolophosaurus* was its crest. Other meat-eating dinosaurs had crests or horns on their heads, but nothing quite like that of *Monolophosaurus*. The single fat crest ran from the tip of its nose to just above its eyes. The bones of this crest were hollow, but it was not connected to the windpipe, so it couldn't be used to make sounds the way that some duckbills could. Instead, this crest was probably hollow so that it didn't weigh down the dinosaur's head too much.

What could this crest have been for? Many modern animals have horns or fan tails or other features that are used for display, to show off in order to win mates or defend territory. It seems likely that *Monolophosaurus* did the same thing with its crest.

MONOLOPHOSAURUS'S CREST MAY HAVE BEEN BRIGHTLY COLOURED, BUT THIS IS JUST A SPECULATION. COLOURS ARE ONLY VERY RARELY PRESERVED IN THE FOSSIL RECORD.

FUN FACT!

MANY DINOSAUR FOSSILS ARE FOUND BY ACCIDENT. *MONOLOPHOSAURUS*, FOR EXAMPLE, WAS FOUND BY GEOLOGISTS SEARCHING FOR OIL DEPOSITS.

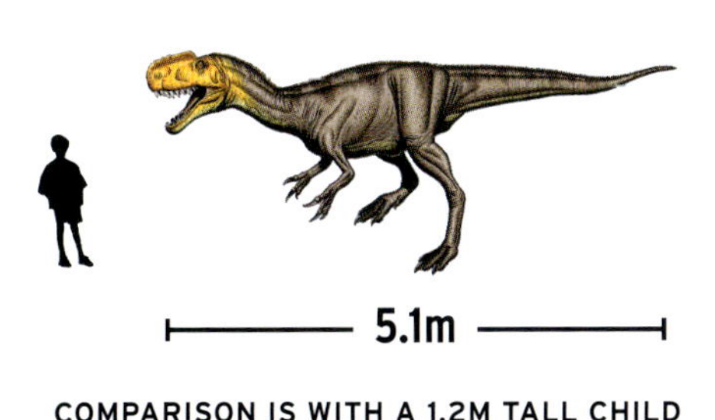

COMPARISON IS WITH A 1.2M TALL CHILD

TIME PERIOD:

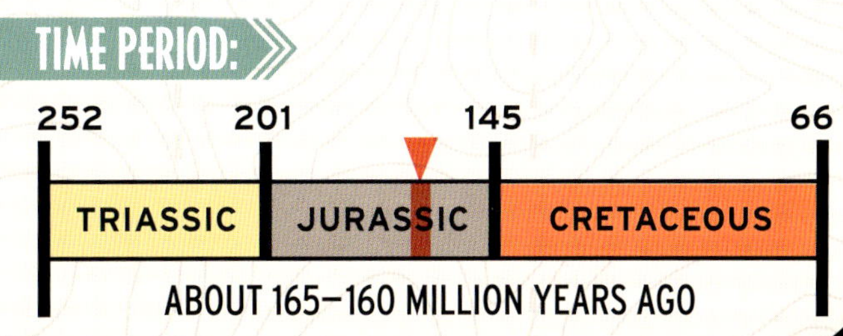

ABOUT 165–160 MILLION YEARS AGO

MUTTABURRASAURUS

mutt-ah-BUR-ah-SOAR-us

LOCATION:

Australia

WHAT WE KNOW:

YEAR NAMED: 1981

DIET: HERBIVORE
Conifers, cycads, ginkgos

SIZE: 8m long, about 3m high at the hips

WEIGHT: 3,000kg

FRIENDS: *Minmi*

ENEMIES: Theropods, or meat-eating dinosaurs

FUN FACT!

BECAUSE THIS DINOSAUR CANNOT BE CONFIDENTLY PLACED WITHIN ANY KNOWN ORNITHOPOD FAMILY, IT IS CONSIDERED A 'FREE AGENT'.

Muttaburrasaurus ('lizard from Muttaburra') has a stocky, well-muscled body. Although the only mounted skeleton in the world is shown with a thumb spike as big as *Iguanodon's,* some scientists question the restoration of this feature. That's because the original 'spike' bone in *Muttaburrasaurus* is only partially preserved.

One feature *Muttaburrasaurus* has in common with later ornithopods, or two-legged plant-eating dinosaurs, is its large nose. It is not known if this nose allowed *Muttaburrasaurus* to communicate, as the hadrosaurs are believed to have done. The nose is closer to the tip of the snout than in hadrosaurs, but it is still large enough to block any stereoscopic vision directly ahead. Humans and predators have stereoscopic vision, which allows them to see in depth. Plant-eating dinosaurs and other prey have non-overlapping fields of vision, which gives them the ability to see more widely but hinders depth perception.

THE ORIGINAL SPECIMEN OF *MUTTABURRASAURUS* WAS FOUND IN MARINE ROCKS. THE DINOSAUR'S BODY MAY HAVE FLOATED OUT TO SEA BEFORE FOSSILISATION.

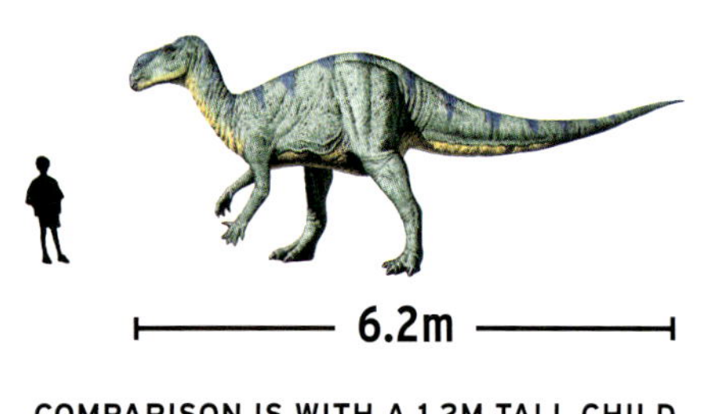

COMPARISON IS WITH A 1.2M TALL CHILD

TIME PERIOD:

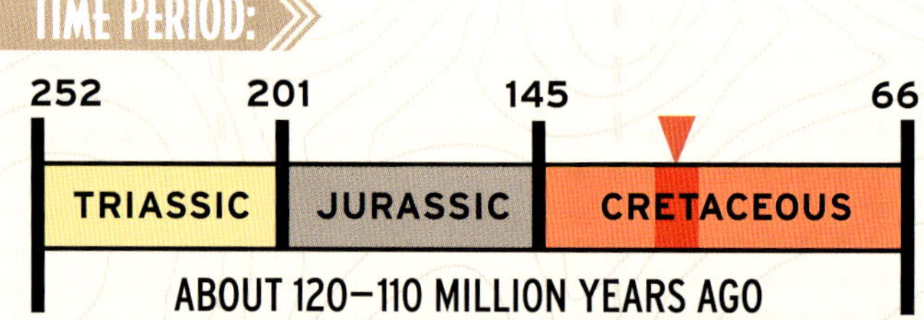

ABOUT 120–110 MILLION YEARS AGO

NQWEBASAURUS

en-KWEB-ah-SOAR-us

LOCATION:

South Africa

WHAT WE KNOW:

YEAR NAMED: 2000

DIET: OMNIVORE
Plants, possibly small mammals and reptiles, possibly insects

SIZE: 80cm long, about 33.3cm high at the hips

WEIGHT: 580g

FUN FACT!

'KIRKY' WAS FOUND WITH GIZZARD STONES IN ITS BELLY. ALTHOUGH IT IS WELL KNOWN THAT PLANT-EATERS USED 'STOMACH STONES' TO HELP THEM GRIND UP FOOD, SOME MEAT-EATING DINOSAURS, SUCH AS THE SPINOSAUR *BARYONYX*, AND CROCODILES ALSO USED THEM.

Nqwebasaurus ('Nqweba lizard') is one of the smallest of all dinosaurs, except for birds. It seems to be related to ostrich dinosaurs such as *Pelicanimimus* and *Gallimimus*.

Two South African palaeontologists, William De Klerk and Callum Ross, discovered the incomplete skeleton of this dinosaur in 1996. The fossil clearly showed a small theropod (or meat-eating dinosaur), about 80cm long, with long hind legs built for running fast. Like many theropods, it had a three-fingered hand. The palaeontologists teamed up with American scientists in 2000 to describe this dinosaur and they gave it the name *Nqwebasaurus* (Nqweba is the Xhosa name of the Kirkwood region of South Africa—where this dinosaur was found).

Nqwebasaurus is about the size of a chicken, as are *Compsognathus* and *Sinosauropteryx*. But unlike these other dinosaurs, its arms are relatively big. It probably could grab food with them. Its gizzard stones and very small teeth suggest that it mostly ate plants.

THE FIRST (AND SO FAR ONLY) SPECIMEN OF *NQWEBASAURUS* WAS NICKNAMED 'KIRKY' FOR THE KIRKWOOD FORMATION OF ROCK IN WHICH IT WAS FOUND.

COMPARISON IS WITH A 1.2M TALL CHILD

TIME PERIOD:

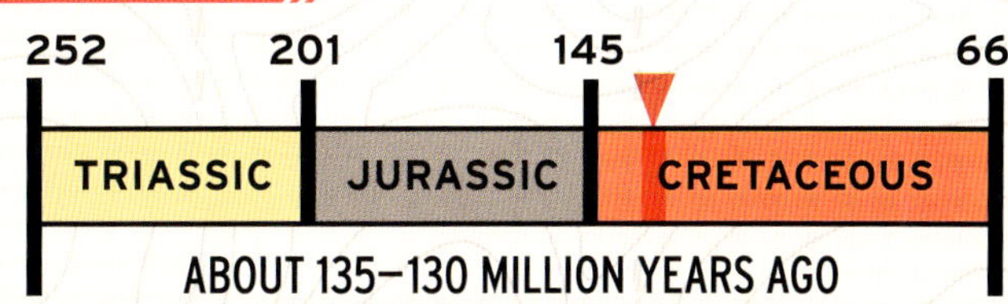

ABOUT 135–130 MILLION YEARS AGO

ORNITHOLESTES

or-NITH-oh-LES-teez

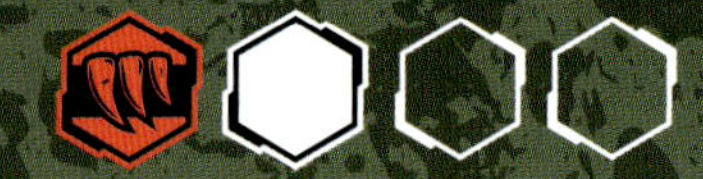

LOCATION:

Wyoming, USA

WHAT WE KNOW:

YEAR NAMED: 1903

DIET: CARNIVORE
Small mammals and reptiles, possibly including little dinosaurs

SIZE: 2.1m long, 47cm high at the hips

WEIGHT: 12.6kg

FUN FACT!

A FAMOUS PAINTING BY CHARLES R. KNIGHT SHOWED AN *ORNITHOLESTES* LEAPING AFTER AN *ARCHAEOPTERYX*. *ORNITHOLESTES* MAY HAVE EATEN EARLY BIRDS, BUT *ARCHAEOPTERYX* LIVED IN A DIFFERENT PART OF THE WORLD, AND IT IS UNLIKELY THAT EVEN AN AGILE HUNTER LIKE *ORNITHOLESTES* COULD HAVE CAUGHT A BIRD IN MIDAIR.

Ornitholestes ('bird thief') is the best-known small theropod, or meat-eating dinosaur, from the famous Morrison Formation. The formation is a series of rocks in the western United States in which the best Late Jurassic dinosaur fossils in the world are found. The Morrison is well known for its sauropods (giant long-necked dinosaurs), impressive stegosaurs (plated dinosaurs), and giant meat-eaters such as *Allosaurus* and *Ceratosaurus*. However, small predators are also found in these rocks.

Ornitholestes is a small dinosaur, about 2.1m long, half of which is tail. It has long arms—some palaeontologists suggest that it could use these arms to catch birds. There is no evidence of this behaviour, but primitive birds would have been about the proper size for this dinosaur to eat. More common victims may have been mammals, lizards and baby dinosaurs.

The only known skull of *Ornitholestes* is damaged near the tip of its snout. It may have had a small horn over its nose.

ORNITHOLESTES IS NOT THE ONLY SMALL THEROPOD FROM THE MORRISON FORMATION; ANOTHER SUCH DINOSAUR IS CALLED *COELURUS*.

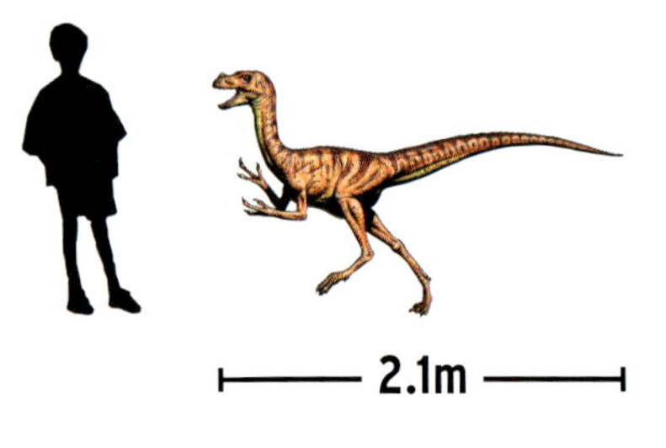

COMPARISON IS WITH A 1.2M TALL CHILD

TIME PERIOD:

252 — TRIASSIC — 201 — JURASSIC — 145 — CRETACEOUS — 66

ABOUT 150–140 MILLION YEARS AGO

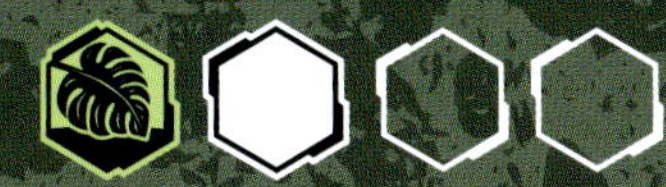

LOCATION:

Colorado, Utah, Wyoming, USA

WHAT WE KNOW:

YEAR NAMED: 2007

DIET: HERBIVORE
Ground plants and soft parts of conifers, cycads, ginkgos

SIZE: Less than 1.1m long, 30cm high at the hips

WEIGHT: 22.7kg

FRIENDS: *Dryosaurus, Camptosaurus*

ENEMIES: Juvenile theropods

Othnielosaurus (after Othniel C. Marsh) was originally found in the 1870s at Garden Park near Canyon City, Colorado. This is one of the most famous Jurassic quarries in the world and has given the world such dinosaurs as *Allosaurus, Ceratosaurus* and *Stegosaurus.*

Despite years of searching, scientists have not found many ornithopods from the Late Jurassic Period. What we do know is that most of these were small, fast, agile plant-eaters with a single row of leaf-cutting teeth. The arms were proportionally small, making these dinosaurs back-heavy. This gave them better balance while running on their well-muscled hind limbs. *Othnielosaurus's* teeth have a short crown with a root that extends four times longer. The dinosaur must have eaten soft plants, because the whole tooth is too small to eat any of the hard plant parts (this left hard, fibrous plants to be eaten by the larger sauropods). As one of the smallest dinosaurs, *Othnielosaurus* made good eating for the juveniles of bigger theropods. *Othnielosaurus* fossils have been found from hatchling to juvenile sizes. No adult skeletons have yet been found.

FRAGMENTS OF A SIMILAR DINOSAUR WERE NAMED *OTHNIELIA* IN 1977.

THE YOUNG OF THIS SMALL DINOSAUR WOULD FIT IN YOUR HAND.

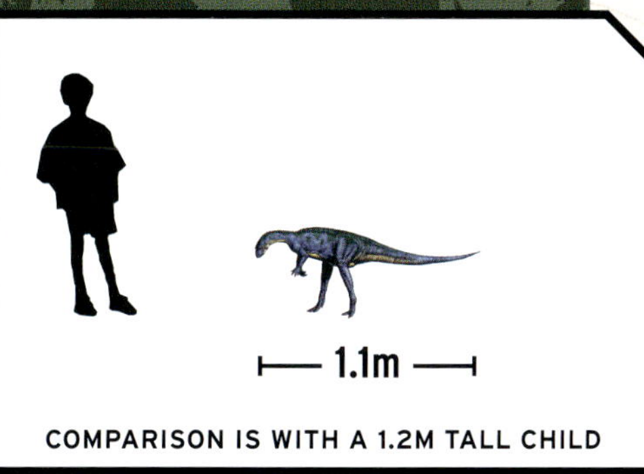

COMPARISON IS WITH A 1.2M TALL CHILD

TIME PERIOD:

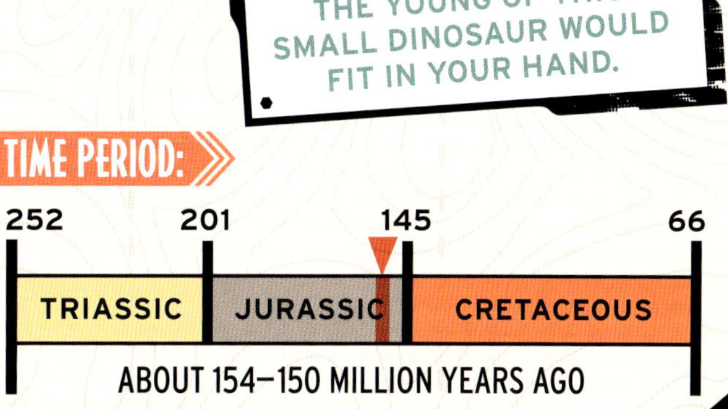

ABOUT 154–150 MILLION YEARS AGO

OVIRAPTOR

OH-vi-RAP-tor

LOCATION:

Mongolia; China

WHAT WE KNOW:

YEAR NAMED: 1924

DIET: OMNIVORE
Small reptiles (including baby dinosaurs), possibly also plants and eggs

SIZE: 2.3m long, almost 75cm high at the hips

WEIGHT: 32.4kg

FUN FACT!

OVIRAPTOR WAS ORIGINALLY GOING TO BE NAMED *FENESTROSAURUS* ('WINDOW LIZARD') BECAUSE OF THE OPENINGS IN ITS SKULL, BUT THE PALAEONTOLOGIST WHO NAMED IT THOUGHT THAT 'EGG HUNTER' WAS A MORE INTERESTING NAME.

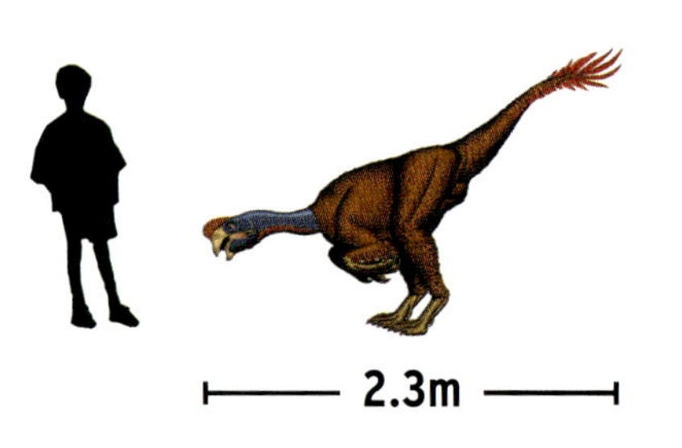

COMPARISON IS WITH A 1.2M TALL CHILD

Oviraptor ('egg hunter') is a dinosaur once thought to have been an egg hunter. It is now known to have been an egg protector!

When palaeontologists first found this little meat-eater in the Mongolian desert, it was sitting on top of a bunch of fossilised eggs. The scientists thought these eggs were from the horned dinosaur *Protoceratops*. Knowing that *Oviraptor* was a theropod, or meat-eating dinosaur, the scientists guessed that *Oviraptor* was about to eat the eggs. Many decades later, however, palaeontologists discovered that these eggs were actually *Oviraptor* eggs, and that (like birds) *Oviraptors* sat on their eggs before they hatched. Since then, many *Oviraptor* nests (and nests of related dinosaurs) have been found with parents on top.

TIME PERIOD:

252 | 201 | 145 | 66

TRIASSIC | JURASSIC | CRETACEOUS

ABOUT 110–100 MILLION YEARS AGO

MEAT OR VEGGIE?

The exact diet of *Oviraptor* is debated by palaeontologists. The first skeleton of *Oviraptor* contained a lizard skeleton in its belly, so it definitely ate some meat. Some palaeontologists, however, think that it may have eaten plants.

Oviraptor is one of the oviraptorosaur dinosaurs. Like other Late Cretaceous oviraptorosaurs, *Oviraptor* had a deep, toothless beak. It also had long, grasping hands, which would have been useful for clutching food.

PACHYCEPHALOSAURUS

PAK-ee-SEF-ah-lo-SOAR-us

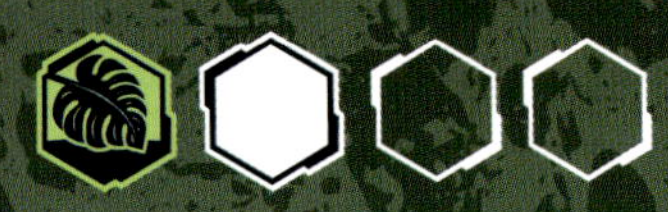

LOCATION:

Montana,
South Dakota,
Wyoming, USA

WHAT WE KNOW:

YEAR NAMED: 1931

DIET: **HERBIVORE**
Low-growing conifers, cycads, ginkgos, flowering plants

SIZE: About 4m long, 1.6m high at the hips

WEIGHT: 364kg

FRIENDS: Hadrosaurs, small ceratopsians (horned dinosaurs)

ENEMIES: *Acheroraptor*, *Troodon*, *Tyrannosaurus*

FUN FACT!

THE TEETH OF *PACHYCEPHALOSAURUS* ARE SMALLER THAN THE FIRST TEETH OF A HUMAN BABY!

MALE PACHYCEPHALOSAURUS HAD LARGER AND MORE ORNAMENTED BUMPS ON THE BACK OF THEIR SKULLS THAN THE FEMALES.

Pachycephalosaurus ('thick-headed lizard') is the last and most famous member of the Pachycephalosauria, or thick-headed dinosaurs. In the 1970s, palaeontologist Peter Galton proposed that male pachycephalosaurs used their domed heads as battering rams, like bighorn sheep. The idea caught the public's imagination.

But by the 1990s, scientists began to question Galton's head-butting theory. It was pointed out that animals who do butt heads have a wide surface area where the heads come into contact to prevent 'head slippage'. This happens when two animals butt heads at high speed and do not hit straight on. They risk breaking their necks when their heads suddenly snap to one side. *Pachycephalosaurus* has a domed, or rounded, head, which would minimise surface contact and therefore increase the risk of head slippage.

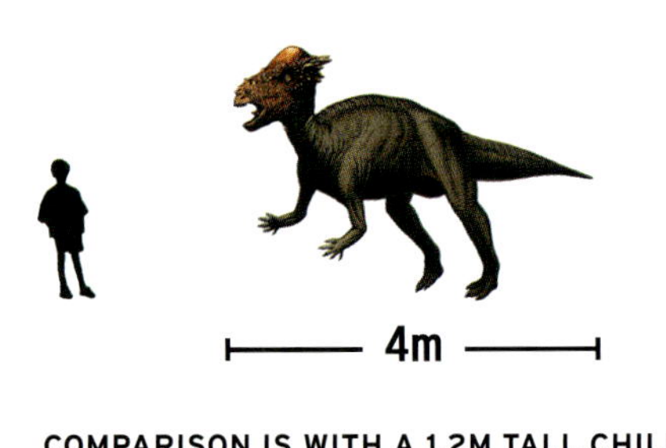

COMPARISON IS WITH A 1.2M TALL CHILD

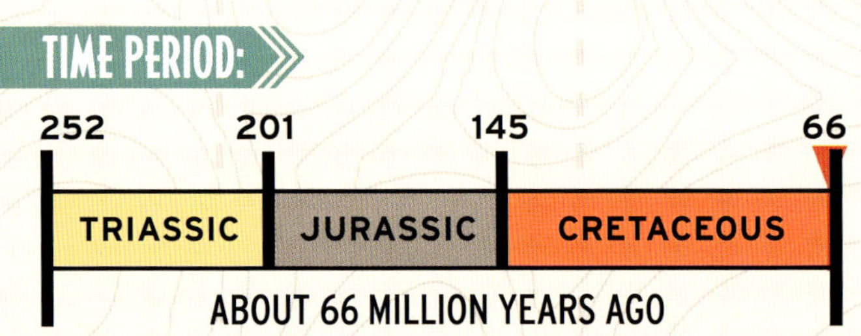

This throws doubt on the idea of any high-speed head-butting between pachycephalosaurs, but it does not exclude 'head-pushing' or 'head-ramming' against non-pachycephalosaurs. It just so happens that if a pachycephalosaur lowered its head and charged at a theropod, the impact would be right at the level of the theropod's head or pelvis—the perfect place to stop an attacker. Since *Pachycephalosaurus* had a skull up to 23cm thick, guess who'd lose?

HEADS & TAILS

Defensive measures can come from either end of the dinosaur. Whilst *Pachycephalosaurus'* unique head structure lends itself to the theory it was used as a defensive battering ram, *Ankylosaurus* likely also used its large tail club as a form of weaponry.

JURASSIC WORLD APPEARANCE

PARASAUROLOPHUS

PAR-ah-saw-ROL-oh-fus

LOCATION:

Montana, New Mexico, Utah, USA; Alberta, Canada

CHARONOSAURUS

ka-RO-no-SOAR-us

LOCATION:

China

WHAT WE KNOW:

YEAR NAMED:
Parasaurolophus: 1922
Charonosaurus: 2000

DIET: HERBIVORE
Conifers, cycads, ginkgos, flowering plants

SIZE: Over 12m long, about 2.8m high at the hips

WEIGHT: 2,000kg

FRIENDS: *Edmontosaurus*

ENEMIES: *Daspletosaurus, Tarbosaurus*

FUN FACT!

COMPUTER STUDIES OF *PARASAUROLOPHUS* CRESTS SUGGEST THEY SOUNDED LIKE A DEEP BASSOON.

The *Parasaurolophus* ('like *Saurolophus*') and *Charonosaurus* ('Charon's lizard') are two very closely related duckbill dinosaurs. They have one major feature in common: a long nasal tube. This hollow tube has up to three paired chambers that connect the nostrils with the back of the throat. Scientists Thomas Williamson and Robert Sullivan have studied these chambers with a computer axial tomography (CAT) scan. They theorise that these dinosaurs could not only make sounds within the range of human hearing but also in 'infra-sound', or below the range of human hearing, like modern elephants!

The nasal tube also served other purposes and is the perfect example of a multi-function device. It aided species recognition during mating, enhanced the dinosaur's sense of smell, humidified the air it breathed and indicated how old it was.

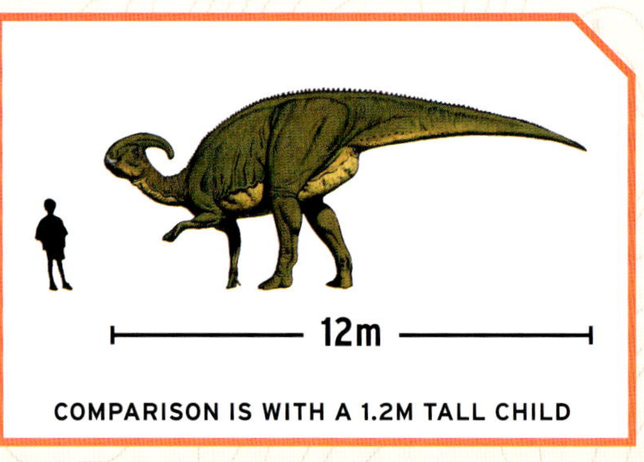

COMPARISON IS WITH A 1.2M TALL CHILD

FRILLS & WHISTLES

Just as the *Parasaurolophus'* head tube had multiple functions, the frilled and three-horned *Triceratops* could have used their head ornaments for multiple uses including warning off predators.

Charonosaurus is from China and *Parasaurolophus* is from western North America. This indicates that these areas were connected by a land bridge at the end of the Cretaceous Period. They are both lambeosaurs, or crested duckbills. Lambeosaurs made up a larger percentage of the herbivore communities in Asia than in North America, where flat-headed hadrosaurs and horned dinosaurs are more common. This means that although the two areas were connected, they had different fauna.

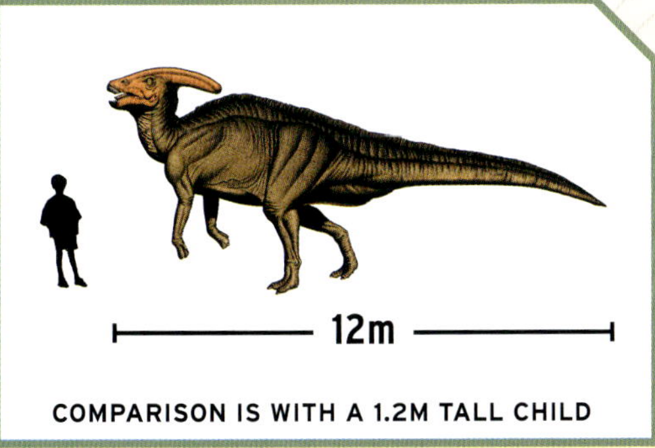

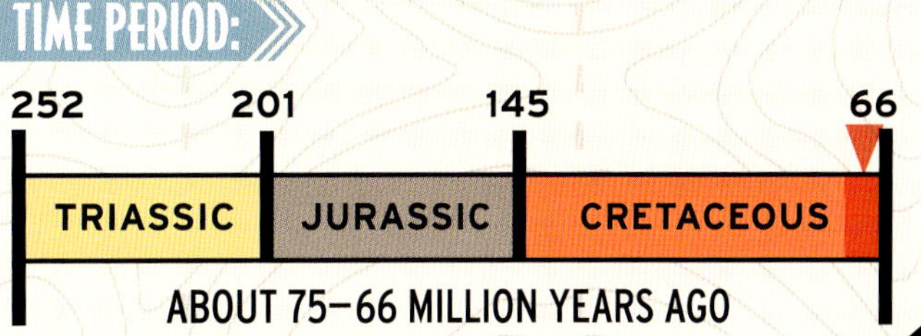

PELECANIMIMUS

pel-e-KAN-ee-MIME-us

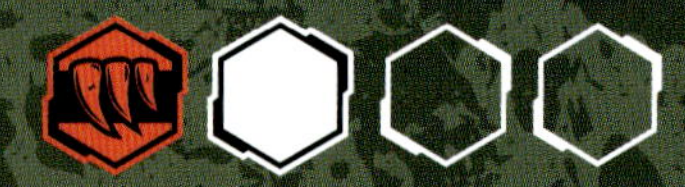

LOCATION:

Spain

WHAT WE KNOW:

YEAR NAMED: 1994

DIET: CARNIVORE
Possibly fish, possibly small reptiles and mammals

SIZE: 2m long, about 50cm high at the hips

WEIGHT: About 12kg

FRIENDS: None

ENEMIES: Larger theropods

PELECANIMIMUS HAS MORE TEETH THAN ANY OTHER KNOWN THERAPOD DINOSAUR.

FUN FACT!

PELECANIMIMUS WAS PRESERVED IN THE MUD OF AN ANCIENT LAGOON. REMAINS OF MANY PLANTS, INSECTS, FISH, LIZARDS, CROCODILES AND AT LEAST THREE BIRD SPECIES WERE ALSO FOUND.

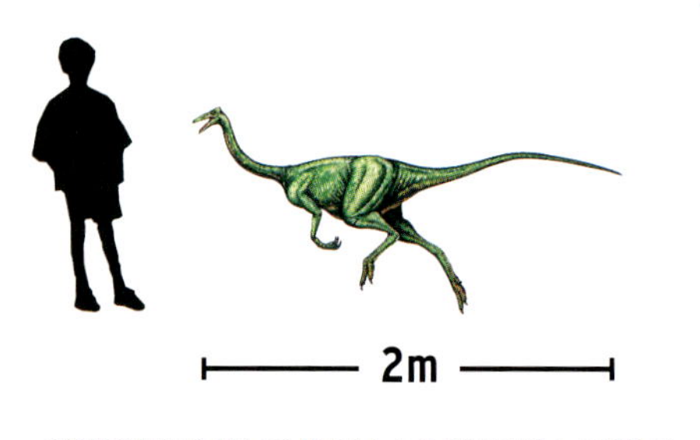

COMPARISON IS WITH A 1.2M TALL CHILD

Pelecanimimus ('pelican mimic') is the earliest known ornithomimosaur, or 'bird mimic', often called an ostrich dinosaur. It lived during the early part of the Cretaceous Period, whereas most ostrich dinosaurs lived millions of years later, during the Late Cretaceous Period.

Like other ornithomimosaurs, *Pelecanimimus* has a small, pointed head at the end of a long neck. Its arms end in typical ostrich dinosaur hands—three fingers of the same length, all curving in the same direction. But unlike the Late Cretaceous ostrich dinosaurs, which have toothless beaks, *Pelecanimimus* has jaws filled with over 220 tiny teeth. It is also the smallest known ostrich dinosaur, being only 2m long.

Pelecanimimus is known only from a single skeleton from Spain. On that skeleton, an impression of skin was found around some of the bones. The impression indicated that there was a pouch underneath the lower jaw, like that of a pelican. However, when scientists examined these impressions more closely, they realised that these were not the outside surface of the skin but the inside tissue! This was one of the first times that a dinosaur's muscle tissue had been preserved. Unfortunately, because the fossilisation process turned this tissue into rock, none of its DNA was preserved.

TIME PERIOD:

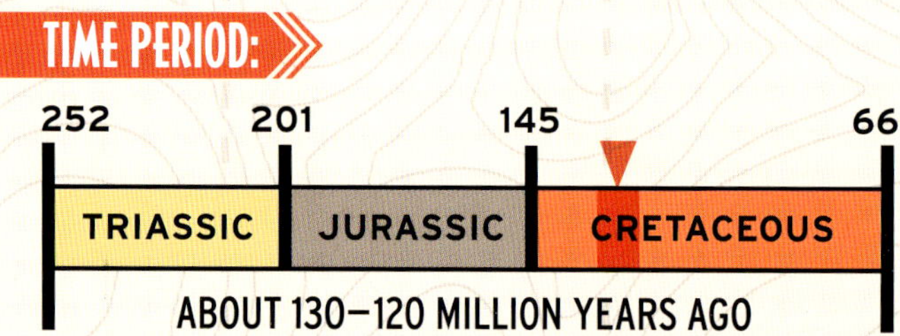

PLATEOSAURUS

PLAT-ee-oh-SOAR-us

LOCATION:

France;
Germany;
Switzerland

WHAT WE KNOW:

YEAR NAMED: 1837

DIET: **HERBIVORE**
Conifers, cycads, ginkgos

SIZE: 8m long, over 2m high at the hips

WEIGHT: 1,000kg

FRIENDS: *Sellosaurus*

ENEMIES: *Liliensternus*

PLATEOSAURUS WAS NAMED IN 1837, BEFORE THE WORD 'DINOSAUR' WAS COINED!

FUN FACT!

OVER A HUNDRED *PLATEOSAURUS* SKELETONS HAVE BEEN FOUND.

Plateosaurus ('flat lizard') is an early dinosaur from the Triassic Period. It was the first dinosaur that was much larger than a human, and the first with a long sauropod-like neck. *Plateosaurus* was heavily built, and its long muzzle was filled with teeth designed for chopping. The feet were clawed, and the hands had some grasping ability. The hand claw was relatively small compared to that of *Massospondylus* (see page 90). Many outdated skeletons show *Plateosaurus* walking on two feet. But that is unlikely because *Plateosaurus* was big and front-heavy and likely walked on all four feet.

Plateosaurus has been studied many times, mainly by the German palaeontologist Friedrich von Huene in the early 1900s and by Peter Galton in the late 1900s. Galton challenged the theory that *Plateosaurus* was an omnivore, or plant- and meat-eater. He showed that its teeth and jaw action were more like that of a true plant-eater, where the lower jaws meet the upper jaws like a nutcracker, with all the teeth coming together at the same time. In an omnivore, the jaws come together more like scissors, with the teeth meeting first at the back of the jaw, then finally at the front of the jaw.

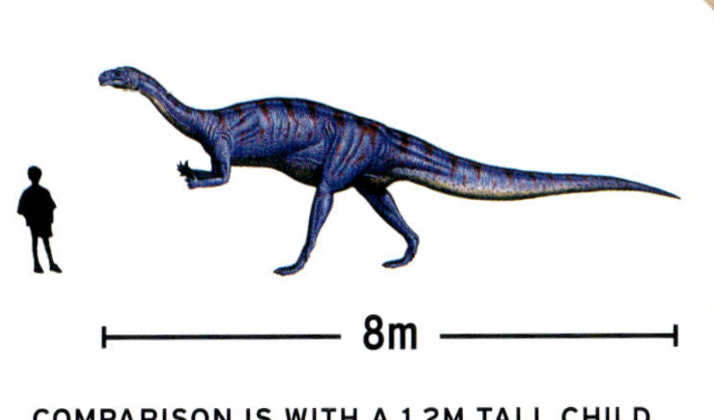

COMPARISON IS WITH A 1.2M TALL CHILD

TIME PERIOD:

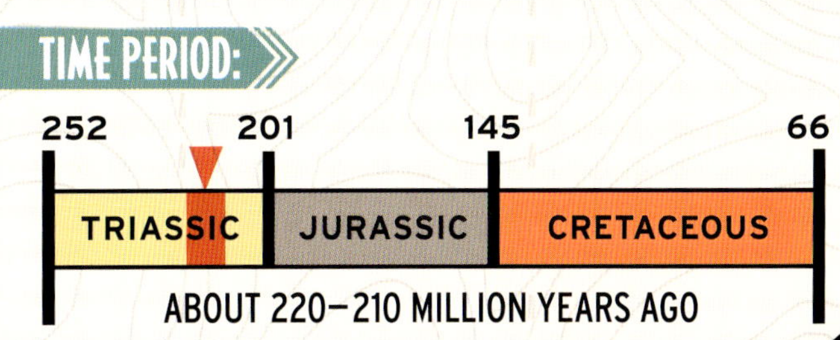

ABOUT 220–210 MILLION YEARS AGO

PROCOMPSOGNATHUS

pro-komp-SOG-na-thus

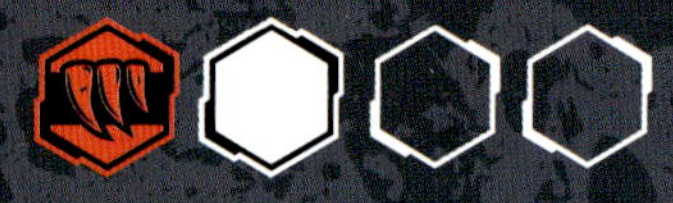

LOCATION:

Germany

WHAT WE KNOW:

YEAR NAMED: 1914

DIET: CARNIVORE
Possibly small mammals, reptiles and insects

SIZE: Less than 90cm long, 26cm high at the hips

WEIGHT: 1kg

FRIENDS: None

ENEMIES: Crocodile relatives

FUN FACT!

***PROCOMPSOGNATHUS* WAS SO SMALL THAT A SMALL DOG OR A HOUSE CAT WOULD HAVE BEEN A DANGER TO IT. GOOD THING FOR *PROCOMPSOGNATHUS* THAT DOGS AND CATS DID NOT EVOLVE UNTIL 200 MILLION YEARS AFTER IT WAS GONE!**

Procompsognathus ('before *Compsognathus'*) is a very small dinosaur from the Late Triassic Period. The only known skeleton of this dinosaur is incomplete but shows that it was less than 90cm long. It is a small theropod, or meat-eating dinosaur, and ran on long hind legs.

The palaeontologists who first discovered this fossil thought it reminded them of *Compsognathus,* the little theropod from the Late Jurassic of Germany. More recent studies of this dinosaur show that it was more closely related to *Coelophysis* and *Dilophosaurus* than to *Compsognathus.* Also, these studies show that the skull that was originally thought to be from *Procompsognathus* was actually from an early land-living crocodile relative.

There is no evidence that *Procompsognathus* (or *Compsognathus)* ran around in packs, attacking much larger animals.

PROCOMPSOGNATHUS IS ONE OF THE SMALLEST DINOSAURS KNOWN FROM THE TRIASSIC PERIOD.

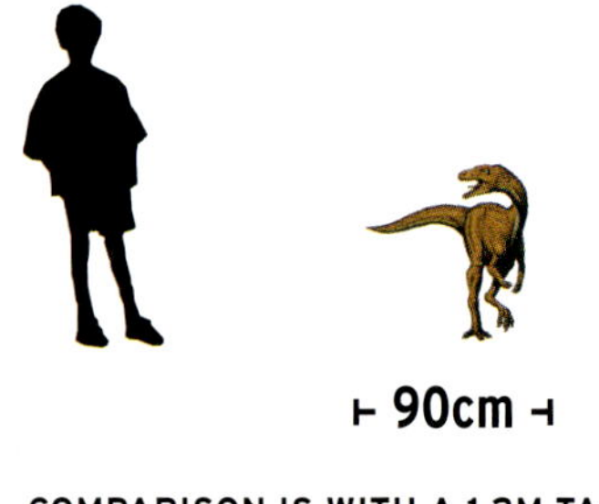

COMPARISON IS WITH A 1.2M TALL CHILD

TIME PERIOD:

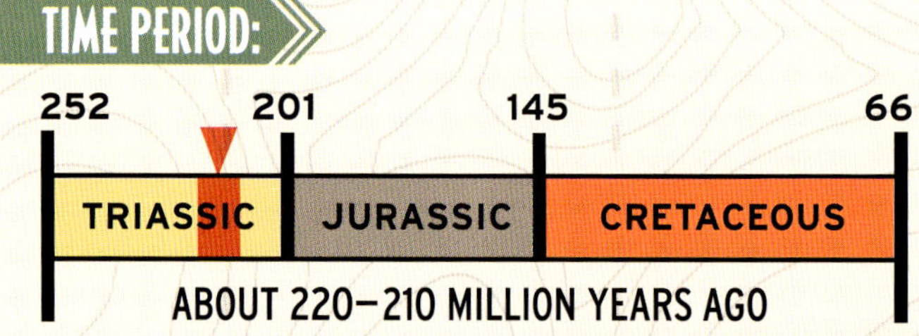

ABOUT 220–210 MILLION YEARS AGO

PROSAUROLOPHUS

PRO-soar-oh-LO-fus

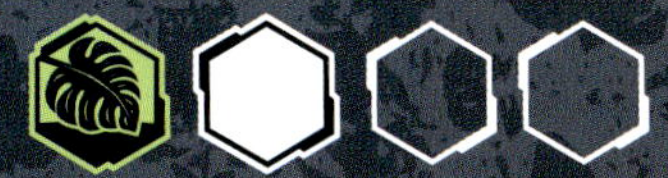

LOCATION:

Montana, USA; Alberta, Canada

WHAT WE KNOW:

YEAR NAMED: 1916

DIET: **HERBIVORE**
Conifers, cycads, ginkgos, flowering plants

SIZE: About 10m long, 1.8m high at the hips

WEIGHT: 2,000kg

Prosaurolophus ('before *Saurolophus*') is a duckbill dinosaur, one of the two-legged herbivorous dinosaurs known as ornithopods. It is a relatively unknown dinosaur, in need of a publicist. The first specimen was collected by the greatest dinosaur field palaeontologist of the twentieth century, Barnum Brown of the American Museum of Natural History in New York. During World War I, Brown led an expedition along the Red Deer River in Alberta, Canada, where he collected some of the most perfect duckbill skeletons ever found—including this one.

Prosaurolophus (and its probable descendant, *Saurolophus*) belongs to a subgroup of duckbills known as the Saurolophini, the rarest of all duckbills. These dinosaurs are sometimes hard to place in the 'big picture' of duckbill evolution because they have features from both the hadrosaurines, or non-crested duckbills, and the lambeosaurines, or crested duckbills.

FUN FACT!

THERE ARE TWO SPECIES OF *PROSAUROLOPHUS*. ONE WAS NAMED BY JACK HORNER, THE DUCKBILL EXPERT.

THERE ARE FEWER DUCKBILL EXPERTS THAN THERE ARE SPECIMENS OF *PROSAUROLOPHUS*!

10m

COMPARISON IS WITH A 1.2M TALL CHILD

TIME PERIOD:

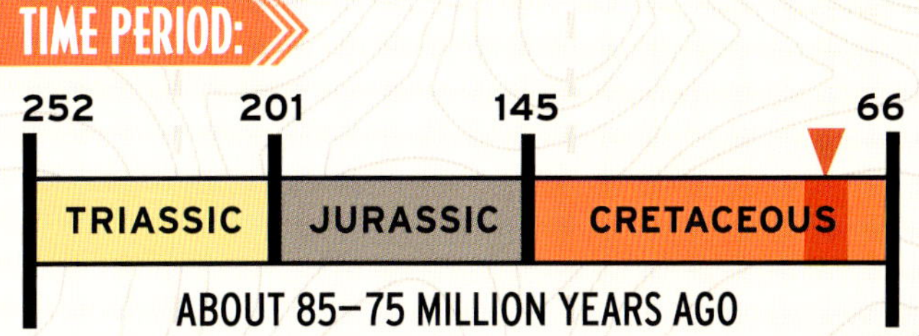

ABOUT 85–75 MILLION YEARS AGO

PSITTACOSAURUS

sih-TAK-oh-SOAR-us

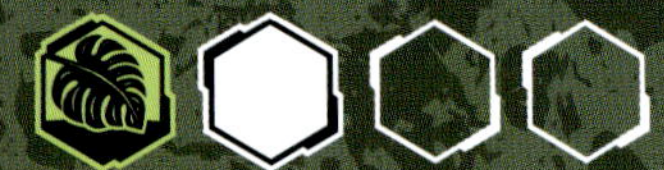

LOCATION:

China;
Mongolia;
Thailand

WHAT WE KNOW:

YEAR NAMED: 1931

DIET: HERBIVORE
Conifers, cycads, ginkgos

SIZE: 2m long, almost 50cm high at the hips

WEIGHT: 23kg

FRIENDS: *Shamosaurus, Altirhinus*

ENEMIES: *Dilong, Yutyrannus, Repenomamus* (a mammal known to eat baby *Psittacosaurus)*

FUN FACT!

CERATOPSIANS ARE SO POPULAR THAT THEY HAVE THEIR OWN BOOK, *THE HORNED DINOSAURS*, BY PETER DODSON.

2m

COMPARISON IS WITH A 1.2M TALL CHILD

Psittacosaurus ('parrot lizard') was one of the first to appear of the last great group of dinosaurs: ceratopsia, the horned dinosaurs. *Psittacosaurus* has two features common to all ceratopsians: an extra upper beak bone on top of the upper lip bone, and the beginnings of what will become the ceratopsian frill.

Over eleven species of *Psittacosaurus* have been named—more than in 99 percent of all other dinosaurs. But are they all valid? Some scientists will name a new species based on very slight differences in the skull. These differences can be the result, however, of sex, age, health and normal variation within populations. There are also stratigraphic differences. This means that over time, later populations can evolve larger features than their ancestors.

Psittacosaurus remains have been found with gastroliths, or stomach stones. Because most herbivorous dinosaurs could not chew their food, they swallowed a lot of unprocessed plants. To aid their digestion, they also swallowed small stones.

PSITTACOSAURUS HAS HORNS ON ITS CHEEKS, CALLED JUGAL HORNS.

TIME PERIOD:

252 | 201 | 145 | 66

TRIASSIC | JURASSIC | CRETACEOUS

ABOUT 135–120 MILLION YEARS AGO

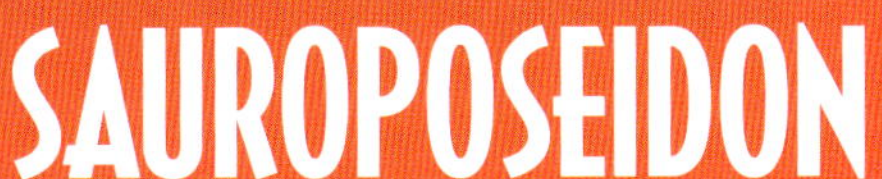

SAUROPOSEIDON

SOAR-oh-po-SIE-don

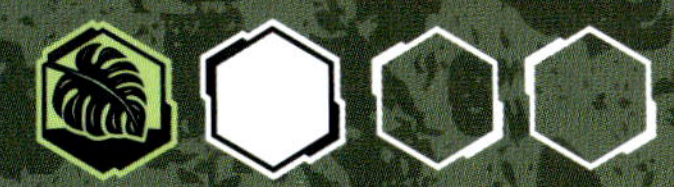

LOCATION:

Oklahoma, Texas, USA

WHAT WE KNOW:

YEAR NAMED: 2000

DIET: HERBIVORE
Conifers, cycads, ginkgos

SIZE: Over 31m long, 4m high at the hips

WEIGHT: 50,000kg

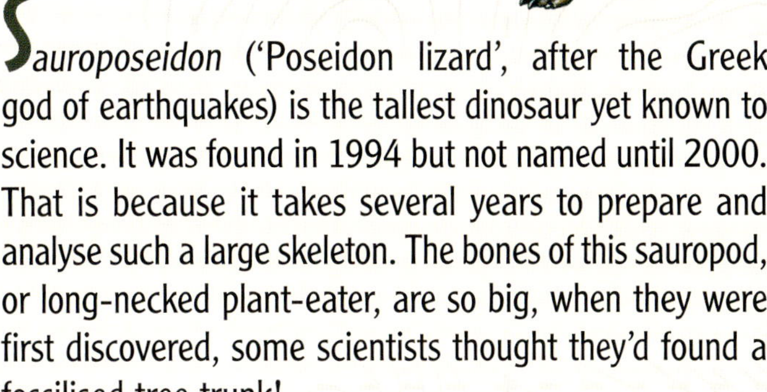

Sauroposeidon ('Poseidon lizard', after the Greek god of earthquakes) is the tallest dinosaur yet known to science. It was found in 1994 but not named until 2000. That is because it takes several years to prepare and analyse such a large skeleton. The bones of this sauropod, or long-necked plant-eater, are so big, when they were first discovered, some scientists thought they'd found a fossilised tree trunk!

Sauroposeidon's neck is about 12m long! A single neck bone is over 1.6m! These neck bones are so hollow that when X-rayed, they show more space than bone. This is a biological phenomenon called 'structural lightening'. It is designed to allow large bones to support great weights without weighing too much themselves. An adult human standing next to *Sauroposeidon* would not even come up to its elbow!

FUN FACT!

THE LARGEST LIVING MAMMALS ARE STILL NOT AS WELL ENGINEERED AS THE DINOSAURS. MAMMAL BONES ARE MORE SOLID AND LESS ABLE TO HANDLE LARGER WEIGHT LOADS.

SAUROPOSEIDON WAS THE LAST MEMBER OF THE FAMILY BRACHIOSAURIDAE BEFORE THEY WENT EXTINCT. THIS IS THE TALLEST KNOWN ANIMAL (SO FAR) IN EARTH'S HISTORY.

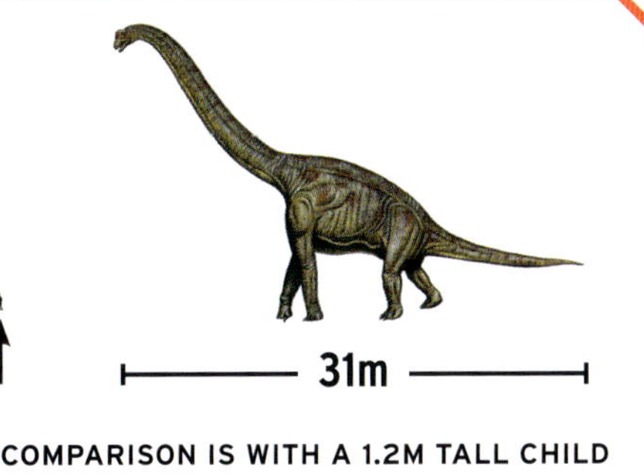

COMPARISON IS WITH A 1.2M TALL CHILD

TIME PERIOD:

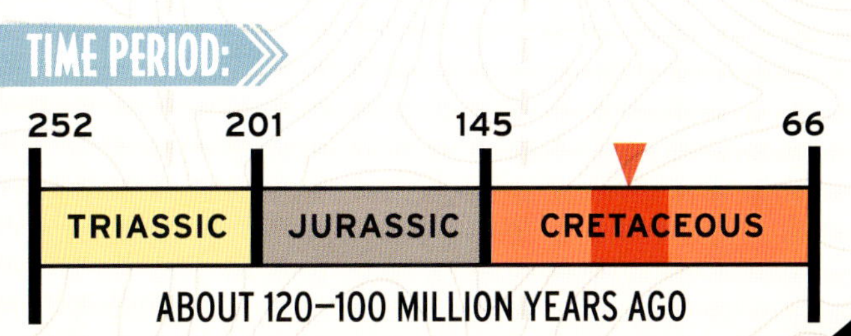

ABOUT 120–100 MILLION YEARS AGO

SHUVUUIA

shu-VOO-ee-ah

LOCATION:

Mongolia

WHAT WE KNOW:

YEAR NAMED: 1998

DIET: CARNIVORE
Possibly insects, possibly small mammals and reptiles

SIZE: About 88cm long, 30cm high at the hips

WEIGHT: About 2.5kg

FRIENDS: None

ENEMIES: *Velociraptor*

A FULL-GROWN *SHUVUUIA* WAS ONLY THE SIZE OF A CHICKEN, BUT IT WAS BIGGER THAN MOST OF THE MAMMALS THAT LIVED IN ITS ENVIRONMENT.

FUN FACT!

A SKELETON OF *SHUVUUIA* IS ON DISPLAY AT THE AMERICAN MUSEUM OF NATURAL HISTORY IN NEW YORK CITY.

Shuvuuia ('bird') is one of the strangest theropods, or meat-eating dinosaurs, ever found. It is one of the alvarezsaurs, a group of small bird-like dinosaurs of the Late Cretaceous Period.

Shuvuuia has a pointed, beaky snout, with jaws holding many very tiny teeth. It has a long neck, a compact body, a fairly short tail (for a dinosaur) and long legs built for running fast.

One of the oddest parts about it is its arms. While most advanced theropods had three working fingers, and the tyrant dinosaurs had two, alvarezsaurs had only one working finger—the thumb. Also, although the arms of *Shuvuuia* are short—like its larger relatives—they were extremely strong. Scientists do not know how *Shuvuuia* used these arms, but they certainly had some function. Perhaps it used them to dig into insect nests?

Shuvuuia and the other alvarezsaurs are a bit of a puzzle in the dinosaur family tree. In some ways they seem like the ostrich dinosaurs, in others they are similar to primitive birds, and in still other ways they are like troodonts. Palaeontologists are still trying to determine the closest relatives to these bizarre little dinosaurs.

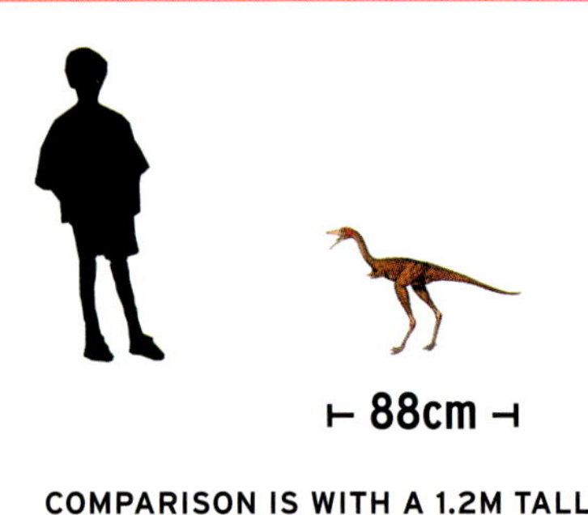

COMPARISON IS WITH A 1.2M TALL CHILD

TIME PERIOD:

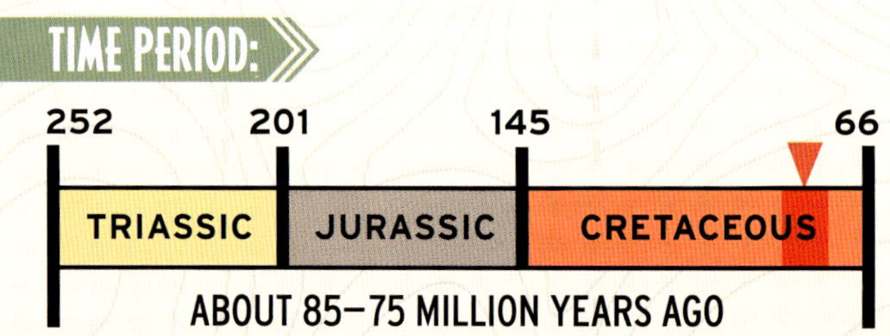

SINORNITHOIDES

sie-NOR-ni-THOI-deez

LOCATION:

Inner Mongolia, China

WHAT WE KNOW:

YEAR NAMED: 1993

DIET: CARNIVORE
Mammals, lizards, smaller dinosaurs, possibly insects, possibly plants

SIZE: About 1.1m long, almost 45cm high at the hips

WEIGHT: About 5.5kg

FRIENDS: None

ENEMIES: Larger theropods

FUN FACT!

UNTIL *SINORNITHOIDES* WAS FOUND, MANY PALAEONTOLOGISTS THOUGHT THAT TROODONTS HAD LONG ARMS LIKE RAPTORS.

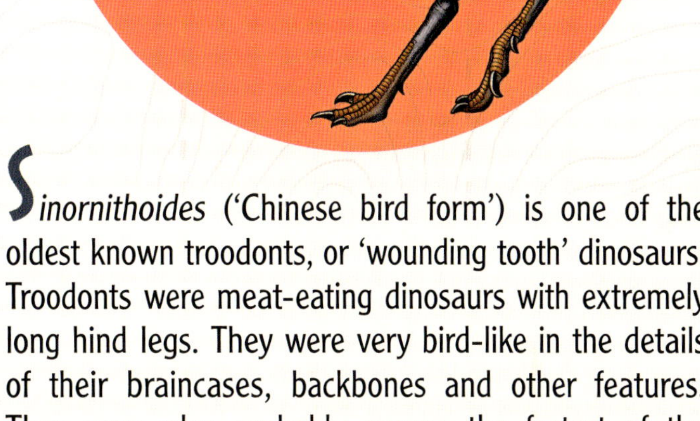

Sinornithoides ('Chinese bird form') is one of the oldest known troodonts, or 'wounding tooth' dinosaurs. Troodonts were meat-eating dinosaurs with extremely long hind legs. They were very bird-like in the details of their braincases, backbones and other features. They were also probably among the fastest of the smaller dinosaurs.

Before *Sinornithoides* was discovered, troodonts were only known from incomplete fossils. Then, in 1988, the skeleton of this little dinosaur was found in the region of China called Inner Mongolia. This dinosaur had been buried by a sandstorm while lying on its belly. Its head and neck were tucked under its arm, and its tail was wrapped around its body. Because it was covered over so quickly and so completely, nearly the entire skeleton was preserved in fine detail.

Sinornithoides was about the size of a wild turkey. It could easily chase down mammals, lizards, smaller dinosaurs (including babies), and similar creatures for their meat. Because the teeth of troodonts are similar to those of plant-eating dinosaurs, some scientists think that troodonts like *Sinornithoides* also ate insects and plants.

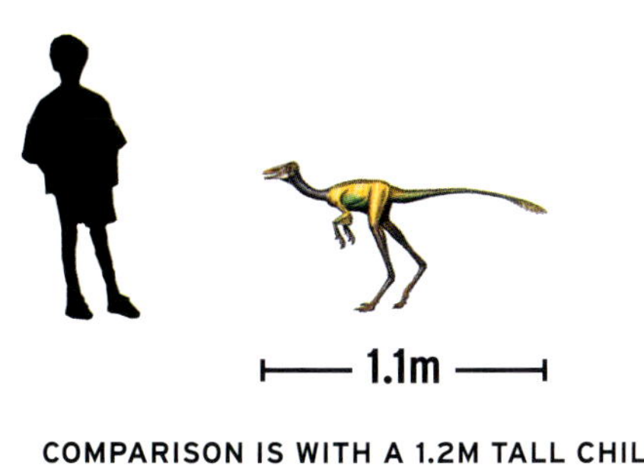

COMPARISON IS WITH A 1.2M TALL CHILD

TIME PERIOD:

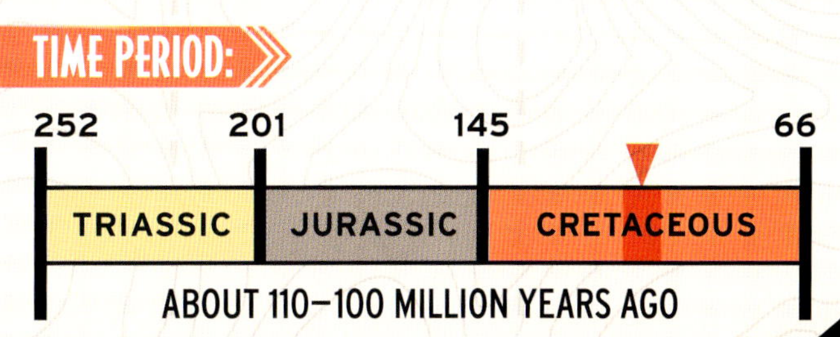

ABOUT 110–100 MILLION YEARS AGO

SINORNITHOSAURUS

SIEN-or-nith-oh-SOAR-us

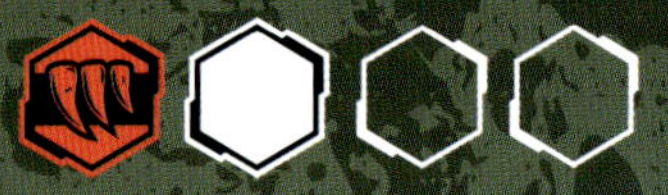

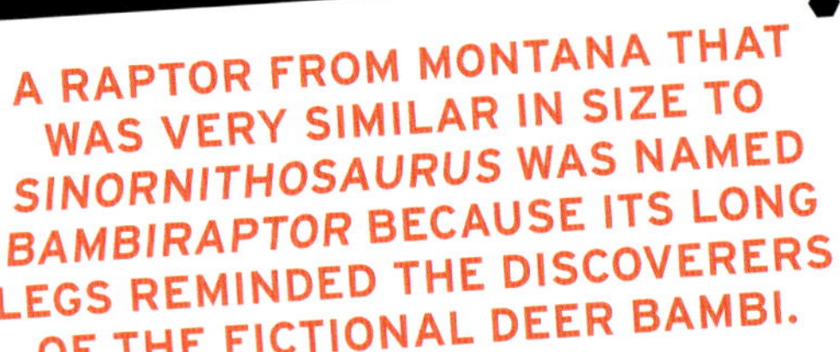

LOCATION:

Liaoning Province, China

A RAPTOR FROM MONTANA THAT WAS VERY SIMILAR IN SIZE TO *SINORNITHOSAURUS* WAS NAMED *BAMBIRAPTOR* BECAUSE ITS LONG LEGS REMINDED THE DISCOVERERS OF THE FICTIONAL DEER BAMBI.

WHAT WE KNOW:

YEAR NAMED: 1999

DIET: CARNIVORE
Beipiaosaurus, Caudipteryx, Confuciusornis, Psittacosaurus, Sinosauropteryx

SIZE: About 1.25m long, over 45cm high at the hips

WEIGHT: 6.4kg

FRIENDS: None

ENEMIES: *Dilong, Yutyrannus*

Sinornithosaurus ('Chinese bird lizard') is one of the oldest known dromaeosaurs, or raptors. This was an early relative of *Velociraptor* and *Deinonychus.* Like *Velociraptor,* it was a fairly small dinosaur, but it was probably very dangerous. It had sharp, curved teeth in its jaws, long grasping hands at the end of long arms, and a killer sickle claw on the second toe of each foot. What makes *Sinornithosaurus* more famous, though, is that fact that it was 'fuzzy'!

All over the body of *Sinornithosaurus* were long filaments. These structures were protofeathers, a fuzzy body covering that eventually evolved into true feathers. Both protofeathers and true feathers are 'soft' features that do not fossilise easily. But the fine-grained mud of the Yixian Formation, where *Sinornithosaurus* was found, was able to preserve the soft features of the dinosaurs, other animals and plants that died there.

FUN FACT!

SINORNITHOSAURUS IS CLASSIFIED AS A RAPTOR BECAUSE OF THE SINGLE, OVERSIZED, SICKLE-SHAPED SINGLE CLAWS ON EACH OF ITS HIND FEET, USED TO TEAR AT ITS PREY.

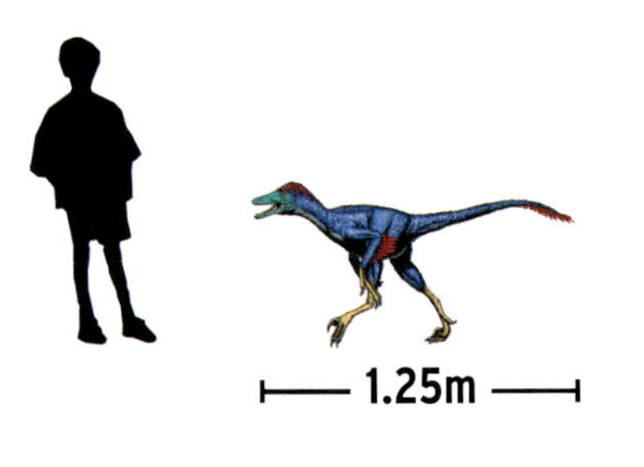

COMPARISON IS WITH A 1.2M TALL CHILD

TIME PERIOD:

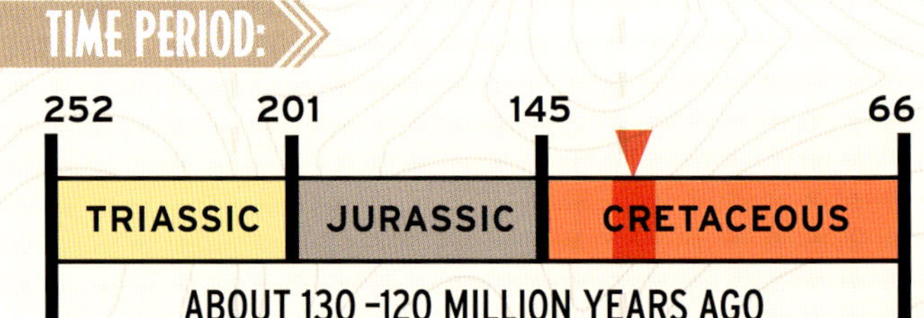

Other theropods found in the Yixian Formation include *Beipiaosaurus, Caudipteryx, Confuciusornis* and *Sinosauropteryx*. They all were found to have either protofeathers or true feathers.

With the discovery of *Sinornithosaurus* (and the other theropods found in the Yixian), we now know that raptors and all the other advanced, bird-like meat-eating dinosaurs were covered with either fuzzy protofeathers or true feathers.

'FUZZY' FINDS

Prior to the discovery of *Sinornithosaurus*, scientists thought that raptor dinosaurs like *Deinonychus* (pictured below) and *Velociraptor* (pictured above) were covered only in scales. This is because the rocks where they were found did not preserve their soft body coverings.

SINOSAUROPTERYX

SIEN-oh-soar-ROP-te-riks

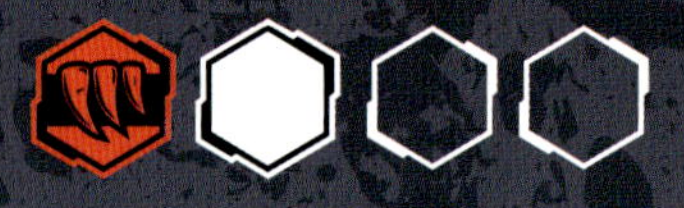

LOCATION:

Liaoning Province, China

WHAT WE KNOW:

YEAR NAMED: 1996

DIET: CARNIVORE
Small mammals and lizards

SIZE: 1.25m long, 29cm high at the hips

WEIGHT: 2.5kg

FRIENDS: *Psittacosaurus, Caudipteryx, Beipiaosaurus, Confuciusornis*

ENEMIES: *Sinornithosaurus*

FUN FACT!

ALTHOUGH ITS NAME MEANS 'CHINESE LIZARD WING', *SINOSAUROPTERYX* DID NOT HAVE WINGS, NOR COULD IT FLY. IN FACT, ITS ARMS WERE SO SHORT THAT THEY COULD BARELY SCRATCH ITS KNEE!

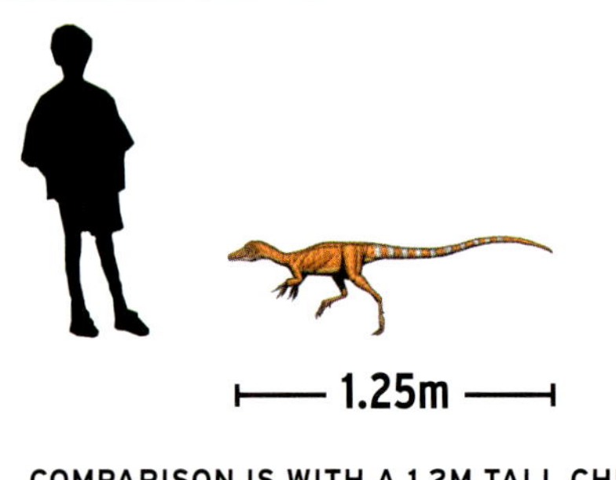

COMPARISON IS WITH A 1.2M TALL CHILD

Sinosauropteryx ('Chinese lizard wing') was probably the most important dinosaur discovered in the 1990s. Before it was found, palaeontologists had shown that birds were the descendants of theropods, meat-eating dinosaurs. However, they did not know when certain bird-like features first appeared. That's because many of the things that make birds special among all living animals are soft features that don't fossilise well.

One of these soft features is feathers. Some palaeontologists suspected that many of the theropod dinosaurs were actually covered by feathers or fuzz, but they could not find proof. Then, in 1996, an amazing discovery was made in northeastern China. In a series of rocks called the Yixian Formation, the skeleton of a small theropod was found. This little dinosaur was very similar to *Compsognathus,* a slightly older dinosaur from Germany. The bones of the skeleton were complete, but the most interesting thing about the fossil was the traces of small fibres surrounding the bones. These fibres turned out to be protofeathers, a simple type of body covering that developed into feathers in birds and their closest relatives.

THE SCIENTISTS WHO DISCOVERED *SINOSAUROPTERYX* AT FIRST THOUGHT THAT DINOSAURS COULD NOT HAVE FEATHERS, SO THEY CALLED IT A BIRD.

TIME PERIOD:

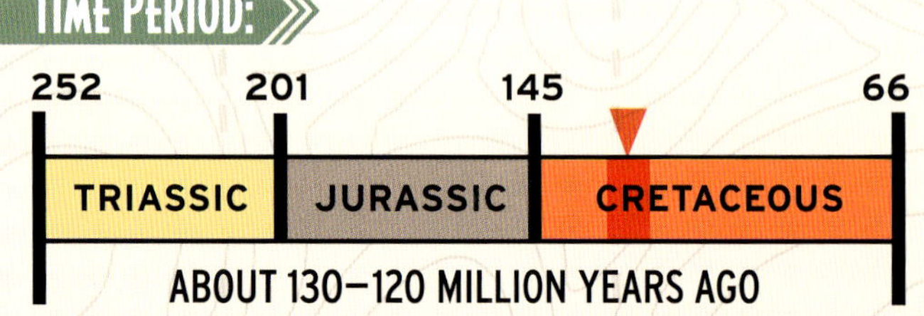

ABOUT 130–120 MILLION YEARS AGO

Since 1996, many feathered dinosaurs have been found in the Yixian Formation, but *Sinosauropteryx* is the most primitive of the feathered dinosaurs found to date. Because the Yixian dig has revealed that *Sinosauropteryx,* as well as its more advanced relatives, had feathers or protofeathers, palaeontologists now realise that almost all the advanced meat-eating dinosaurs had this covering. This includes not only little dinosaurs like troodonts (see *Sinornithoides)* and alvarezsaurs (see *Shuvuuia),* but also medium-sized forms like ostrich dinosaurs (see *Pelecanimimus* and *Gallimimus),* oviraptorosaurs (see *Oviraptor* and *Caudipteryx)* and dromaeosaur raptors (see *Sinornithosaurus, Velociraptor* and *Deinonychus).* Even *Tyrannosaurus, Gorgosaurus* and the other tyrant dinosaurs (which are more advanced than *Sinosauropteryx)* probably had proto-feathers when they were hatchlings, but some scientists think that they might have shed these as they grew up.

MUDDY IMPRINTS

You might wonder why the Yixian Formation was able to preserve the soft features of these dinosaurs, while other rocks did not. The mud that became the Yixian Formation is very fine-grained—that is, the particles that make it up are very small. Because of this, small details were not blurred out. Also, because these dinosaurs were preserved in a quiet lake-like environment, rather than in muds dumped by a flooding river or sands blown around by sandstorms, the bodies of the dinosaurs were not damaged before they were covered over with mud. Thanks to this lucky circumstance, we now know much more about the outsides of these dinosaurs!

SPINOSAURUS

SPINE-o-SOAR-us

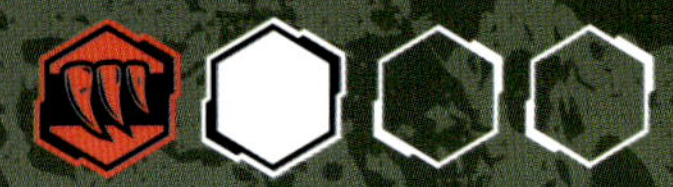

LOCATION:

Egypt;
Morocco

WHAT WE KNOW:

YEAR NAMED: 1915

DIET: CARNIVORE
Other dinosaurs, large fish

SIZE: Perhaps over 14m long, 5.6m high (including sail)

WEIGHT: Perhaps 8,000kg

OLD PICTURES OF SPINOSAURUS SHOWED IT INCORRECTLY WITH A TYRANNOSAURUS-LIKE SKULL.

Spinosaurus ('spine lizard') is one of the most spectacular dinosaurs ever found. It was an enormous meat-eating dinosaur, as big as *Tyrannosaurus rex*. But its jaws and teeth were very different from *T. rex's*. The jaws were long and slender, and the teeth were cone-shaped, like those of a crocodile.

Its most distinctive feature, however, was the huge sail-like fin on its back. This sail was made from the spines that come out of the top of the backbones of dinosaurs and all other backboned animals. If you feel down your spine from the bottom of your head, you'll feel a series of bumps (especially at the base of the neck). These bumps are the same bumps on the top of backbones of dinosaurs. The spines of *Spinosaurus*, though, were tremendous: the longest one found was over 1.7m tall!

What would have been the purpose of such a sail? Although *Spinosaurus* lived in a swampy coastal environment, the sail would not have been used like the sail of a boat. Instead, it may have served to let *Spinosaurus* cool itself down if it got too hot. The skin on the sail, like all skin, would have been filled with blood vessels. Hot blood pumped into the sail would be cooled off, especially if there was a breeze; African elephants use blood vessels in their ears for this purpose. Also, the sail might have been used to show off to other *Spinosaurus*, either to attract a mate or to defend its territory.

FUN FACT!

SPINOSAURUS IS NOT THE ONLY DINOSAUR WITH A SAIL. *OURANOSAURUS* (A RELATIVE OF *IGUANODON*) ALSO HAD A SAIL.

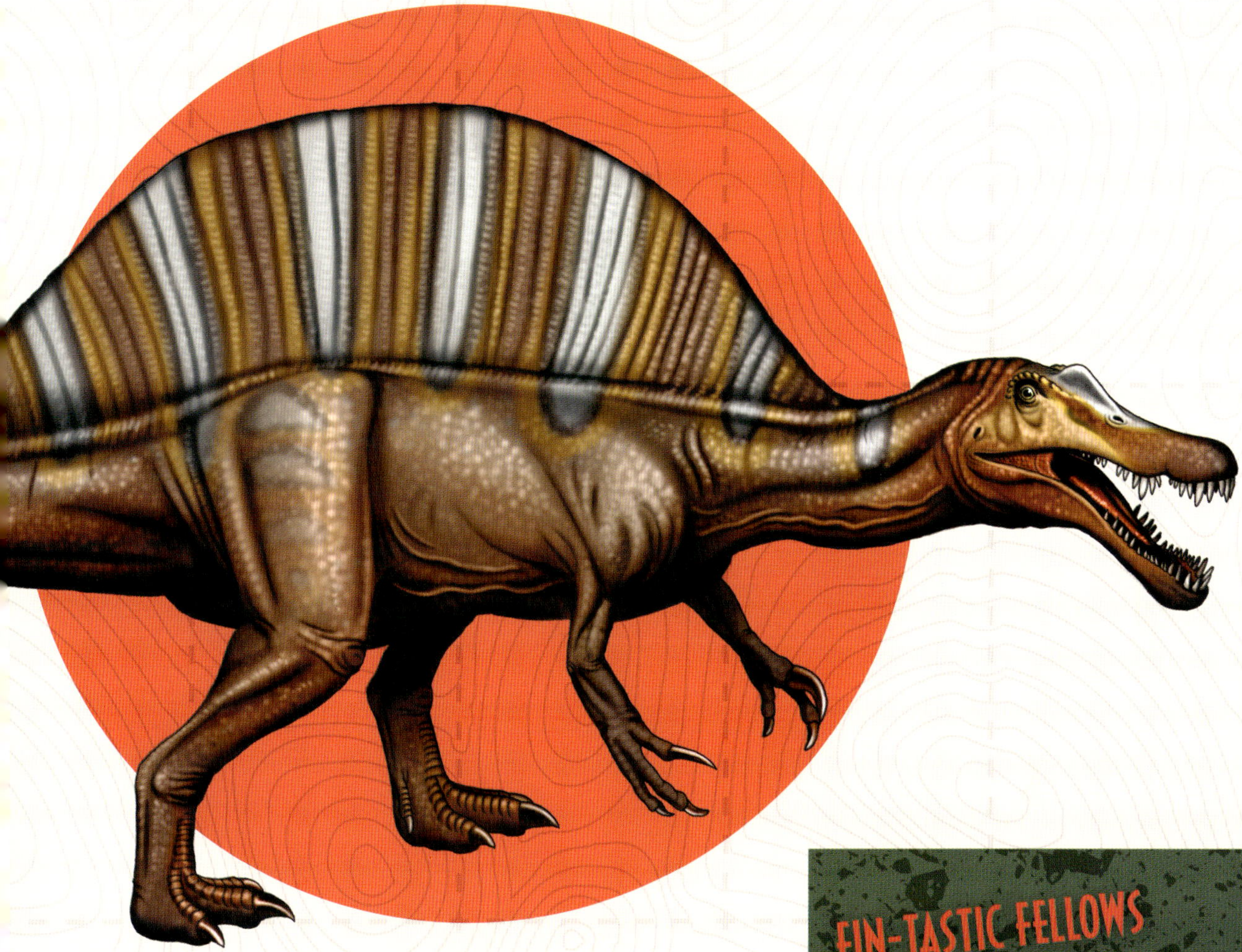

Additionally, the dinosaur may have used its sail to make itself look bigger. Living in the same environment as *Spinosaurus* were a couple of other giant predators, *Carcharodontosaurus* and *Deltadromeus*. If a *Spinosaurus* turned itself sideways towards an attacker, it would suddenly look much larger, and so the other predator might think twice about attacking. Modern cats do something similar: when they get scared, they puff up their fur to make themselves look larger.

FIN-TASTIC FELLOWS

Whilst not classed as a dinosaur, the sail-backed *Dimetrodon* (pictured below) of the Permian Period also boasted a sail-like fin, similar to that of *Spinosaurus*. *Dimetrodon* was, in fact, a primitive synapsid (or protomammal), more closely related to the ancestors of mammals.

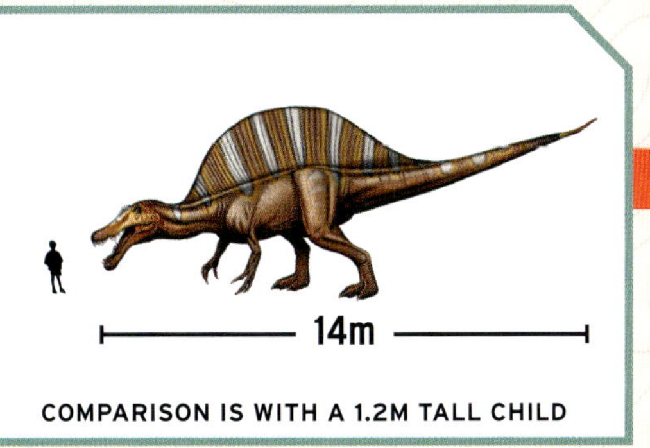

COMPARISON IS WITH A 1.2M TALL CHILD

TIME PERIOD:

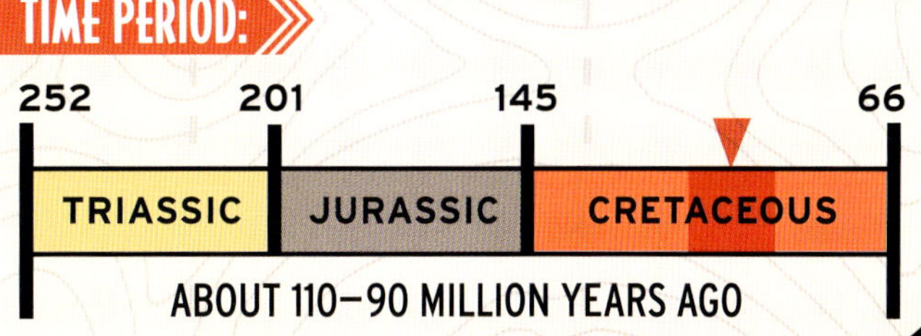

ABOUT 110–90 MILLION YEARS AGO

STEGOSAURUS

STEG-oh-SOAR-us

LOCATION:

Colorado, Utah, Wyoming, USA

WHAT WE KNOW:

YEAR NAMED: 1877

DIET: HERBIVORE
Plants

SIZE: About 7.5m long, 2.1m high at the hips

WEIGHT: 3,000kg

FUN FACT!

***STEGOSAURUS* COMES IN TWO VARIETIES: A LARGE-PLATED SPECIES WITH FOUR LONG TAIL SPIKES AND A RARER, SMALLER-PLATED SPECIES WITH SHORTER TAIL SPIKES (POSSIBLY EIGHT OF THEM). THE SECOND SPECIES IS BASED ON A PARTIAL SPECIMEN AND MAY NOT BE VALID.**

Stegosaurus ('roofed lizard') is the best known 'plated' dinosaur. It was a favourite food of *Allosaurus* and has been well studied by palaeontologists for over 125 years. It has also been the subject of many false 'dinosaur myths'—among them that it had a brain no bigger than a walnut (it was, in fact, more than twice as big as a walnut), a second brain in its hips and plates that could flap on command.

Several questions about *Stegosaurus* have received a lot of study by scientists in the 1990s. It has been proposed at various times that *Stegosaurus* had either one or two rows of plates along its back. A specimen found by Ken Carpenter, Bryan Small and a team at the Denver Museum of Natural History shows that *Stegosaurus* did have a double row of alternating plates down its back. This new specimen also shows that the tail spikes did not point upward—as in most museum exhibits—but instead pointed sideways.

ALMOST EVERYTHING IN POPULAR BOOKS DURING THE 20TH CENTURY ABOUT *STEGOSAURUS* WAS BASED ON THE SPECIMEN AT THE SMITHSONIAN INSTITUTION.

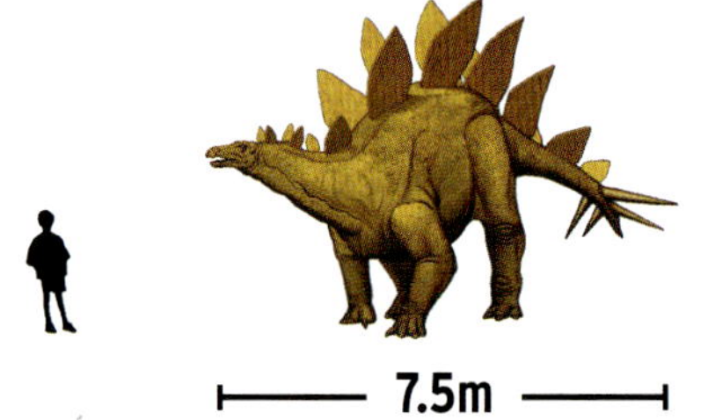

COMPARISON IS WITH A 1.2M TALL CHILD

TIME PERIOD:

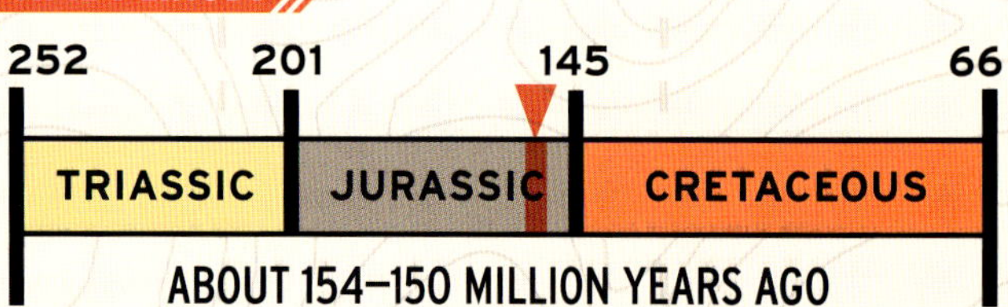

ABOUT 154–150 MILLION YEARS AGO

SUCHOMIMUS

SOOK-oh-MY-mus

LOCATION:

Niger;
Northern
Africa

WHAT WE KNOW:

YEAR NAMED: 1998

DIET: CARNIVORE
Large fish, dinosaurs

SIZE: 11m long, 3.6m high at the hips

WEIGHT: 5,000kg

FRIENDS: None

ENEMIES: *Eocarcharia*, *Kryptops*

FUN FACT!

ANOTHER DINOSAUR FROM THE SAME ROCK FORMATION AS *SUCHOMIMUS* IS THE SAIL-BACKED *OURANOSAURUS*, A RELATIVE OF *IGUANODON*.

11m

COMPARISON IS WITH A 1.2M TALL CHILD

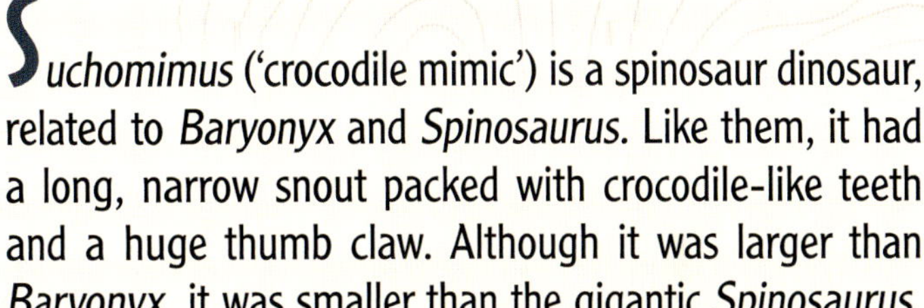

Suchomimus ('crocodile mimic') is a spinosaur dinosaur, related to *Baryonyx* and *Spinosaurus.* Like them, it had a long, narrow snout packed with crocodile-like teeth and a huge thumb claw. Although it was larger than *Baryonyx,* it was smaller than the gigantic *Spinosaurus.*

Suchomimus was given the name 'crocodile mimic' because, like a crocodile, its skull was long and slender and its teeth were shaped like cones (unlike many of the meat-eaters, which had blade-like teeth). Some palaeontologists think that this means they ate mostly fish. It is true that *Suchomimus* lived near water, and that the remains of 3m fish were found with it in the same rocks. This suggests that *Suchomimus* waded into the water and grabbed fish with its jaws, or hooked them with its thumb claw.

Today's big crocodilians eat both large fish and land animals. *Suchomimus* too, could have hunted the big land animals of its day—other dinosaurs. Its jaws could kill a dinosaur as easily as they could a fish.

THE THUMB CLAW WAS ONE OF THE FIRST BONES FOUND FOR BOTH BARYONYX AND SUCHOMIMUS.

TIME PERIOD:

252 | 201 | 145 | 66

TRIASSIC | JURASSIC | CRETACEOUS

ABOUT 110–100 MILLION YEARS AGO

THER-ih-ZEE-no-SOAR-us

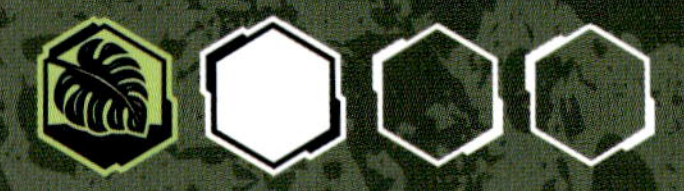

LOCATION:
Mongolia

WHAT WE KNOW:

YEAR NAMED: 1954

DIET: HERBIVORE
Conifers, ginkgos, possibly flowering plants

SIZE: About 7m long, over 3m high at the hips

WEIGHT: 3,000kg

FRIENDS: *Saurolophus*

ENEMIES: *Tarbosaurus* (a relative of *Tyrannosaurus*)

FUN FACT!

WHEN FIRST DISCOVERED, PALAEONTOLOGISTS THOUGHT *THERIZINOSAURUS* WAS SOME KIND OF GIANT TURTLE!

7m

COMPARISON IS WITH A 1.2M TALL CHILD

Therizinosaurus ('scythe lizard') is enormous. It is also one of the most bizarre dinosaurs. Although it is a theropod (or meat-eating) dinosaur, it most likely ate just plants! It had gigantic claws, the largest over 70cm long. But these claws were not curved and hooked like the claws of a predator. Instead, they were flat and straight.

Therizinosaurus was a giant relative of *Beipiaosaurus*. That earlier dinosaur was covered by protofeathers, a simple body covering that in some other dinosaurs (including oviraptorosaurs and birds) became true feathers. Because the earlier therizinosaur *Beipiaosaurus* had these protofeathers, palaeontologists suspect that *Therizinosaurus* had them too.

It may seem strange to think of a plant-eater as a member of a group of meat-eating animals, but this is not the only case of that happening. For example, the modern giant panda eats almost nothing except bamboo, but it is a member of the carnivorous mammal group.

THERIZINOSAURUS HAS THE LARGEST FINGER BONES OF ANY KNOWN ANIMAL IN EARTH'S HISTORY.

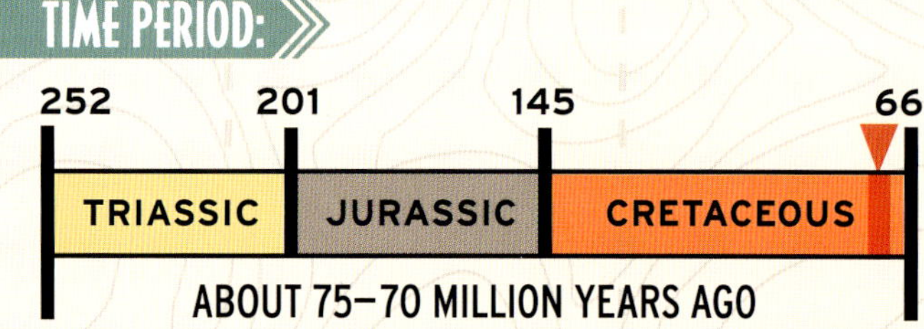

THESCELOSAURUS

THES-sel-oh-SOAR-us

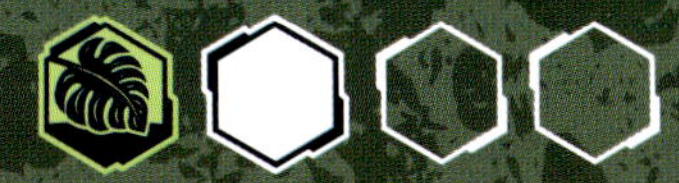

LOCATION:

Montana, South Dakota, Wyoming, USA; Alberta, Saskatchewan, Canada

WHAT WE KNOW:

YEAR NAMED: 1913

DIET: HERBIVORE
Ground cover, such as cycads and flowering plants

SIZE: Over 3m long, over 1m high at the hips

WEIGHT: 68kg

FRIENDS: *Edmontosaurus, Pachycephalosaurus, Triceratops*

ENEMIES: *Acheroraptor, Ornithomimus, Troodon*

Thescelosaurus ('marvellous lizard') was originally collected in Wyoming in 1891 by legendary field palaeontologist John Bell Hatcher. He shipped it back to his employer, Professor Othniel C. Marsh, at Yale University. It stayed packed up and ignored until the turn of the century. It was then given to the Smithsonian Institution as a part of the Marsh Collection. And there it remained, still packed up, until 1913. When Charles Gilmore finally unpacked it, he immediately knew the specimen was a new dinosaur. He named it *Thescelosaurus* neglectus, or 'marvellous but neglected lizard'!

Thescelosaurus is part of the ornithopod family Hypsilophodontidae. All its members have relatively small arms, well-muscled legs and a stiffened tail. Most known specimens are from juveniles.

One rare adult *Thescelosaurus* specimen made worldwide headlines in 2000. It was sold by a commercial collector and nicknamed 'Willo'.

FUN FACT!

THE ORIGINAL SPECIMEN WAS ON DISPLAY AT THE SMITHSONIAN INSTITUTION IN WASHINGTON, D.C.

SKIN SAMPLES (WHICH ARE VERY RARE!) HAVE BEEN FOUND FOR THIS DINOSAUR.

COMPARISON IS WITH A 1.2M TALL CHILD

TIME PERIOD:

252 | 201 | 145 | 66

TRIASSIC | JURASSIC | CRETACEOUS

ABOUT 70–66 MILLION YEARS AGO

TOROSAURUS

TOR-oh-SOAR-us

LOCATION:

Colorado, New Mexico, South Dakota, Texas, Utah, Wyoming, USA; Saskatchewan, Canada

WHAT WE KNOW:

YEAR NAMED: 1981

DIET: HERBIVORE
Conifers, cycads, ginkgos, flowering plants

SIZE: Over 11m long, over 2m high at the hips

WEIGHT: 4,000kg

Torosaurus ('pierced lizard') is one of the last of the ceratopsians, or horned dinosaurs. It is best known for one major feature: its frill, which is larger than its skull—which, at 3m, is one of the longest skulls of any land animal in Earth's history! *Torosaurus's* frill is so long that it severely restricted movement of the skull. The result is that *Torosaurus* would have had to move its whole body, and not just its head, when confronting an attacker. That is why its forelegs were so powerful and highly muscled. Its horns point up and out to the side—directly at the height of an adult *Tyrannosaurus's* belly.

Torosaurus lived at the same time as *Triceratops,* but the *Torosaurus* population appears to have been much smaller. In *Torosaurus,* the frill is much longer and thinner than in *Triceratops,* and the frill has two fenestrae, or windows, that make it much lighter.

FUN FACT!

THE ORIGINAL SPECIMEN WAS COLLECTED BY JOHN BELL HATCHER, WHO WAS NICKNAMED 'THE SKULL FINDER'. HE IS FAMOUS FOR FINDING OVER FIFTY *TRICERATOPS* SKULLS IN JUST TWO SUMMERS.

THE FRILL IS COMPOSED OF THE SAME KIND OF BONE MATTER FOUND IN HUMAN SKULLS.

11m

COMPARISON IS WITH A 1.2M TALL CHILD

TIME PERIOD:

252 | 201 | 145 | 66

TRIASSIC | JURASSIC | CRETACEOUS

ABOUT 70–66 MILLION YEARS AGO

TORVOSAURUS

TOR-vo-SOAR-us

LOCATION:

Colorado, Utah, Wyoming, USA; Portugal

WHAT WE KNOW:

YEAR NAMED: 1979

DIET: CARNIVORE
Sauropods, stegosaurs

SIZE: 10m long, 2.5m high at the hips

WEIGHT: 3,000kg

FUN FACT!

JAMES 'DINOSAUR JIM' JENSEN FOUND A GIANT SPECIMEN OF *BRACHIOSAURUS* (WHICH HE CALLED *'ULTRASAURUS'*) AND A GIANT RELATIVE OF *DIPLODOCUS* (WHICH HE CALLED *'SUPERSAURUS'*) IN THE SAME QUARRY IN WHICH HE DISCOVERED *TORVOSAURUS*.

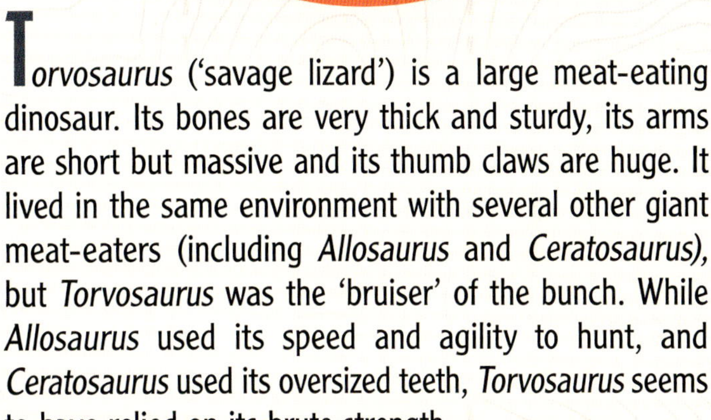

Torvosaurus ('savage lizard') is a large meat-eating dinosaur. Its bones are very thick and sturdy, its arms are short but massive and its thumb claws are huge. It lived in the same environment with several other giant meat-eaters (including *Allosaurus* and *Ceratosaurus),* but *Torvosaurus* was the 'bruiser' of the bunch. While *Allosaurus* used its speed and agility to hunt, and *Ceratosaurus* used its oversized teeth, *Torvosaurus* seems to have relied on its brute strength.

Torvosaurus was first found by legendary fossil hunter 'Dinosaur Jim' Jensen in the Morrison Formation of Colorado. This formation contains many kinds of plant-eating dinosaurs but is especially known for sauropods or giant long-necks, like *Apatosaurus, Brachiosaurus* and *Camarasaurus,* and stegosaurs like *Stegosaurus. Torvosaurus* might have been well suited for attacking young sauropods. It was probably not very fast, but neither were they.

THE STRONG ARMS OF *TORVOSAURUS* ARE PECULIAR: THE FOREARMS ARE LESS THAN HALF THE LENGTH OF THE UPPER ARM!

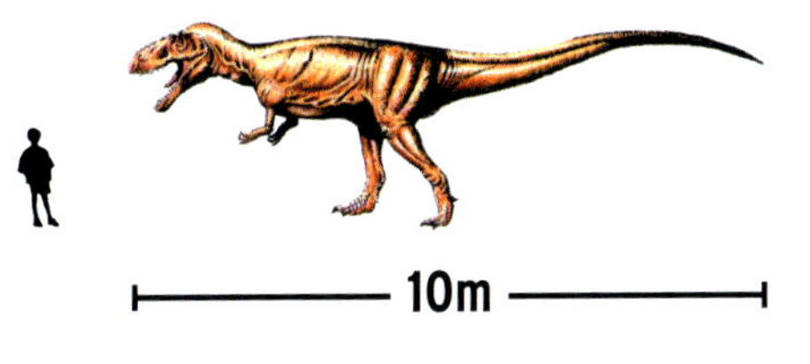

COMPARISON IS WITH A 1.2M TALL CHILD

TIME PERIOD:

252 | 201 | 145 | 66

TRIASSIC | JURASSIC | CRETACEOUS

ABOUT 154–140 MILLION YEARS AGO

TRICERATOPS

try-SAIR-ah-tops

LOCATION:

Colorado, Montana, South Dakota, Wyoming, USA; Canada

WHAT WE KNOW:

YEAR NAMED: 1889

DIET: HERBIVORE
Plants

SIZE: Over 9m long, over 3m high at the hips

WEIGHT: 5,500kg

FUN FACT!

TRICERATOPS HAD ANYWHERE BETWEEN 400 AND 800 TEETH!

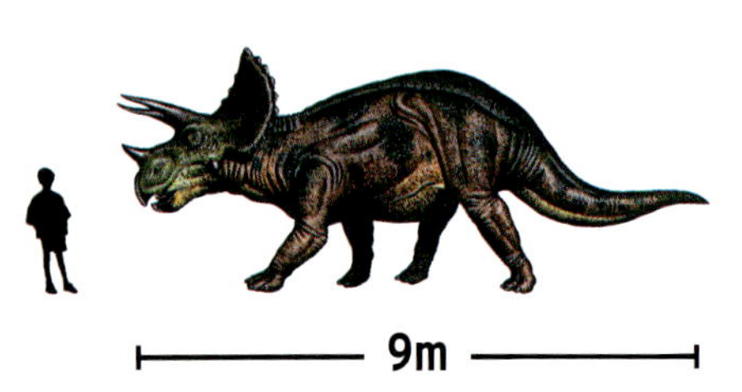

COMPARISON IS WITH A 1.2M TALL CHILD

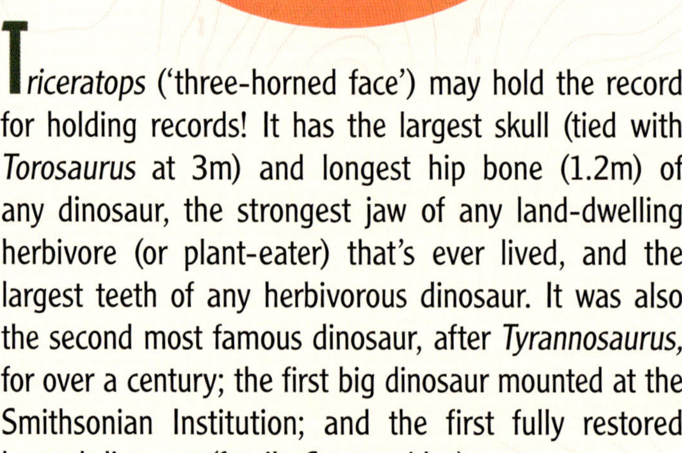

Triceratops ('three-horned face') may hold the record for holding records! It has the largest skull (tied with *Torosaurus* at 3m) and longest hip bone (1.2m) of any dinosaur, the strongest jaw of any land-dwelling herbivore (or plant-eater) that's ever lived, and the largest teeth of any herbivorous dinosaur. It was also the second most famous dinosaur, after *Tyrannosaurus,* for over a century; the first big dinosaur mounted at the Smithsonian Institution; and the first fully restored horned dinosaur (family Ceratopsidae).

With its parrot-like beak, self-sharpening and ever-replacing teeth, massive jaw muscles, 1m horns and body more powerful than a rhino, *Triceratops* was the only dinosaur that could (and sometimes did) outfight a *T. rex!*

IN 1999, *TRICERATOPS* BECAME THE WORLD'S FIRST FULLY 'DIGITAL DINOSAUR'. THE SMITHSONIAN'S COMPLETE MOUNTED SKELETON—AS WELL AS EACH INDIVIDUAL BONE—WAS SCANNED INTO A COMPUTER AND MADE AVAILABLE ON THEIR WEBSITE, WHERE YOU CAN MOVE ITS INDIVIDUAL BONES.

TIME PERIOD:

252 | 201 | 145 | 66

TRIASSIC | JURASSIC | CRETACEOUS

ABOUT 66 MILLION YEARS AGO

TROODON

TRO-oh-don

LOCATION:

Montana, Wyoming, USA; Alberta, Canada

WHAT WE KNOW:

YEAR NAMED: 1856

DIET: OMNIVORE
Possibly small mammals and reptiles, baby dinosaurs, insects, plants

SIZE: 3m long, 94cm high at the hips

WEIGHT: 50kg

WHEN THE FIRST *TROODON* TOOTH WAS FOUND, PALAEONTOLOGISTS THOUGHT IT WAS FROM A LIZARD!

FUN FACT!

PALAEONTOLOGIST DALE RUSSELL ONCE MADE A MODEL OF WHAT HE THOUGHT A MODERN, INTELLIGENT, TOOL-USING DESCENDANT OF *TROODON* WOULD LOOK LIKE. HE NAMED THIS CREATURE A 'DINOSAUROID'.

Troodon ('wounding tooth') is a small bird-like theropod. It has very long legs with specialised feet, in which the middle long bone was pinched out at the top to form a shock-absorbing wedge. This allowed it to run very fast. *Troodon* had very large eyes that faced mostly forward, so that it could focus better. It is famous for having one of the largest brains (for its body size) of any dinosaur.

Troodon had a jaw full of many small teeth, but they were not like the teeth of typical meat-eaters. Instead of little serrations running up and down the back of the teeth (as in most meat-eaters), there were much bigger bumps running along the side, as in many plant-eating dinosaurs and lizards. Some palaeontologists speculate that *Troodon* may have eaten not only small mammals, lizards, and baby dinosaurs, but also insects, eggs and even plants.

Palaeontologist Dave Varricchio discovered the first *Troodon* nests. Like oviraptorosaurs and ground-dwelling birds, *Troodon* would make a nest on the ground. It would then curl up on top of the nest to brood its eggs.

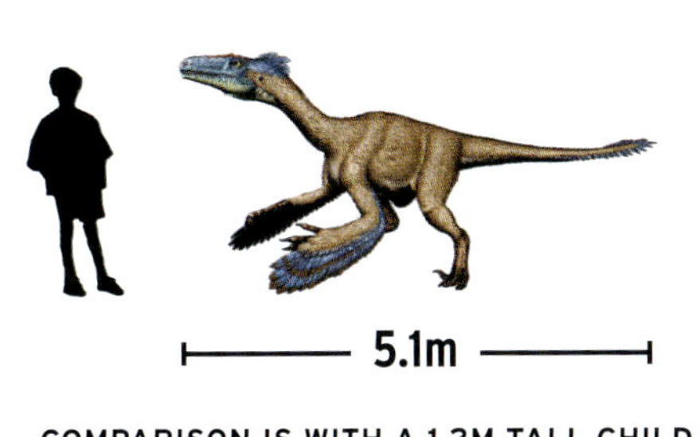

COMPARISON IS WITH A 1.2M TALL CHILD

TIME PERIOD:

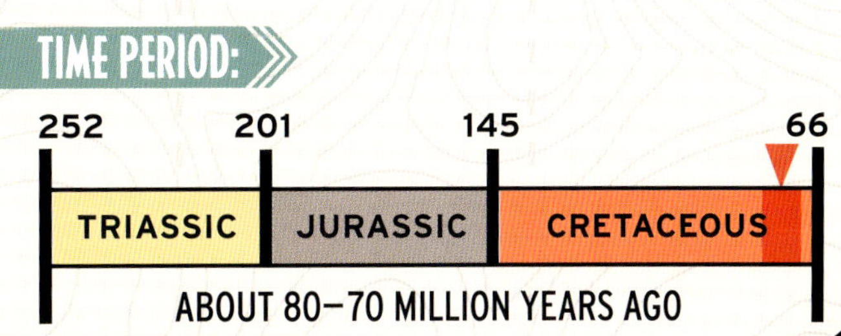

ABOUT 80–70 MILLION YEARS AGO

TYRANNOSAURUS

tie-RAN-oh-SOAR-us

LOCATION:

Colorado, Montana, New Mexico, South Dakota, Texas, Wyoming, USA; Alberta, Saskatchewan, Canada

WHAT WE KNOW:

YEAR NAMED: 1905

DIET: CARNIVORE
Ankylosaurus, Edmontosaurus, Thescelosaurus, Triceratops

SIZE: 12.5m long, 3.9m high at the hips

WEIGHT: 7,000kg

FRIENDS: None

ENEMIES: None

FUN FACT!

A FOSSILISED *T. REX* DROPPING WAS FOUND IN SASKATCHEWAN, CANADA, IN 1995. IT WAS FILLED WITH THE BROKEN AND DIGESTED BONES OF A PLANT-EATING DINOSAUR. THE DROPPING WAS THE SIZE OF A LOAF OF BREAD!

TYRANNOSAURUS HAD THE BIGGEST BRAIN OF ANY DINOSAUR KNOWN.

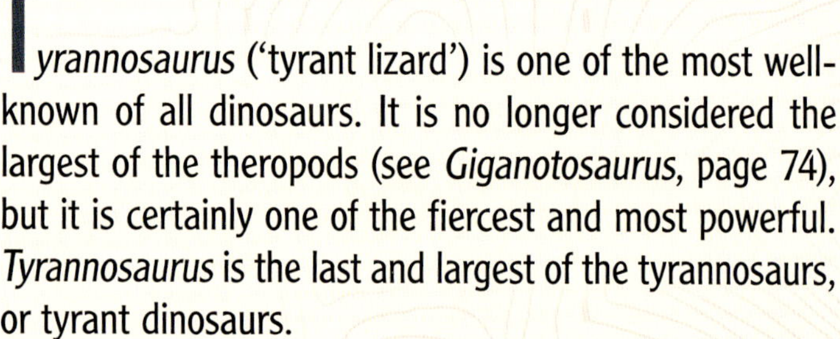

Tyrannosaurus ('tyrant lizard') is one of the most well-known of all dinosaurs. It is no longer considered the largest of the theropods (see *Giganotosaurus*, page 74), but it is certainly one of the fiercest and most powerful. *Tyrannosaurus* is the last and largest of the tyrannosaurs, or tyrant dinosaurs.

Like other tyrant dinosaurs, *Tyrannosaurus* has very short arms with only two fingers. Although these were probably useless while hunting, its jaws were not: *Tyrannosaurus* has an enormous skull armed with teeth the size of bananas! Unlike the teeth of most meat-eaters, tyrant dinosaur teeth are very thick and capable of crushing bones. The skull and neck bones show that *T. rex* had the largest neck muscles of any meat-eating dinosaur. It probably used its strong neck to twist and pull off big chunks of meat that it grasped with its jaws. *Tyrannosaurus* could bite with extremely strong force—one fossilised skeleton shows that it crushed and swallowed the bones of a smaller plant-eating dinosaur.

Most dinosaurs, in general, had eyes facing sideways, which allowed them to see all around themselves. The eyes of *Tyrannosaurus*, though, faced forwards so it could focus better on a single object and tell precisely how far away it was. This would be very useful for a hunter—especially one that had to fight *Triceratops*, one of the most dangerous plant-eating dinosaurs of all.

The legs of the tyrant dinosaurs were long and slender for their size, allowing them to chase down the horned dinosaurs and duckbills that were the most common plant-eaters of their time. In fact, a specimen of the duckbill *Edmontosaurus* shows a bite mark taken out of its tail that matches the bite of *Tyrannosaurus*. Because this bite was healed, we know that the *Edmontosaurus* managed to get away from its attacker!

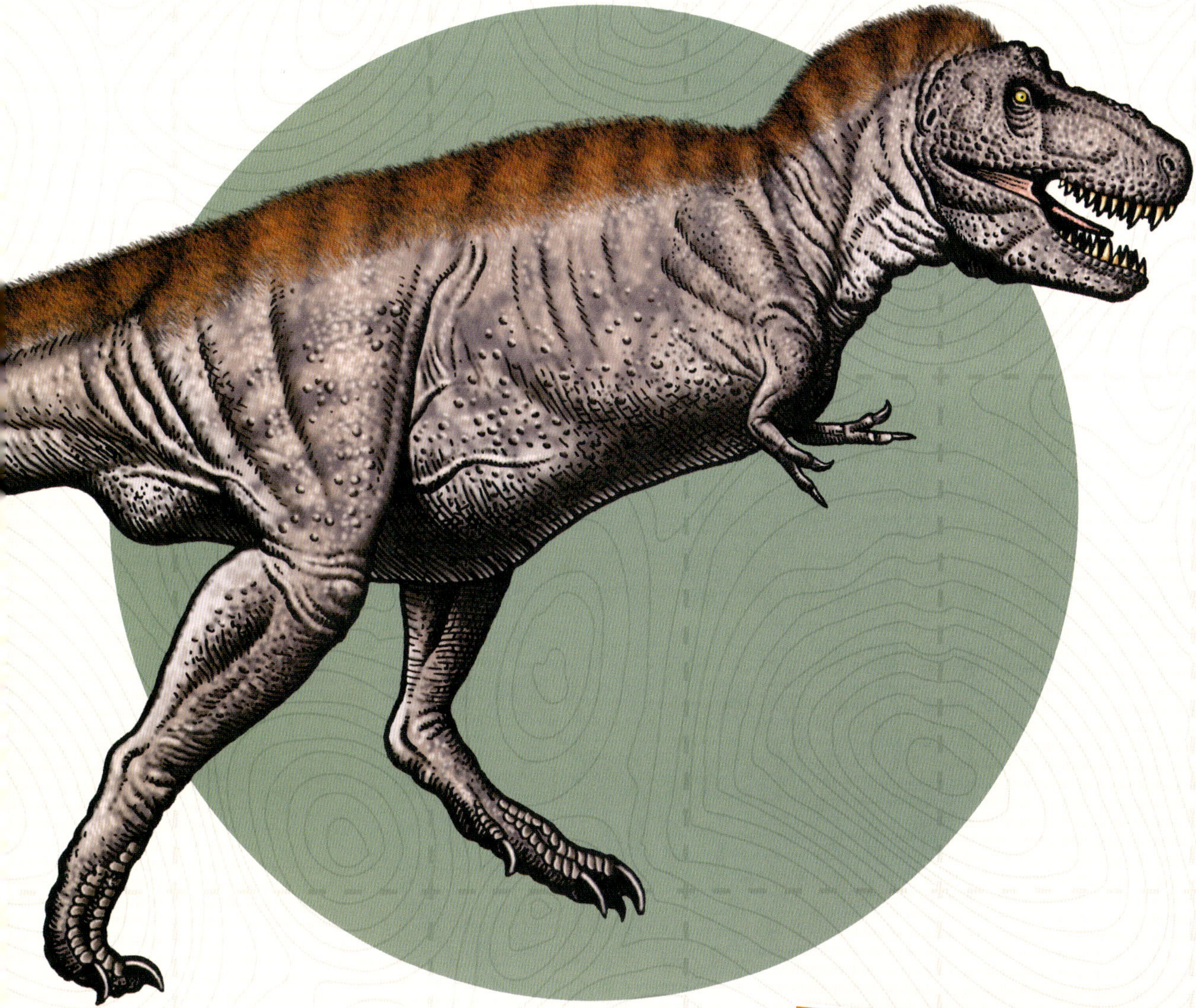

Although some people think that the female *Tyrannosaurus* was larger than the male, there is no real evidence for this. Indeed, palaeontologists do not yet know how to tell a male *Tyrannosaurus* from a female from just the skeleton. It is known, though, that *Tyrannosaurus* led a rough life. Some specimens show many broken bones that had healed over.

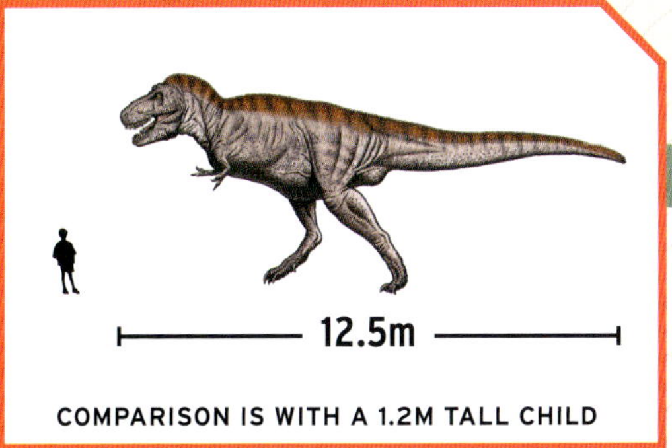

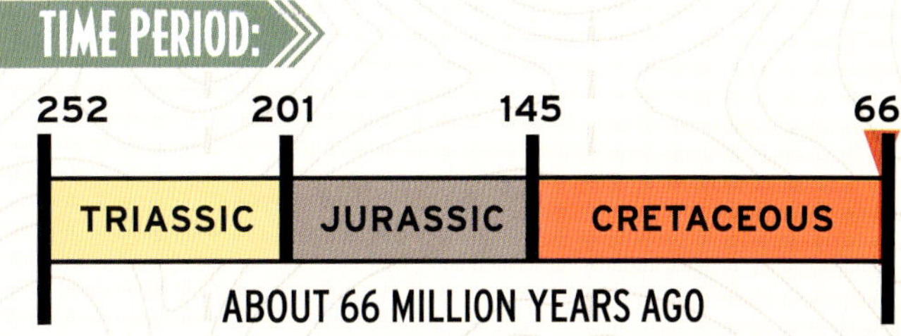

VELOCIRAPTOR

vuh-LOS-ih-RAP-tor

LOCATION:

Mongolia;
China

WHAT WE KNOW:

YEAR NAMED: 1924

DIET: CARNIVORE
Protoceratops, Oviraptor, Shuvuuia, other dinosaurs

SIZE: About 2m long, 50cm high at the hips

WEIGHT: 7kg

FUN FACT!

VELOCIRAPTORS ARE KNOWN ONLY FROM ASIA!

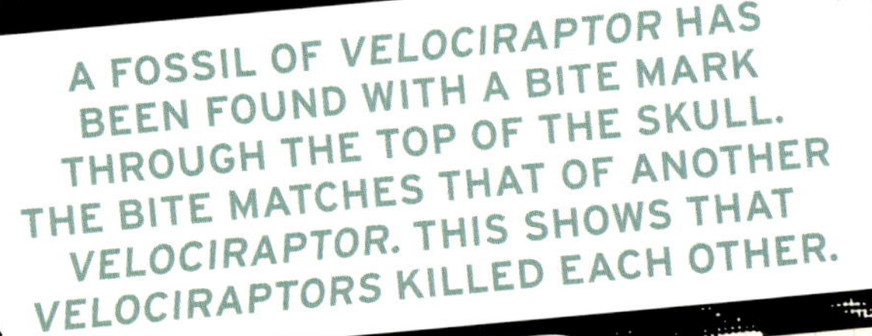

Velociraptor ('swift hunter') is probably the most famous meat-eating dinosaur after *Tyrannosaurus*. Although it was first described in 1923, it was made famous to most people by its starring role in *Jurassic World* and *Jurassic Park*.

Velociraptor is one of the dromaeosaurs, or raptor dinosaurs. It is actually a pretty small, but fierce, dinosaur, with a skull only 18cm long. Its arms are long and end in powerful grasping claws. Its feet have huge sickle-shaped claws, which could retract when not in use.

A spectacular fossil from Mongolia shows exactly how these claws were used. The fossil shows a *Velociraptor*

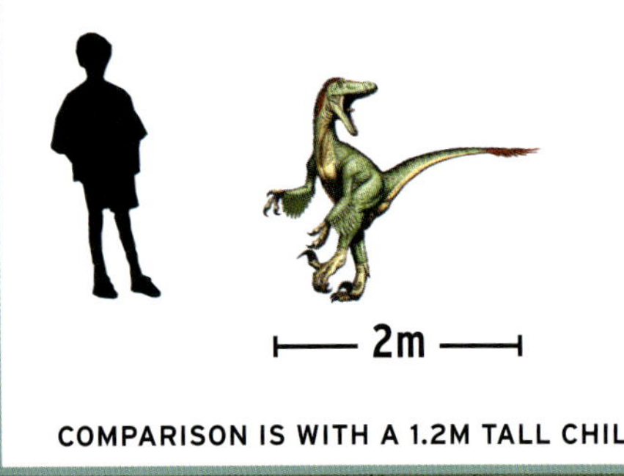

COMPARISON IS WITH A 1.2M TALL CHILD

TIME PERIOD:

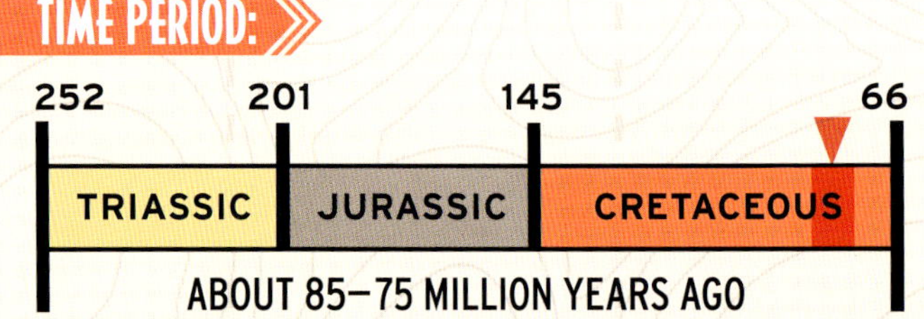

ABOUT 85–75 MILLION YEARS AGO

and a little horned dinosaur—*Protoceratops*—locked in their final battle. The hands of the *Velociraptor* are clutching the skull of the *Protoceratops,* while the left foot claw of the raptor is buried deep in the horned dinosaur's neck. The *Velociraptor* was apparently in the midst of ripping out the throat of the *Protoceratops* when the two were buried in a sand dune. (The little horned dinosaur seems to have had its revenge, however, as the *Velociraptor's* right arm was in its beak. The *Protoceratops* no doubt bit it off with its final bite!)

Like all raptor dinosaurs, the real *Velociraptor* was covered with feathers. There are even bumps on its arms to show where big feathers were attached.

WUERHOSAURUS

woo-AIR-ho-SOAR-us

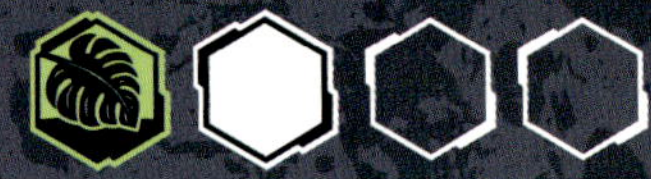

LOCATION:

Mongolia; China

WHAT WE KNOW:

YEAR NAMED: 1994

DIET: HERBIVORE
Conifers, cycads, ginkgos

SIZE: 8.1m long, 1.8m high at the hips

WEIGHT: 4,000kg

FUN FACT!

STEGOSAURS WERE PROBABLY THE SLOWEST OF ALL DINOSAURS. THE THIGHBONE IS ALMOST TWICE AS LONG AS THE SHIN BONE–THE OPPOSITE OF WHAT YOU'D FIND IN HIGH-SPEED ANIMALS. IN *WUERHOSAURUS*, WE SEE ANOTHER DINOSAUR THAT GAVE UP ANY CHANCE AT SPEED TO PUT ALL OF ITS EFFORT INTO DEFENCE.

COMPARISON IS WITH A 1.2M TALL CHILD

Wuerhosaurus ('lizard from Wuerho') is a rare type of stegosaur from the Cretaceous Period. Well before the final extinction of the dinosaurs, stegosaurs became extinct and were replaced by ankylosaurs. The reason this occurred may be found by comparing their features. Although stegosaurs were well covered with plates on their backs and tails, their sides were less protected. Ankylosaurs were fully armoured, and this may help explain why stegosaurs became extinct first. The presence of this stegosaur *(Wuerhosaurus)* in China—well into the Cretaceous—suggests that an isolated group survived in that area.

There are two major features that separate *Wuerhosaurus* from a typical *Stegosaurus*. *Wuerhosaurus* has a shorter body and a wide, flaring hip bone. In stegosaurs in general, the hip bone is so large that it grows up, outwards and over the thighbone.

STEGOSAURS, IN GENERAL, ARE ONE OF THE RAREST OF ALL THE DINOSAUR GROUPS BECAUSE NOT MANY SPECIES EVOLVED.

TIME PERIOD:

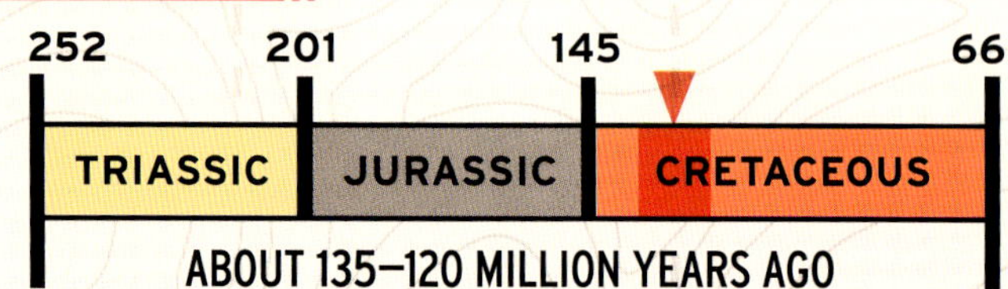

ABOUT 135–120 MILLION YEARS AGO

ZUNICERATOPS

ZOO-nee-SAIR-ah-tops

LOCATION:

New Mexico, USA

WHAT WE KNOW:

YEAR NAMED: 1998

DIET: HERBIVORE
Ground cover of cycads, flowering plants

SIZE: 3m long, about 1m high at the hips

WEIGHT: 250kg

FRIENDS: Hadrosaurs

ENEMIES: Dromaeosaurs

Zuniceratops ('Zuni horned face') was the first ceratopsian, or horned dinosaur, to appear with horns over the eyes (an advanced feature) as well as several primitive features. It is older than all the classic horned dinosaurs of western North America, like *Centrosaurus* and *Triceratops.* So maybe long horns first appeared in North America? But science can be complicated: another dinosaur of just about the same age, *Turanoceratops,* is known from central Asia, and it also has eyebrow horns. Did these horns first appear in Asia and move to North America, or vice versa? We are still looking for the answer.

Zuniceratops also has single-rooted teeth (all the later ceratopsians have double-rooted teeth). This shows that in ceratopsians, the frill and horns evolved first, followed by changes in the teeth.

FUN FACT!

TEETH OF AN EVEN EARLIER CERATOPSIAN, POSSIBLY RELATED TO *ZUNICERATOPS,* WERE FOUND IN MARYLAND IN 1991.

THE FIRST KNOWN PERSON TO DISCOVER THE FOSSIL OF A *ZUNICERATOPS* WAS JUST EIGHT YEARS OLD! HIS NAME WAS CHRISTOPHER JAMES WOLFE AND HE WAS THE SON OF THE PALAEONTOLOGIST DOUGLAS G. WOLFE.

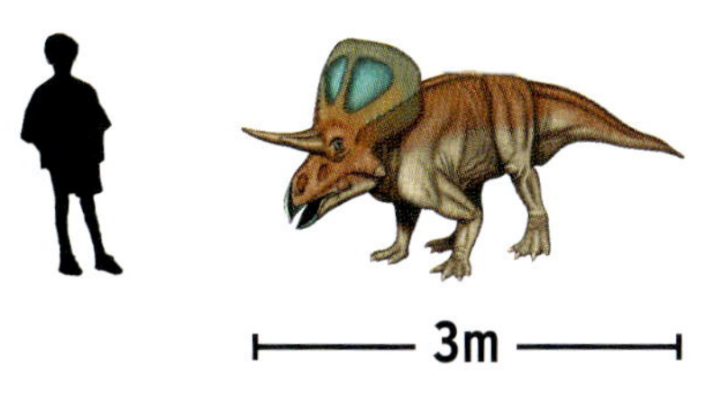

COMPARISON IS WITH A 1.2M TALL CHILD

TIME PERIOD:

252 | 201 | 145 | 66

TRIASSIC | JURASSIC | CRETACEOUS

ABOUT 93–89 MILLION YEARS AGO

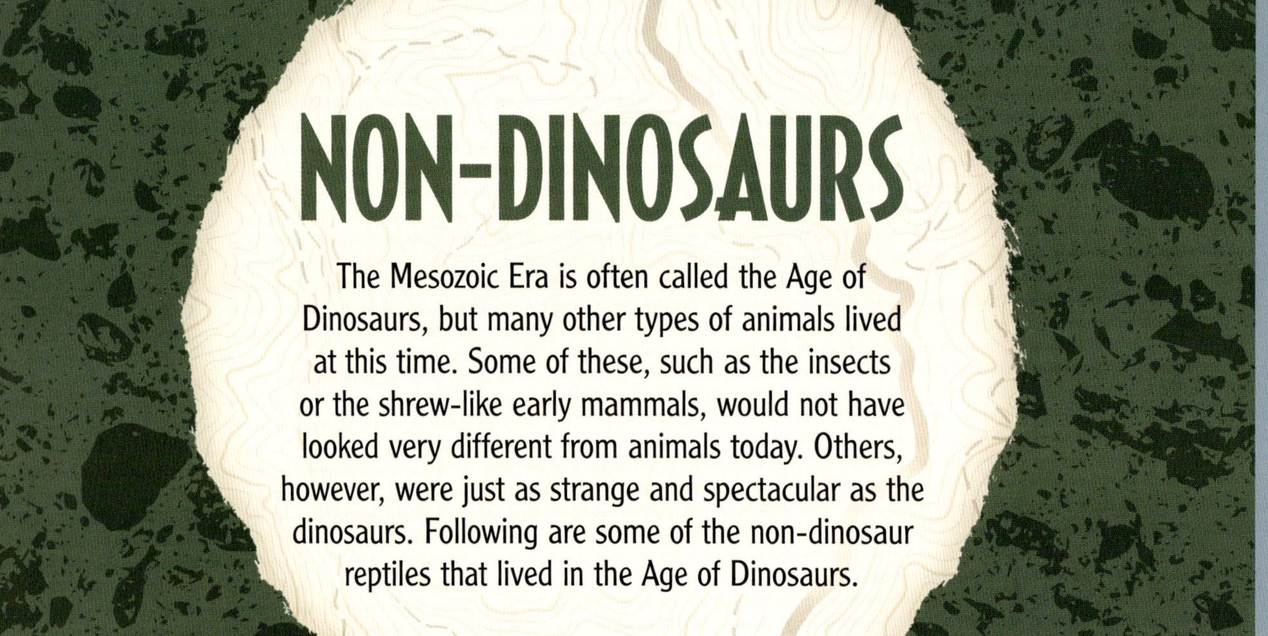

NON-DINOSAURS

The Mesozoic Era is often called the Age of Dinosaurs, but many other types of animals lived at this time. Some of these, such as the insects or the shrew-like early mammals, would not have looked very different from animals today. Others, however, were just as strange and spectacular as the dinosaurs. Following are some of the non-dinosaur reptiles that lived in the Age of Dinosaurs.

MARINE REPTILES

During the Age of Dinosaurs, many groups of reptiles that once had land-living ancestors evolved into swimming reptiles. Most of the groups still spent a lot of time on shore—as do the marine iguanas of the Galápagos Islands today—and had hands and feet that ended in fingers and toes. Others, however, spent almost their whole lives in the water. In these groups, the hands and feet evolved into flippers. Three of the more amazing groups of marine reptiles are plesiosaurs, ichthyosaurs and mosasaurs.

MOSASAURUS

Mosasaurs are a genus of large aquatic carnivorous lizards from the Late Cretaceous about 70–66 million years ago. This giant reptile, shown below, is seen in the *Mosasaurus Feeding Show* in *Jurassic World.*

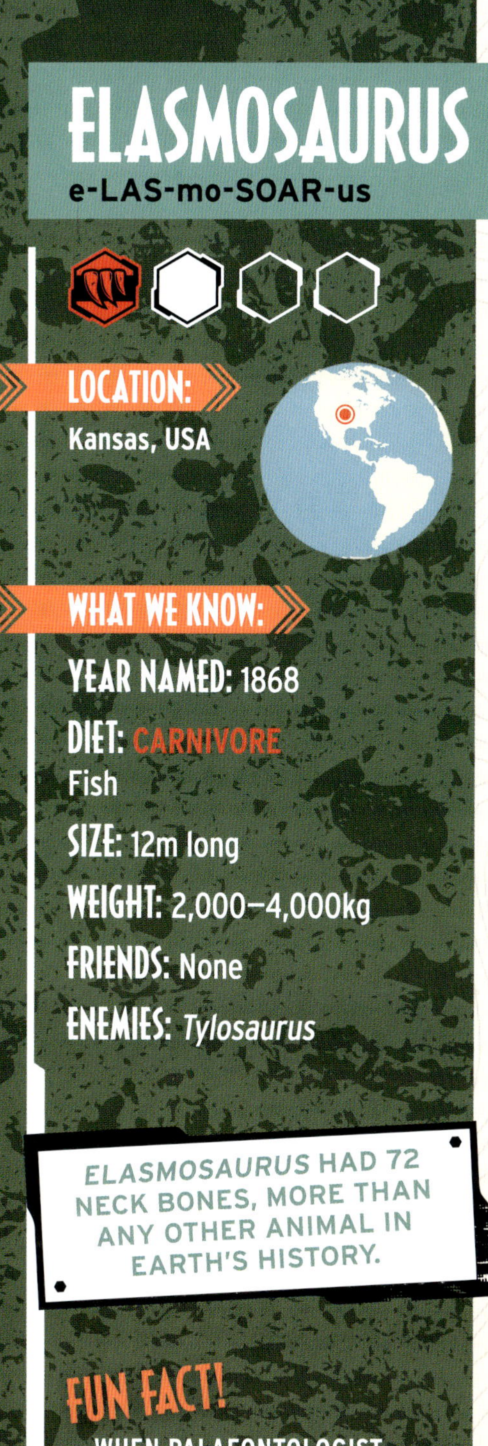

Elasmosaurus ('plate lizard') is one of the more famous members of the plesiosaurs, or near lizards, a major group of Mesozoic Era marine reptiles. All plesiosaurs had compact bodies with four powerful flippers, which they used to swim through the water. Their tails were generally short, and they may have crawled up onto beaches to lay their eggs, the way sea turtles do today.

Elasmosaurus, like many plesiosaurs, had a small head at the end of a long neck and a mouth full of needle-like teeth. It could swim into schools of fish, moving its head back and forth to catch them. At up to 12m long, *Elasmosaurus* was among the largest of the long-necked plesiosaurs.

Other plesiosaurs had bodies similar to *Elasmosaurus's,* but instead of small heads and long necks, they had big heads and short necks! These plesiosaurs had large, conical teeth for catching larger prey. Some of these short-necked plesiosaurs were small, but others grew as big as a sperm whale! These giant plesiosaurs had skulls much bigger than those of the biggest meat-eating dinosaurs, like *Tyrannosaurus, Giganotosaurus* and *Spinosaurus.*

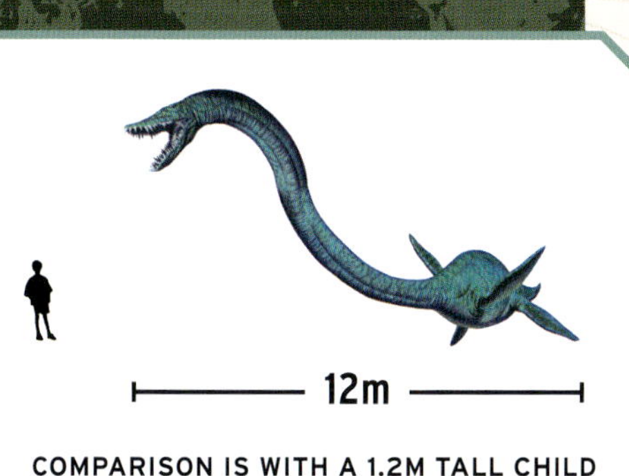

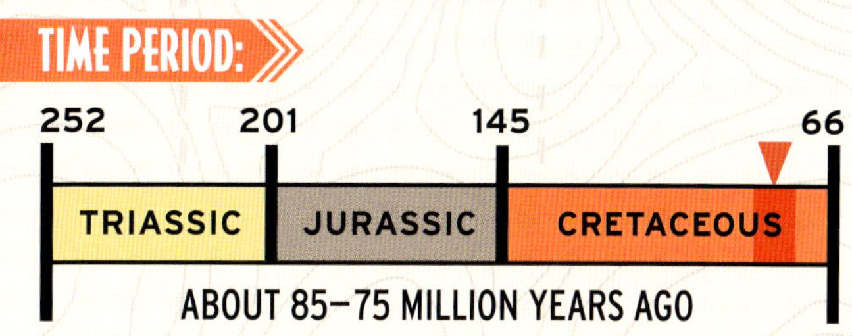

OPHTHALMOSAURUS

op-THAL-mo-SOAR-us

LOCATION:

England

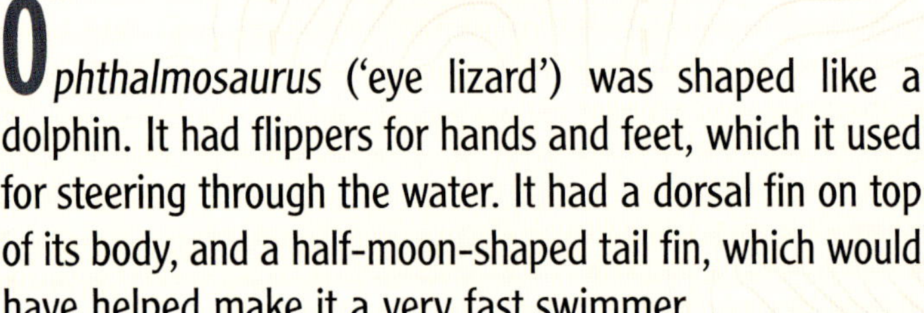

WHAT WE KNOW:

YEAR NAMED: 1874

DIET: CARNIVORE
Squid and squid-like shellfish, fish

SIZE: 4m long

WEIGHT: 1,000kg

FRIENDS: None

ENEMIES: *Liopleurodon* (a giant short-necked plesiosaur)

Ophthalmosaurus (‘eye lizard’) was shaped like a dolphin. It had flippers for hands and feet, which it used for steering through the water. It had a dorsal fin on top of its body, and a half-moon-shaped tail fin, which would have helped make it a very fast swimmer.

Ophthalmosaurus was one of the ichthyosaurs, or fish lizards. They were neither fish nor lizards, but were related to the plesiosaurs.

Although dolphins and ichthyosaurs look similar, there are many important differences. Dolphins are a kind of mammal, whereas ichthyosaurs were reptiles. Dolphins primarily use sonar (sending out and listening for special sound waves) to tell where objects are underwater. There is no evidence that ichthyosaurs used sonar, but they did have enormous eyes to see their prey.

Ichthyosaurs would not have been able to support themselves on land to lay their eggs. Instead, as fossils show us, their babies grew inside the body of the mother until they were large enough to swim on their own. Then, like dolphins, they were born tail first.

FUN FACT!

THE LARGEST ICHTHYOSAUR HAD EYES OVER 26CM ACROSS–THE LARGEST EYES OF ANY KNOWN ANIMAL IN THE HISTORY OF THE EARTH!

OPHTHALMOSAURUS MAY HAVE BEEN ABLE TO DIVE ALMOST A THOUSAND FEET DOWN IN THE WATER WHILE CHASING AFTER ITS FOOD.

4m

COMPARISON IS WITH A 1.2M TALL CHILD

TIME PERIOD:

252 | 201 | 145 | 66

TRIASSIC | JURASSIC | CRETACEOUS

ABOUT 165–150 MILLION YEARS AGO

TYLOSAURUS

TIE-lo-SOAR-us

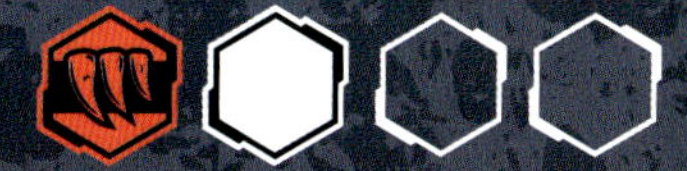

LOCATION:

Kansas, USA; South Africa; Angola; Japan

WHAT WE KNOW:

YEAR NAMED: 1872

DIET: CARNIVORE
Turtles, plesiosaurs, other mosasaurs, large fish, shellfish

SIZE: 12m long

WEIGHT: 5,000kg

FRIENDS: Unknown

ENEMIES: Unknown

FUN FACT!

MOSASAURS WERE THE FIRST GROUP OF EXTINCT REPTILES KNOWN TO SCIENCE.

Tylosaurus ('knob lizard') has a large, strong chest and arms, big hands, a long body with weak legs and a strong tail for swimming. It has a ram-shaped snout and big conical teeth for catching prey. It is a mosasaur, or 'Meuse River lizard', a true marine lizard. The mosasaurs are related to the modern monitor lizards (like the Komodo dragon), Gila monsters, and snakes. Mosasaurs, however, lived their whole lives in the water. As in ichthyosaurs, their young developed inside the mother and were born live into the water.

Mosasaurs were probably not as fast as the earlier ichthyosaurs had been, and instead ambushed their prey the way many sharks do today. Some mosasaurs had flatter teeth than *Tylosaurus,* which they used for cracking open shellfish.

A FOSSIL OF A GIANT SEA TURTLE HAS BEEN FOUND WITH A FLIPPER BITTEN OFF– PROBABLY BY A *TYLOSAURUS.*

COMPARISON IS WITH A 1.2M TALL CHILD

TIME PERIOD:

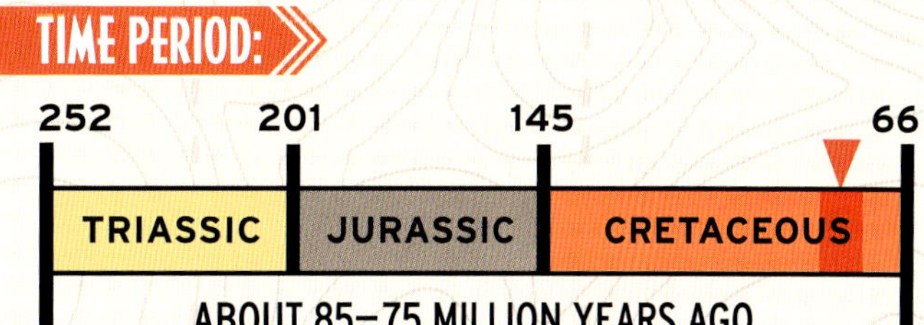

ABOUT 85–75 MILLION YEARS AGO

ARCHOSAURS AND RELATIVES

Archosaurs, or 'ruling lizards', is the name given by scientists to a large group of both extinct and modern reptiles. Crocodilians and birds are living archosaurs. Various extinct groups of dinosaurs and pterosaurs are also archosaurs.

Each particular group of archosaurs has its own distinct features. All dinosaurs are archosaurs, but not all archosaurs are dinosaurs (remember, to be a dinosaur an animal has to be a descendant of the most recent common ancestor of *Iguanodon* and *Megalosaurus*). Following are some non-dinosaurian archosaurs that lived during the Age of Dinosaurs, including some extinct crocodilians. Also included is *Tanystropheus,* an archosaur relative.

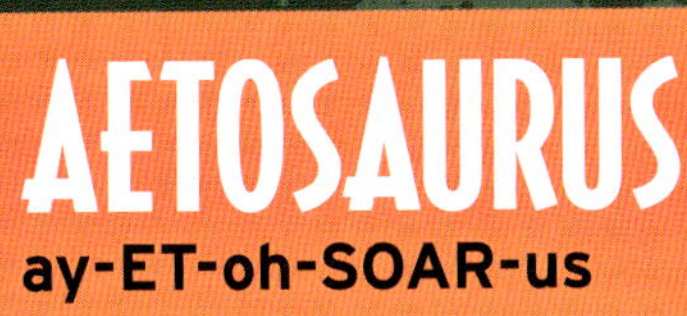

AETOSAURUS

ay-ET-oh-SOAR-us

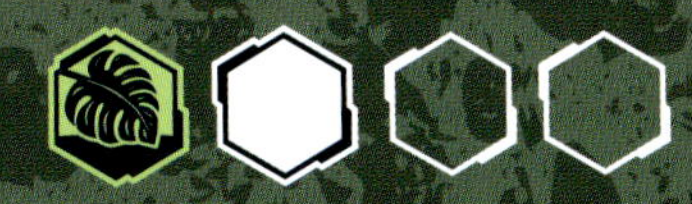

LOCATION:

Germany

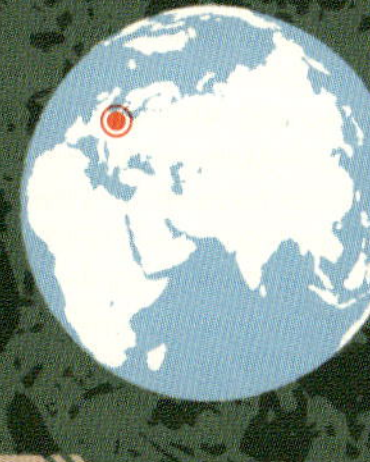

WHAT WE KNOW:

YEAR NAMED: 1877

DIET: HERBIVORE
Ferns, cycads

SIZE: 1.5m long, 30cm high at the hips

WEIGHT: 45kg

Aetosaurus ('eagle lizard') was a plant-eater built low to the ground. It had legs that sprawled out to the side and heavy armour protecting its back.

Aetosaurus had a pig-like snout, which it might have used to sniff out tasty plants. Its hands, however, do not seem to have been specialised for digging. The armour on its back was jointed so that it could roll itself up to protect its belly, like a modern armadillo.

During the Late Triassic, the armoured dinosaurs had not yet evolved. Perhaps this was because the aetosaurs were already present and there wasn't a place in the environment for a new group of armoured plant-eating reptiles.

At the end of the Late Triassic, there was a series of extinctions among the animals and plants on land and in the sea. These extinctions may have been caused by volcanic eruptions, though other factors may have helped. Whatever the cause, aetosaurs (and many other groups) died out at the end of the Late Triassic.

FUN FACT!

THE FIRST AETOSAUR FOSSILS DISCOVERED WERE OF THEIR ARMOUR. BECAUSE THESE PLATES RESEMBLED THE ARMOUR OF EXTINCT FISH THAT WERE FOUND IN SIMILAR ROCKS, PALAEONTOLOGISTS THOUGHT THEY HAD FOUND A NEW KIND OF EXTINCT FISH. IT WASN'T UNTIL AN AETOSAUR'S BONES WERE DISCOVERED THAT THEY REALISED THEY HAD FOUND A NEW KIND OF REPTILE.

AETOSAURS WERE FOUND IN NORTH AMERICA, SOUTH AMERICA AND EUROPE.

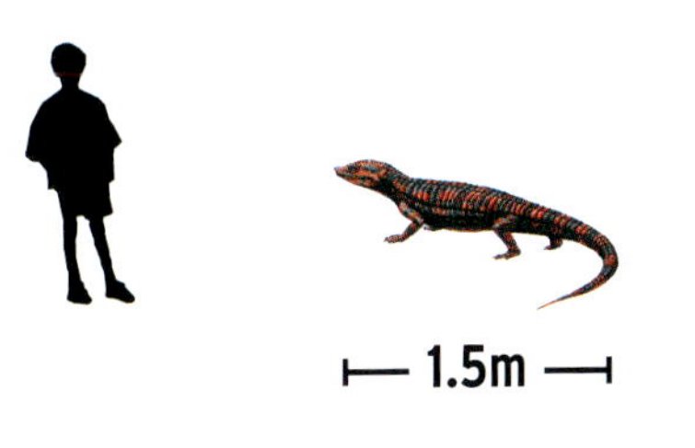

COMPARISON IS WITH A 1.2M TALL CHILD

TIME PERIOD:

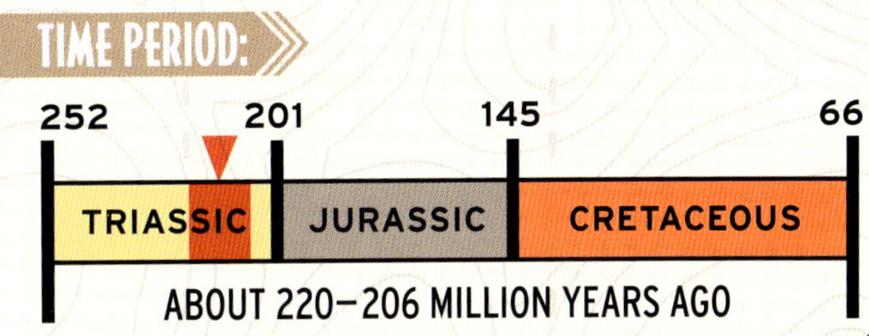

ABOUT 220–206 MILLION YEARS AGO

DEINOSUCHUS

DI-no-SOO-kus

LOCATION:

Alabama, Georgia, Mississippi, Montana, New Jersey, North Carolina, Texas, USA

WHAT WE KNOW:

YEAR NAMED: 1909

DIET: CARNIVORE
Large turtles, possibly large fish and dinosaurs

SIZE: 12m long, 2.4m high, maybe more, at the hips

WEIGHT: 9,000–10,000kg

Deinosuchus ('terrible crocodile') is a giant crocodilian, closely related to the modern alligators and caimans (Central and South American crocodilians).

Deinosuchus is a gigantic predator, up to 12m long. Because crocodilians are more heavily built than theropods, or meat-eating dinosaurs, the largest *Deinosuchus* would have been larger than the largest *Tyrannosaurus, Giganotosaurus* or *Spinosaurus.*

Deinosuchus is sometimes pictured as eating dinosaurs. While it most likely would have eaten a dinosaur if one came close, it probably hunted prey that was more common in the swamps where it lived. Some palaeontologists speculate that it was mostly a hunter of large turtles.

Although crocodilians survived the extinction at the end of the Cretaceous Period, *Deinosuchus* did not.

FUN FACT!

MOST SPECIMENS OF *DEINOSUCHUS* CONSIST OF INDIVIDUAL TEETH OR ARMOURED PLATES.

NO MODERN CROCODILES ARE AS BIG AS *DEINOSUCHUS*, BUT THE SALTWATER CROCODILE OF AUSTRALIA AND THE INDIAN OCEAN REGION GROWS UP TO 6M LONG, BIGGER THAN ANY LAND-LIVING PREDATOR IN THE MODERN WORLD!

COMPARISON IS WITH A 1.2M TALL CHILD

TIME PERIOD:

252	201	145	66
TRIASSIC	JURASSIC	CRETACEOUS	

ABOUT 80–70 MILLION YEARS AGO

LAGOSUCHUS

law-go-SOOK-us

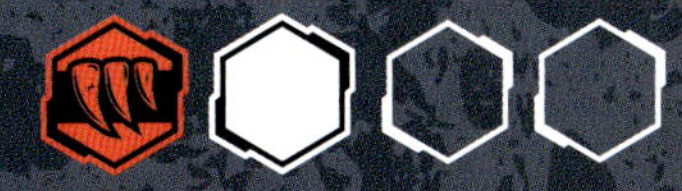

LOCATION:

Argentina

WHAT WE KNOW:

YEAR NAMED: 1971

DIET: CARNIVORE
Insects, possibly small reptiles

SIZE: 50cm long, 15cm high at the hips

WEIGHT: 220g

FRIENDS: Herbivorous reptiles

ENEMIES: *Rauisuchus*

FUN FACT!

SOME PALAEONTOLOGISTS CALL THIS ARCHOSAUR *MARASUCHUS*, AFTER THE MARA–A RODENT FROM SOUTH AMERICA THAT LOOKS AND ACTS LIKE A RABBIT.

Lagosuchus ('rabbit crocodile') is a little archosaur the size of a rabbit. It had a small, pointed snout, long hind legs and a long tail.

There were many larger and more interesting creatures living in the Middle Triassic, but *Lagosuchus* is important to palaeontologists for a good reason: It helps us understand where dinosaurs came from.

Lagosuchus had long shins and feet. Its legs were not sprawled out at the side (as in most reptiles) but were held directly underneath the body. This would have allowed it to run fast for a long time. Dinosaurs also have these features. In fact, *Lagosuchus* seems either to be the ancestor of the dinosaurs or a close relative of that ancestor.

Dinosaurs were not always giant creatures. The earliest dinosaurs were small. Having legs directly underneath the body helped early dinosaurs run after insects and small reptiles, and run away from bigger meat-eaters. The same trait helped the later dinosaurs become giants because legs like that could better support their weight.

THIS POSSIBLE ANCESTOR OF THE GIANT DINOSAURS WAS SMALL ENOUGH TO HAVE BEEN THREATENED BY A CAT!

50cm

COMPARISON IS WITH A 1.2M TALL CHILD

TIME PERIOD:

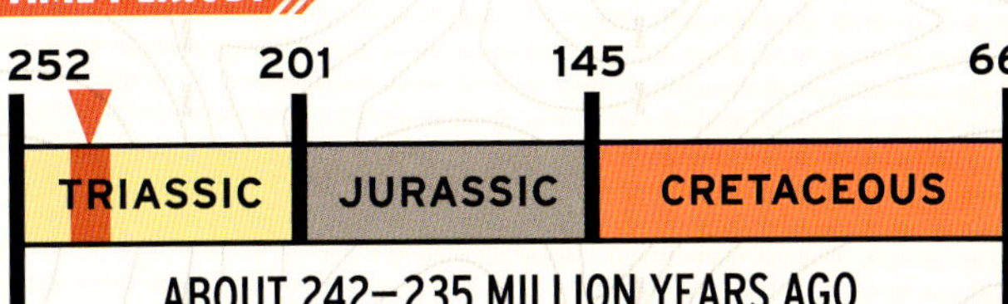

ABOUT 242–235 MILLION YEARS AGO

RAUISUCHUS

ROW-ee-SOO-kus

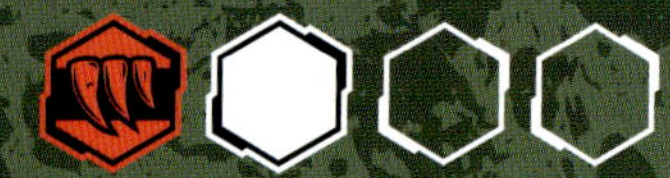

LOCATION:

Brazil

WHAT WE KNOW:

YEAR NAMED: 1942

DIET: CARNIVORE
Other reptiles

SIZE: 4m long, 90cm high at the hips

WEIGHT: 250kg

FRIENDS: Unknown

ENEMIES: Unknown

Rauisuchus ('Rau's crocodile'—named after fossil collector Dr Wilhelm Rau) is one of a group of land-dwelling relatives of the crocodilians called the rauisuchians. These creatures were the top predators on land during the Triassic Period (the beginning of the Age of Dinosaurs).

Rauisuchus and its relatives had heads that looked a lot like those of theropods, or meat-eating dinosaurs. Rauisuchians, however, walked on all fours, while theropods walked on their hind legs. Like a dinosaur's, *Rauisuchus's* legs were directly underneath its body, but unlike a dinosaur, it walked on the soles of its feet. Dinosaurs walked only on their toes, like cats and dogs. Because of this, dinosaurs were probably faster than *Rauisuchus* and its kin.

Rauisuchus lived with the very earliest dinosaurs. It may have hunted these early ancestors of *Tyrannosaurus*, *Velociraptor* and *Triceratops*.

FUN FACT!

SOME RAUISUCHIANS GREW UP TO 7M LONG.

THE FOSSIL TRACKWAYS OF RAUISUCHUS AND ITS RELATIVES WERE FIRST THOUGHT TO HAVE COME FROM SOMETHING LIKE A GIGANTIC FROG!

4m

COMPARISON IS WITH A 1.2M TALL CHILD

TIME PERIOD:

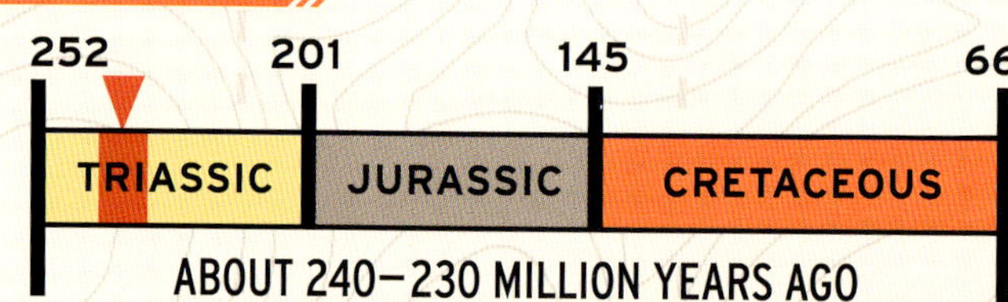

ABOUT 240–230 MILLION YEARS AGO

SIMOSUCHUS

seem-o-SOOK-us

LOCATION:

Madagascar

WHAT WE KNOW:

YEAR NAMED: 2000

DIET: **HERBIVORE**
Ferns, cycads, possibly flowering plants

SIZE: 1m long, 25cm high at the hips

WEIGHT: 23kg

FRIENDS: None

ENEMIES: *Majungasaurus*

Simosuchus ('pug-nosed crocodile') is a crocodilian—a member of the group that contains living crocodiles, alligators, caimans, gavials, and their extinct relatives—with a short snout. Its teeth are almost identical to those of plant-eating dinosaurs. Its body is covered with heavy armour. In fact, *Simosuchus* seems to be part crocodile, part ankylosaur! This is an example of what palaeontologists call 'convergent evolution', where two different groups of animals evolve the same basic features because of a similar lifestyle.

People sometimes say that crocodilians are 'unchanged since the Age of Dinosaurs'. While it is true that some Mesozoic crocodilians look similar to living crocodiles, *Simosuchus* lived on land—in other words, it was not an aquatic predator.

WHEN THREATENED, A *SIMOSUCHUS* WOULD PROBABLY HUNKER DOWN SO THE ATTACKING MEAT-EATER COULD BITE ONLY ITS TOUGH ARMOUR.

FUN FACT!

OTHER PLANT-EATING CROCODILES ARE KNOWN FROM THE LATE CRETACEOUS OF SOUTH AMERICA.

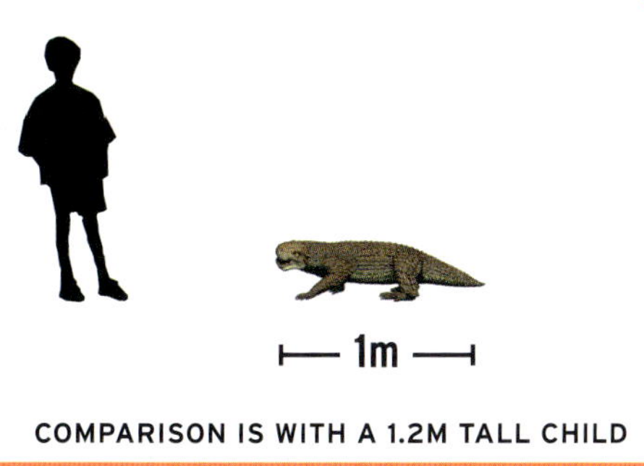

TIME PERIOD:

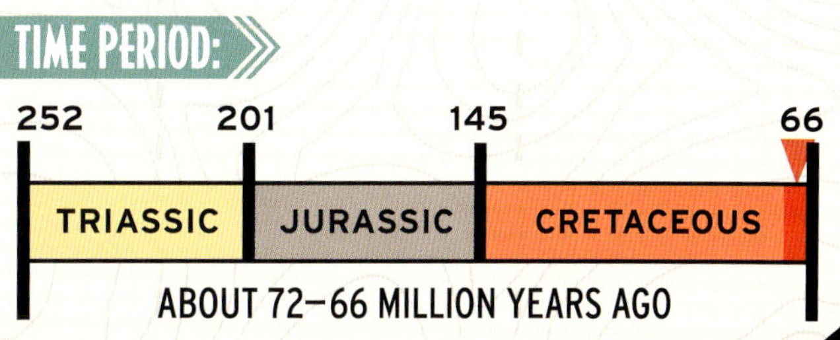

TANYSTROPHEUS

tan-ee-STRO-fee-us

LOCATION:

Italy

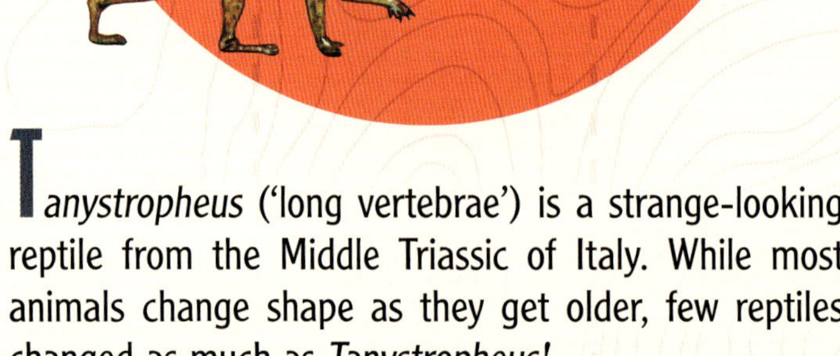

WHAT WE KNOW:

YEAR NAMED: 1852

DIET: CARNIVORE
Fish

SIZE: Over 3m long, more than 1.2m high when the neck was raised

WEIGHT: 18kg

FRIENDS: None

ENEMIES: Predatory reptiles

Tanystropheus ('long vertebrae') is a strange-looking reptile from the Middle Triassic of Italy. While most animals change shape as they get older, few reptiles changed as much as *Tanystropheus!*

The main change was in the size of the neck. Baby *Tanystropheus* had necks shorter than their legs, but adult *Tanystropheus* had necks longer than the rest of their bodies (head, back and tail) combined! Although the neck became very long, no neck vertebrae were added. Instead, each vertebra became longer and longer.

Some palaeontologists think that *Tanystropheus* used its long neck to swim into schools of fish and sweep its jaws through them. Others think that the super-long neck was used as a form of display, like the huge tail of a peacock. Both ideas may be correct.

FUN FACT!

THE FIRST BONES OF *TANYSTROPHEUS* FOUND WERE THOUGHT TO BE PART OF AN EARLY PTEROSAUR.

BEFORE THEY FOUND COMPLETE SKELETONS, PALAEONTOLOGISTS THOUGHT THE NECK VERTEBRAE OF *TANYSTROPHEUS* WERE FROM A DINOSAUR LIKE *COELOPHYSIS*.

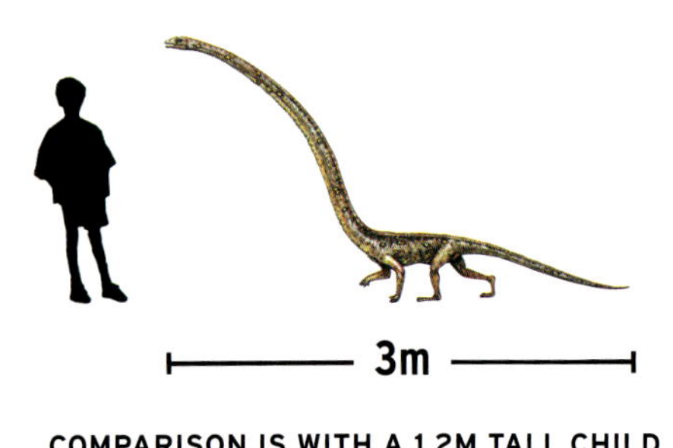

COMPARISON IS WITH A 1.2M TALL CHILD

TIME PERIOD:

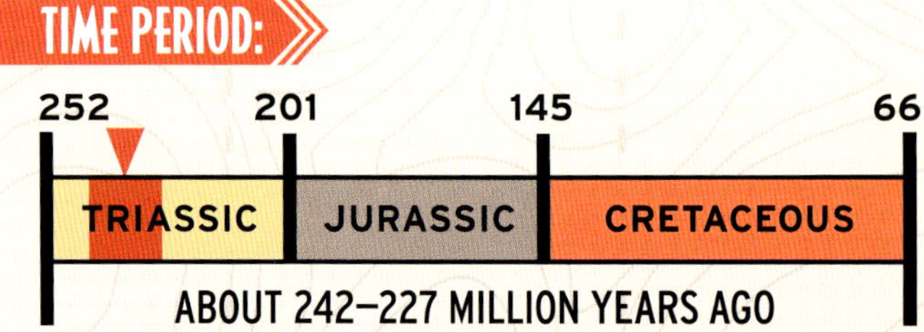

ABOUT 242–227 MILLION YEARS AGO

PTEROSAURS

Other than the dinosaurs, the most well-known reptiles during the Age of Dinosaurs are probably the pterosaurs ('wing lizards'). Pterosaurs are also archosaurs ('ruling reptiles'), just like the dinosaurs. They are not birds, nor are they any other kind of dinosaur (birds are the only known flying dinosaurs).

Like bats and birds, pterosaurs were flyers rather than gliders. Their arms and hands evolved into wings. They did not have feathers but instead had skin attached to long arms with very long fourth fingers. The other three fingers may have been used for grooming or climbing. The skin in these wings was reinforced inside with slender fibers that made the wings stiffer at the edges.

Pterosaurs had a covering of fur on their bodies, probably to keep them insulated. Although some palaeontologists think that pterosaurs walked only on their hind legs, most think they walked something like a gorilla, using their long wings as arms.

Many pterosaurs were small, but some were the largest flying animals of all time. The first pterosaurs appeared in the Late Triassic, around the same time as the first dinosaurs. They died out at the end of the Cretaceous, along with the dinosaurs (except for birds), the marine reptiles, and many other groups of animals. Although it is not certain, the most likely cause for this extinction was the impact of an asteroid with Earth in what is now the Yucatán Peninsula of Mexico. The ash and dust from this explosion would have plunged Earth into darkness and cold, killing off many of the plants that are the base of the food chain both on land and in the sea.

IN *JURASSIC WORLD*

DIMORPHODON

Dimorphodon lived during the early Jurassic. It weighed about 18kg and had a wingspan of 1.5m. This flying reptile, shown below, takes to the sky in *Jurassic World*.

PTERANODON

te-RAN-o-don

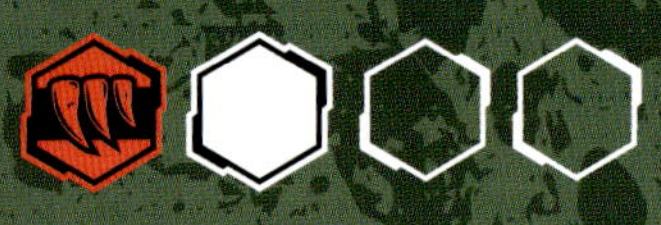

LOCATION:

Kansas, USA

WHAT WE KNOW:

YEAR NAMED: 1876

DIET: CARNIVORE
Fish

WINGSPAN: 8–10m

STANDING HEIGHT: 1.8m

WEIGHT: 25kg

FRIENDS: None

ENEMIES: *Tylosaurus*

FUN FACT!

WHEN *PTERANODON* WAS FIRST DISCOVERED, IT BECAME VERY FAMOUS. WHILE ALL THE PTEROSAURS FOUND PREVIOUSLY WERE THE SIZE OF A SEAGULL OR SMALLER, *PTERANODON* WAS MUCH BIGGER THAN ANY FLYING ANIMAL TODAY.

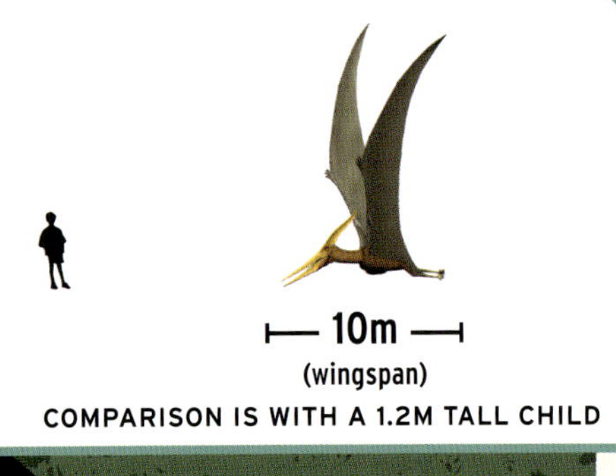

COMPARISON IS WITH A 1.2M TALL CHILD

Pteranodon ('wings without teeth') is probably the best known of the more advanced pterosaurs, called pterodactyls ('winged fingers'). There are several species of *Pteranodon,* each with a distinctive crest on the back of the head. All species of *Pteranodon,* however, had long, slender beaks that were totally toothless. They probably ate fish that they caught while skimming over the water.

Pteranodon is known from thousands of fossils, most of which are just broken fragments but some of which are complete skeletons. It had a wingspan of at least 8m—possibly 10m for the largest specimens—which made it one of the largest of all flying creatures in the history of Earth. For many decades, it was the largest pterosaur known, but larger ones have since been discovered (*Quetzalcoatlus* and *Hatzegopteryx* had a wingspan of 11m).

Pteranodon flew above the seas of Kansas during the Late Cretaceous. Although it must have come to land to roost and lay its eggs, it does not appear to have lived much on the mainland. Therefore, pictures showing it flying over the heads of tyrant dinosaurs, horned dinosaurs and/or duckbill dinosaurs are most likely wrong.

PTERANODON IS OFTEN SHOWN INCORRECTLY WITH TEETH, OR WITH THE TAIL OF A RHAMPHORHYNCHUS.

TIME PERIOD:

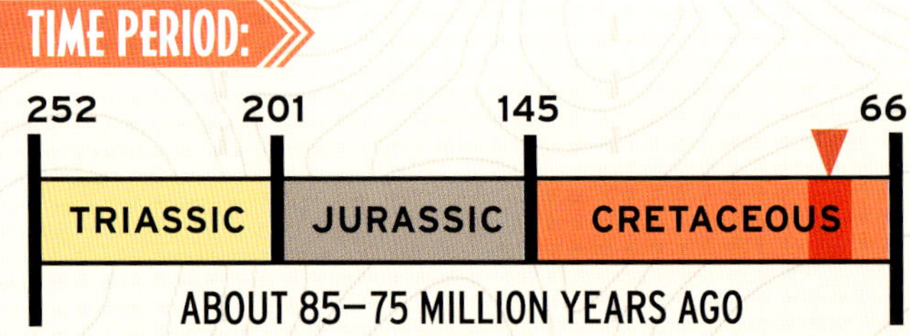

ABOUT 85–75 MILLION YEARS AGO

JURASSIC WORLD
APPEARANCE

QUETZALCOATLUS

KET-sal-ko-AHT-lus

LOCATION:

Texas, USA; possibly Alberta, Canada

WHAT WE KNOW:

YEAR NAMED: 1975

DIET: CARNIVORE
Fish, possibly carrion

WINGSPAN: 11m

STANDING HEIGHT: 3.3m

WEIGHT: Unknown, maybe only 160kg

FUN FACT!

THE FULL NAME OF THIS SPECIES, *QUETZALCOATLUS NORTHROPI*, HONOURS THE NORTHROP AVIATION COMPANY, WHICH BUILT A PLANE CALLED THE FLYING WING THAT LOOKED SOMETHING LIKE A PTEROSAUR.

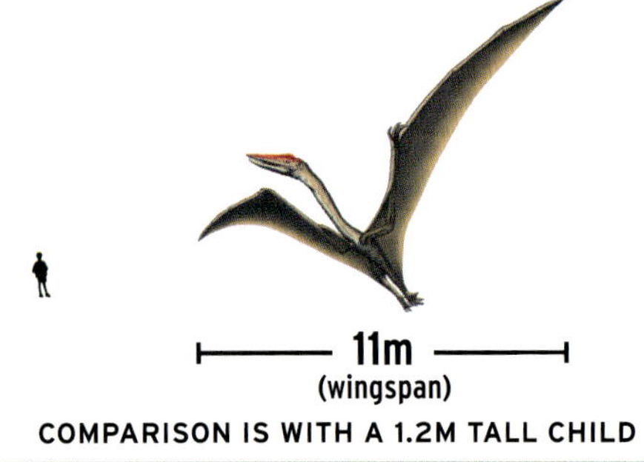

COMPARISON IS WITH A 1.2M TALL CHILD

Quetzalcoatlus (after Quetzalcoatl, the 'feathered serpent' of Aztec mythology) is one of the biggest animals ever to fly. It is an immense animal, with a head possibly 3m long in the biggest individuals. It has a wingspan of 11m, and possibly more.

Like *Tapejara* and *Pteranodon,* this giant pterosaur was a pterodactyl (one of the short-tailed pterosaurs). Unlike *Tapejara* and *Pteranodon,* though, *Quetzalcoatlus* lived on the mainland. Although some palaeontologists have speculated that it was mostly a carrion-eater (like a vulture), others think that it probably ate mostly fish. It had very long legs, so it could wade into the water like an immense stork.

It lived at the very end of the Age of Dinosaurs, flying over the heads of *Tyrannosaurus, Triceratops* and *Edmontosaurus.*

QUEZTALCOATLUS AND RELATED PTEROSAURS WERE PROBABLY PRETTY GOOD AT WALKING ON THE GROUND, UNLIKE MANY EARLY PTEROSAURS.

TIME PERIOD:

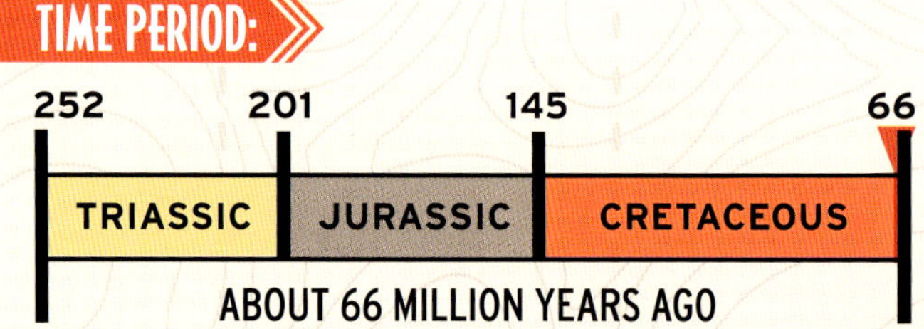

RHAMPHORHYNCHUS

RAM-fo-RING-kus

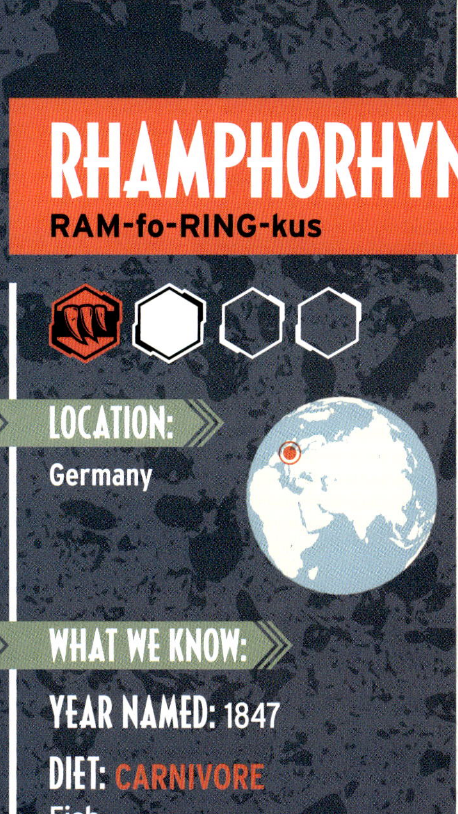

LOCATION:

Germany

WHAT WE KNOW:

YEAR NAMED: 1847

DIET: CARNIVORE
Fish

WINGSPAN: 1.75m

STANDING HEIGHT: 25cm

WEIGHT: 680g

FRIENDS: *Archaeopteryx*

ENEMIES: *Compsognathus*

Rhamphorhynchus ('beak snout') was a primitive long-tailed pterosaur. From skin impressions, we know that the tip of its tail ended in a diamond-shaped fin. This was probably used for steering.

Rhamphorhynchus lived in the tropical islands of Late Jurassic Europe. It ate fish. From the pointed and upturned shape of its snout, palaeontologists think that *Rhamphorhynchus* would fly just above the surface of the water and spear fish with its jaws.

Early pterosaurs rarely got much larger than *Rhamphorhynchus,* although one is known that was probably as big as a bald eagle.

MANY PTEROSAUR FOSSILS HAVE BEEN FOUND IN THE SAME ROCKS AS *RHAMPHORHYNCHUS*. AMONG THESE IS *PTERODACTYLUS*, THE FIRST PTEROSAUR EVER KNOWN (FIRST DESCRIBED IN 1784).

FUN FACT!

PTEROSAUR BONES ARE EVEN THINNER-WALLED THAN BIRD BONES.

COMPARISON IS WITH A 1.2M TALL CHILD

TIME PERIOD:

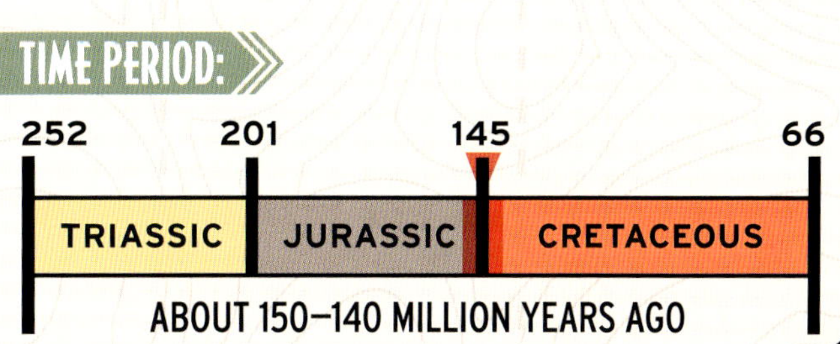

ABOUT 150–140 MILLION YEARS AGO

TAPEJARA

tah-pay-ZHAHR-a

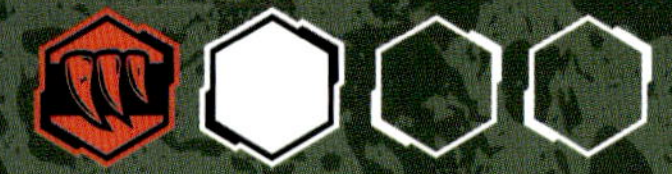

LOCATION:

Brazil

WHAT WE KNOW:

YEAR NAMED: 1989

DIET: CARNIVORE
Probably fish

WINGSPAN: 8m

STANDING HEIGHT: 3.2m

WEIGHT: Unknown, estimated at 25kg

FUN FACT!

MANY OF THE PTEROSAURS, FISH, AND EVEN DINOSAURS FOUND IN THE LIMESTONES WITH *TAPEJARA* HAVE MUSCLE TISSUE THAT HAS PETRIFIED, OR TURNED TO STONE. UNFORTUNATELY, BECAUSE THE MUSCLES HAVE TURNED TO STONE, THEY NO LONGER CONTAIN DNA.

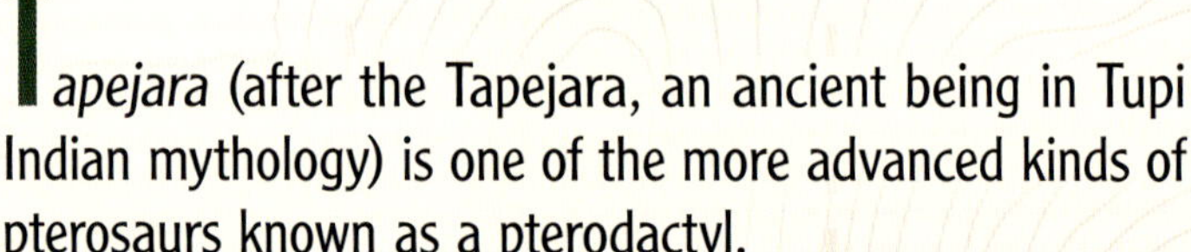

Tapejara (after the Tapejara, an ancient being in Tupi Indian mythology) is one of the more advanced kinds of pterosaurs known as a pterodactyl.

Pterodactyls ('winged fingers') generally had shorter tails than primitive pterosaurs. Although some pterodactyls were small, many were eagle-sized or larger. The bones in the palm of a pterodactyl's hand were much longer than the palm bones in primitive pterosaurs, making their wings even longer.

Each species of pterodactyl had its own distinctive crest on its head. Even within each species, some individuals had bigger and better-developed crests than others. Some scientists think that those with the bigger crests were the males and those with the smaller crests were the females.

The crest in some *Tapejaras* is very strange. There is a single spike near the front of the snout that is taller than the skull is long.

THE SANTANA FORMATION OF BRAZIL CONTAINS THE FOSSILS OF MANY DIFFERENT PTEROSAURS. EACH IS DISTINCT IN ITS OWN WAY: SOME HAVE TALL CRESTS; SOME HAVE SHORT, HEAVY BEAKS; AND SOME (LIKE *TROPEOGNATHUS*) ARE GIGANTIC.

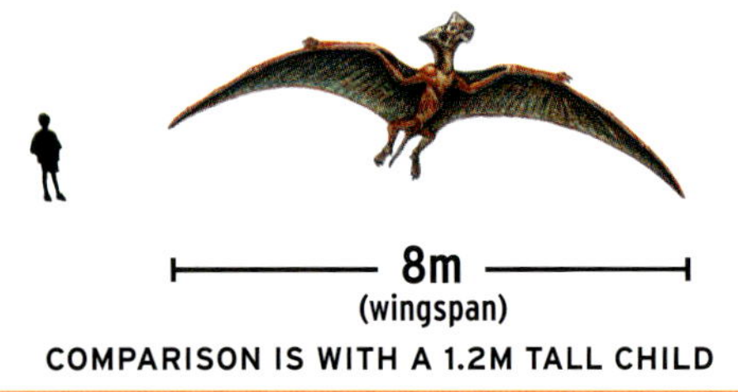

COMPARISON IS WITH A 1.2M TALL CHILD

TIME PERIOD:

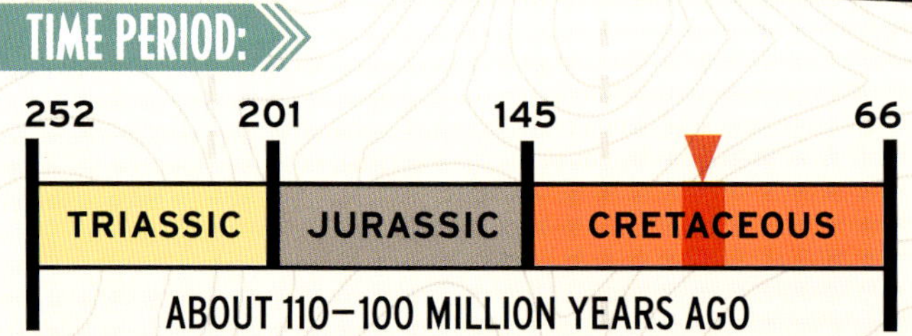

ABOUT 110–100 MILLION YEARS AGO

MAPS OF EARTH IN THE MESOZOIC ERA

TRIASSIC PERIOD / 252–201 MYA

During the Triassic Period, the landmasses of Earth were joined into a supercontinent called Pangaea, which means 'all Earth'.

JURASSIC PERIOD / 201–145 MYA

During the Jurassic Period, Pangaea began to break apart and become separated by water. Notice how North America began to drift away from Africa, forming the very beginnings of the Atlantic Ocean.

CRETACEOUS PERIOD / 145–66 MYA

During the Cretaceous Period, the continents moved closer to their present-day positions. This separation of landmasses increased the differences among the plants and animals that developed on the different continents.

DINOSAUR DISCOVERIES AROUND THE WORLD

KEY

- LT Late Triassic
- EJ Early Jurassic
- MJ Middle Jurassic
- LJ Late Jurassic
- EK Early Cretaceous
- LK Late Cretaceous

Dinosaur fossils have been found on every continent. Indicated on the map below are over thirty of the most important spots on Earth where dinosaur fossils have been discovered. Some of these are important for historical reasons, others are more recent sites where new discoveries are still being made.

(For a more complete listing of sites, see the chapter on dinosaurian distribution in *The Dinosauria,* edited by Weishampel, Dodson and Osmólska.)

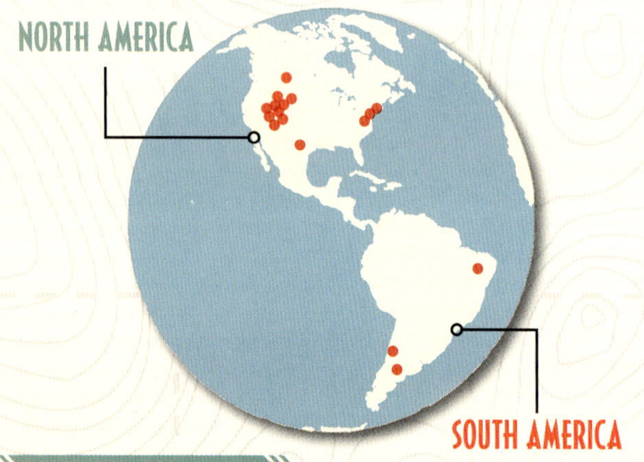

NORTH AMERICA:

- **Ghost Ranch, NM LT:** A site where hundreds of Coelophysis of all ages died and were buried together.
- **Connecticut River Valley, CT & MA LT EJ:** The first dinosaur footprints studied by scientists.
- **Kayenta Formation, AZ EJ:** The rocks of the Kayenta contain the best Early Jurassic fossils in North America, including *Dilophosaurus.*
- **Morrison Formation sites LJ:** This real-life 'Jurassic Park' is a series of rocks that formed along the eastern side of the ancestral Rocky Mountains back in the Late Jurassic. The formation has produced more different kinds of dinosaur fossils than any other known to palaeontology. Some of the most important sites in the Morrison include:
  - **Como Bluff, WY:** One of the best-studied sites. Twenty-six separate quarries here have each produced one or more dinosaur fossils.
  - **Cleveland-Lloyd Dinosaur Quarry, UT:** Over forty *Allosaurus* individuals were found in a single place here.
  - **Dinosaur National Monument, UT-CO border:** Made a National Monument because of the completeness of the fossils found here in an old Jurassic riverbed.
  - **Howe Quarry, WY:** Still producing many excellent dinosaur fossils, and has since the 1930s.
  - **Garden Park, CO:** The type (name-holding) specimens of many of the Morrison's dinosaurs come from here. Several are on display at the Smithsonian Institution.
- **Cloverly Formation, WY-MT border EK:** The most complete Early Cretaceous dinosaur fossils (including *Deinonychus)* in North America.
- **Paluxy River, TX EK:** An important footprint site that recorded a large meat-eater attacking a giant sauropod.
- **Patuxent (Arundel) Clay, MD EK:** Has produced fossils of more dinosaur (and other Mesozoic land vertebrate) species than any other eastern North American Cretaceous site.
- **Moreno Hills Formation, NM LK:** Newly discovered; contains fossils of the oldest horned dinosaurs and therizinosaurs in North America.
- **Two Medicine Formation, MT LK:** Numerous preserved dinosaur nest sites and a bone bed 'graveyard' of thousands of individuals of the duckbill dinosaur *Maiasaura.*
- **Dinosaur Provincial Park, Alberta LK:** The most abundant, diverse, and complete Late Cretaceous dinosaur fossils.
- **Haddonfield, NJ LK:** Site of the discovery of the duckbill *Hadrosaurus,* the first dinosaur named from east of the Mississippi River.

◆ **Hell Creek Formation, MT LC:** Contains the geologically youngest fossils of dinosaurs (other than birds) in North America, including such famous dinosaurs as *Triceratops, Edmontosaurus* and *Tyrannosaurus.*

SOUTH AMERICA:

◆ **Ischigualasto Formation, Argentina LT:** The best site for the oldest dinosaurs known to science, including *Eoraptor* and *Herrerasaurus.*

◆ **Santana Formation, Brazil EK:** Amazingly well preserved fossils that include the remains of dinosaur muscle tissue!

◆ **Neuquen, Argentina LK:** Formations in these badlands of Patagonia have produced many different species of Late Cretaceous dinosaurs, from babies to adults.

AFRICA:

◆ **Upper Elliot Beds, South Africa, Lesotho, and Zimbabwe EJ:** The best Early Jurassic dinosaur skeletons in the Southern Hemisphere.

◆ **Tendaguru Hill, Tanzania LJ:** Giant sauropods like *Brachiosaurus,* as well as stegosaurs and smaller herbivores, make this Jurassic site famous.

◆ **Gadoufaouna, Niger EK:** *Ouranosaurus, Lurdusaurus* and other large dinosaurs from the middle of the Cretaceous have been found in this Sahara Desert location.

◆ **Bahariya Oasis, Egypt LK:** Home of *Spinosaurus!*

◆ **Maevarano Formation, Madagascar LK:** Many new species have been discovered here in the last few years.

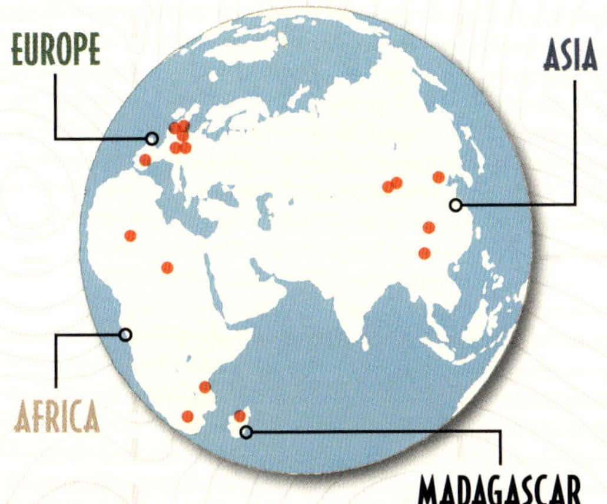

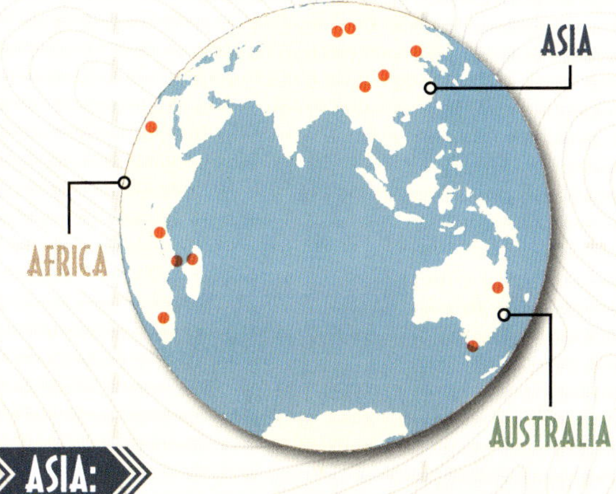

EUROPE:

◆ **Trossingen, Germany LT:** Famous for many specimens of *Plateosaurus* and the remains of one of the oldest known turtles.

◆ **Stonesfield, England MJ:** *Megalosaurus* (the first dinosaur known to science) was discovered here.

◆ **Solnhofen Limestone, Germany LJ:** Most famous as the only known site of the early bird *Archaeopteryx.* Has produced many pterosaur fossils, as well as the little theropod *Compsognathus.*

◆ **Wealden Group in the UK, especially the Isle of Wight EK:** Contains the skeletons of Iguanodon and many other Early Cretaceous European dinosaurs.

◆ **Bernissart, Belgium EK:** The first complete *Iguanodon* skeletons were discovered here.

◆ **Las Hoyas, Spain EK:** Newly discovered, this site has produced many early bird fossils, as well as the early ostrich dinosaur *Pelecanimimus.*

ASIA:

◆ **Lufeng, Yunnan Province, China EJ:** The most completely known dinosaur community of the Early Jurassic.

◆ **Zigong, Sichuan Province, China MJ:** By far the most completely known Middle Jurassic dinosaurs come from Zigong.

◆ **Sihetun, Liaoning Province, China EK:** Site of the discovery of the amazing feathered dinosaur specimens.

◆ **Flaming Cliffs, Ukhaa Tolgod, and Nemegt Valley, Mongolia LK:** Three different sites in Mongolia, containing the (sometimes spectacularly preserved) fossils of dinosaurs from the Late Cretaceous of Asia. Home of *Velociraptor* and *Protoceratops!*

AUSTRALIA:

◆ **Muttaburra, Queensland EK:** Home of *Muttaburrasaurus.*

◆ **Dinosaur Cove, Victoria EK:** Famous for fossils of polar dinosaurs!

WHERE TO SEE DINOSAURS

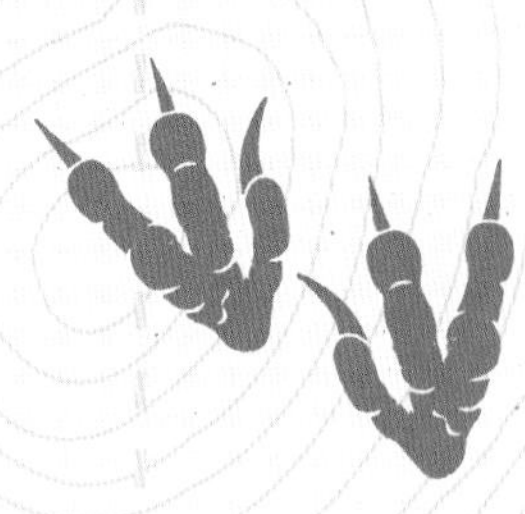

IN THE FIELD

Places where you can see dinosaurs as they have been found—and are being found—in the rock.

BROOME, WA, AUSTRALIA

◆ **Dinosaur Coast**

The Dinosaur Coast has more different types of dinosaur tracks than anywhere else in the world! The 130 million year old dinosaur tracks are preserved in rocks of the Broome Sandstone, and form part of the West Kimberley National Heritage Area.

CANOWINDRA, NSW, AUSTRALIA

◆ **Age of Fishes Fossil Museum**

150 million years before dinosaurs roamed the earth, almost all backboned animals were aquatic and spent their entire lives underwater. This era is known as the Devonian Period or the 'Age of Fishes'. This Canowindra site is listed as part of Australia's National Heritage because of its international scientific importance.

INVERLOCH, VIC, AUSTRALIA

◆ **Dinosaur Dreaming**

More than 15,000 bones, teeth and fossils of small dinosaurs have been found at the Dinosaur Dreaming dig site, along the coastline of Inverloch. When the tide is out, an extensive rock platform is exposed, revealing rock pools and imprints that tell a prehistoric story.

NARRACOORTE, SA, AUSTRALIA

◆ **Victoria Caves**

In 1969, two explorers squeezed through a gap in Victoria Fossil Cave and discovered a massive chamber full of fossilised remains. Since then, this fossil deposit has been a working palaeontological dig—tens of thousands of fossil bones have been recovered. The fossils give us a unique window into the climate and environment of the times when these animals lived.

PATRICIA, ALBERTA, CANADA

◆ **Dinosaur Provincial Park, World Heritage Site**

One of the most productive locations for digging dinosaurs is the Dinosaur Park Formation of Alberta, Canada. In the Dinosaur Provincial Park, you can visit sites where herds of horned dinosaurs (and other Late Cretaceous creatures) are being uncovered, prepared, and removed for study.

DINOSAUR, COLORADO, USA

◆ **Dinosaur National Monument**

On exhibit at this monument is a wall (once the bed of an ancient river) where the fossils of many different Jurassic dinosaurs are exposed.

MORRISON, COLORADO, USA

◆ **Dinosaur Ridge National Landmark**

This is one of the best places in the world to see the footprints of Cretaceous ornithopods.

ROCKY HILL, CONNECTICUT, USA

◆ **Dinosaur State Park**

The dome of this museum is built directly over the fossilised tracks of Triassic dinosaurs and other reptiles; you can actually see the footsteps of ancient dinosaurs as they are preserved in the rock.

GLEN ROSE, TEXAS, USA

◆ **Dinosaur Valley State Park**

This site has footprints of Cretaceous sauropods and theropods in the place where they were discovered.

PRICE, UTAH, USA

◆ **Cleveland-Lloyd Dinosaur Quarry**

The remains of over forty-four individual *Allosaurus,* as well as other dinosaurs, were collected at this world-famous site.

WORLAND, WYOMING, USA

◆ **Red Gulch Dinosaur Tracksite**

This site features thousands of Middle Jurassic theropod footprints.

THERMOPOLIS, WYOMING, USA

◆ **Wyoming Dinosaur Center**

This museum has daily tours of their excavations in the Jurassic Morrison Formation, where you can see the bones of *Stegosaurus, Allosaurus* and *Diplodocus.*

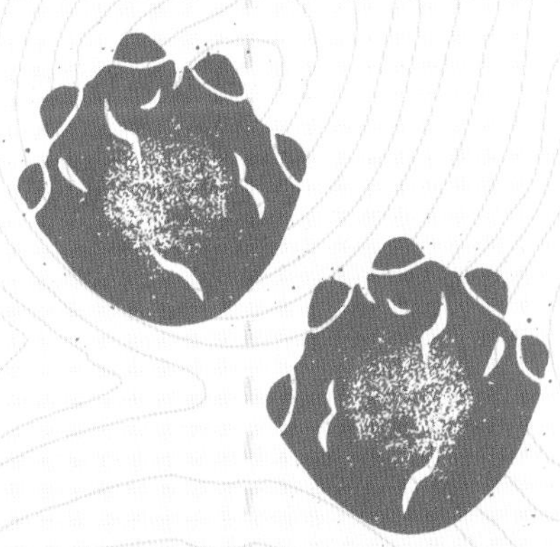

IN MUSEUMS

These are some of the biggest and most famous museums with dinosaur displays around the world.

FIELD MUSEUM

Illinois, USA

Key exhibits:

- SUE, the 12 metres long *Tyrannosaurus rex,* is the largest *Tyrannosaurus rex* specimen yet discovered, and the most complete—around 90 percent.
- Máximo, the titanosaur *Patagotitan mayorum* is the biggest dinosaur that scientists have discovered to date at 37 metres long.

FUKUI DINOSAUR MUSEUM

Katsuyama City, Fukui Prefecture, Japan

Key exhibits:

- *Fukuiraptor* and *Fukuisaurus* skeletons display fossils that were found nearby in the region.
- A hands-on zone where you can touch real fossils!

IZIKO MUSEUM

Cape Town, South Africa

Key exhibits:

- The African Dinosaurs exhibit dioramas dedicated to the mighty creatures inhabiting the continent, like the *Jobaria* from Niger.
- A *Carcharodontosaurus* skull from North Africa, with 14cm long teeth.

NATURAL HISTORY MUSEUM

London, England

Key exhibits:

- The first skeleton of *Iguanodon* known to science!
- The skull of a *Triceratops.*

MUSEUM FÜR NATURKUNDE

Berlin, Germany

Key exhibits:

- *Brachiosaurus brancai* stands 13.27 metres tall and is the tallest mounted dinosaur skeleton in the world
- The Berlin specimen of the primeval bird *Archaeopteryx lithographica* is approximately 150 million years old, and thought to be the best-known fossil in the world.

NATIONAL DINOSAUR MUSEUM

Canberra, Australian Capital Territory, Australia

Key exhibits:

- This museum houses Australia's largest collection of dinosaur fossils.
- Walk through an interactive garden with animatronic dinosaurs.

ROYAL BELGIAN INSTITUTE OF NATURAL SCIENCES

Brussels, Belgium

Key exhibits:

- The Dinosaur Gallery is the largest dinosaur hall in Europe!
- The Bernissart *Iguanadons* are 30 almost complete *Iguanadon* skeletons discovered 322 metres below ground in a coal mine.

ROYAL TYRRELL MUSEUM OF PALEONTOLOGY

Alberta, Canada

Key exhibits:

- The original 'Black Beauty' *Tyrannosaurus* skeleton with its unique dark sheen, casts of this fossil are on display in many museums around the world.
- Visitors can watch palaeontologists at work in the preparation lab to see how they prepare fossilised bones, like those of an *Ankylosaurus* found in a Canadian mine.

WYOMING DINOSAUR CENTER

Wyoming, USA

Key exhibits:

- 'Lori' the *Hesperornithoides,* troodontid dinosaur fossil found in Wyoming.
- 'Jimbo' the 32 metre *Supersaurus* spans the length of the museum, and is the biggest dinosaur fossil in Wyoming.

ZIGONG DINOSAUR MUSEUM

Zigong, China

Key exhibits:

- 18 complete skeletons excavated from the Dashanpu fossil site that lies within the museum.
- Visitors get to see an excavation site firsthand.

RESEARCH RECOMMENDATIONS

BOOKS FOR YOUNGER READERS:

THE BIG GOLDEN BOOK OF DINOSAURS (2013)
by Robert T. Bakker

A modern update of a classic 20th century dinosaur book for children.

CHILDREN'S ENCYCLOPEDIA OF DINOSAURS (2009)
by Michael K. Brett-Surman

Covers 142 species of dinosaurs in detail.

DIGGING FOR BRACHIOSAURUS
DIGGING FOR STEGOSAURUS
DIGGING FOR TRICERATOPS
DIGGING FOR TYRANNOSAURUS REX (2015)
by Thomas R. Holtz Jr.

Four-volume set about our changing knowledge of four 'classic' dinosaur species.

DINOSAUR! DINOSAURS AND OTHER AMAZING PREHISTORIC CREATURES AS YOU'VE NEVER SEEN THEM BEFORE (2014)
by John Woodward

This 'coffee table book' is for the whole family with its lavish artwork and pictures.

DINOSAURS OF THE WORLD, VOLUMES 1-11 (1999)
edited by Chris Marshal

Contains two- and four-page spreads about dinosaurs, the animals and plants of their world, and principles of evolution, extinction and fossilisation.

DINOSAURS: THE MOST COMPLETE UP-TO-DATE ENCYCLOPEDIA FOR DINOSAUR LOVERS OF ALL AGES (2007)
by Thomas R. Holtz Jr.

What it says in the title!

DINO-TREKKING (1995)
by Kelly Milner Halls

Where to find dinosaurs anywhere on display in North America. Lists all museums and expositions with their addresses, hours of operation, and names of dinosaurs on display.

DISCOVERING DINOSAURS (2014)
by Bob Walters and Tess Kissinger

A book on dinosaurs by the artists who illustrated this book!

FIELD GUIDE TO DINOSAURS (2009)
by Steve Brusatte

An excellent review of dinosaurs.

THE LITTLE GIANT BOOK OF DINOSAURS (2001)
by Thomas R. Holtz Jr.

An examination of dinosaur history and evolution. One of the first books on dinosaur cladistics for kids!

BOOKS FOR TEACHERS AND PARENTS:

THE COMPLETE DINOSAUR, 2ND EDITION (2012)
edited by Michael K. Brett-Surman, Thomas R. Holtz and James O. Farlow

This is the best undergraduate book for college students, whether they are non-science majors or pre-palaeontologists.

THE DINOSAURIA, 2ND EDITION (2004)
by David B. Weishampel, edited by Peter Dodson and Halszka Osmólska

Written by and for palaeontologists, this book contains chapters on the anatomy and biology of all the major groups of dinosaurs.

DINOSAUR IMAGERY: THE SCIENCE OF LOST WORLDS AND JURASSIC ART (THE LANZENDORF COLLECTION) (2000)
created by John J. Lanzendorf

Images from the world's largest private collection of dinosaur art, with explanations by leading dinosaur scientists and artists. See Michael Brett-Surman's contribution on pp. 40–42, and Tom Holtz's on pp. 54–56.

DINOSAUR PALEOBIOLOGY (2012)
by Stephen L. Brusatte

An excellent medium-length textbook for the serious student of dinosaurs, written by a leading researcher.

DINOSAURS: THE ENCYCLOPEDIA (1997)
by Donald F. Glut

A massive volume with a photograph or illustration of the original specimen of every dinosaur species, as well as text description of its discovery. A series of supplements updates this book on a regular basis.

SCIENTIFIC AMERICAN BOOK OF DINOSAURS: THE BEST MINDS IN PALEONTOLOGY CREATE A PORTRAIT OF THE PREHISTORIC ERA (2000)
edited by Gregory Paul

A collection of classic papers from *Scientific American* as well as brand-new chapters discussing the origin, evolution, history, and extinction of dinosaurs. Written to give the interested public the latest information on the cutting edge of dinosaur research.

VERTEBRATE PALAEONTOLOGY, 4TH EDITION (2014)
by Michael J. Benton

This is the crown jewel of books on the evolution of all vertebrates.

WEBSITES

AMERICAN MUSEUM OF NATURAL HISTORY
amnh.org

The AMNH has the largest collection and largest exhibits of dinosaurs and other fossil vertebrates anywhere in the world.

ENCYCLOPEDIA OF LIFE
eol.org

GEOLOGIC TIMESCALE FOUNDATION
engineering.purdue.edu/Stratigraphy/charts/educational.html

One of the best places to find educational time charts and posters.

AUSTRALIAN MUSEUM
www.australian.museum/learn/dinosaurs

The Australian Museum's has many pages of dinosaur learning resources, as well as articles dedicated to dinosaurs discovered in Australia.

NATURAL HISTORY MUSEUM, LONDON
nhm.ac.uk

One of the oldest and grandest natural history museums in the world, the Natural History Museum is still a center of dinosaur research.

SCIENCE DAILY
sciencedaily.com

A great place for up-to-the-minute news about fossils.

SMITHSONIAN INSTITUTION NATIONAL MUSEUM OF NATURAL HISTORY
paleobiology.si.edu/dinosaurs/

This is the first museum to have a 'virtual tour' of their entire dinosaur hall—and the home of the first fully 'digital' *Triceratops*.

THE TREE OF LIFE PROJECT: DINOSAURIA
tolweb.org/Dinosauria

An international multi-year project to map out the entire 'Tree of Life', with detailed information on all organisms, past and present. This link is to the dinosaur part of the tree.

GLOSSARY

ANGIOSPERM ('covered seed'):
A group of seed plants in which the seed is surrounded by a fruit; the flowering plants.

ANKYLOSAUR ('fused lizard'):
Any short-legged, plant-eating dinosaur that is armoured with thick, bony scutes (small plates).

ARCHOSAURS ('ruling lizards'):
A group of advanced reptiles including the dinosaurs, pterosaurs and crocodilians.

CARNIVORE ('flesh-eater'):
Any meat-eating animal.

CERATOPSIAN ('horned face'):
A plant-eating dinosaur with horns on its face and a bony frill over its neck.

CLADISTICS:
A method of classifying organisms in which hypotheses about evolutionary relationships are the basis for classification. Organisms are grouped according to their common ancestors, determined by the identification of shared derived characteristics. Higher groups are not ranked. This system has replaced the older Linnaean system of classification.

CRETACEOUS ('chalk age'):
The third geological period in the Age of Dinosaurs, from 145 to 66 million years ago.

CROCODILIAN:
The group of archosaurs including crocodiles, alligators and gavials.

DINOSAUR ('fearfully great lizard'):
Any descendant of the most recent common ancestor of *Iguanodon* and *Megalosaurus*. This group includes the Saurischia and the Ornithischia.

DROMAEOSAURS ('swift-running lizards'– the 'raptors'):
A group of advanced theropods with very stiff tails and a sickle-like claw on the second toe of the foot.

ERA:
A division of geological time composed of geological periods. The Mesozoic Era includes the Triassic, Jurassic and Cretaceous Periods.

EVOLUTION ('unfolding'):
The development of plants and animals through geological time, and the way that this development has come about. This is oversimplified in many books as 'change over time'.

EXTINCTION ('wiping out'):
The death of a group of plants or animals.

FORMATION:
A formally defined, mappable rock unit.

FOSSIL ('dug up'):
The remains of something that once lived. Fossils are often millions of years old and have usually turned to stone over time. It is also defined as 'evidence of life in the geologic past'.

GASTROLITH ('stomach stone'):
A pebble or stone that is swallowed by an animal and kept in the digestive tract. Gastroliths grind up food, making it easier to digest.

GEOLOGIC TIME:
1/ The period of time from the formation of Earth to the beginning of recorded history; prehistoric time.
2/ A very long span of time extending over millions of years.

GONDWANA:
The supercontinent or landmass that fragmented millions of years ago to form modern South America, Africa, Antarctica, Madagascar, India and Australia.

HADROSAUR ('sturdy lizard'):
A group of plant-eating dinosaurs of the Late Cretaceous. Hadrosaurs are often known as 'duckbilled dinosaurs' because of their broad, flat snouts.

HERBIVORE ('plant-eater'):
An organism whose diet consists exclusively or mainly of plants.

JURASSIC (from the Jura Mountains, where rocks from this period were first named):
The second geological period in the Age of Dinosaurs, from 201 to 145 million years ago.

LAURASIA:
The supercontinent or landmass that fragmented millions of years ago to form modern North America, Greenland, Europe and Asia.

LINNAEAN TAXONOMY:
The older system of classifying life based on a hierarchical system. This includes the ranked categories such as Kingdom, Phylum, Class, Order and Family. Palaeontologists now use Cladistics (see above).

MESOZOIC ('middle age'):
The Age of Dinosaurs, the time from 252 to 66 million years ago, which includes the Triassic, Jurassic, and Cretaceous Periods. The Mesozoic Era is the 'middle age' between the Palaeozoic and Cenozoic Eras.

OMNIVORE ('all-eater'):
An animal that eats both other animals and plants.

ORNITHOPOD ('bird-foot'):
A plant-eating dinosaur that has no spines or horns and walks on two legs.

PACHYCEPHALOSAUR ('thick-headed lizard'):
A plant-eating dinosaur with a very thick skull roof, possibly used for head- or flank-butting.

PALAEONTOLOGIST ('expert on ancient life'):
A scientist who studies fossils and the history of life on Earth.

PANGAEA ('all Earth'):
A giant ancient supercontinent, made up of all the land area of Earth, which formed during the late Palaeozoic Era and later divided into the supercontinents of Laurasia and Gondwana, from which the present continents derived. We now know of at least two earlier supercontinents.

PERIOD:
A division of geological time smaller than an Era, such as the Jurassic, Triassic or Cretaceous.

PREDATOR:
An animal that hunts and seizes other animals for food.

PREY:
An animal hunted or seized for food; victim of a predator.

PROTOFEATHERS:
The ancestral form of the feathers of modern birds; simple tubes found covering the bodies of many advanced theropods.

SAUROPOD ('lizard-foot'):
A large plant-eating dinosaur with a long neck and a long tail, such as *Diplodocus* or *Apatosaurus*. Lived in the Jurassic or Cretaceous Periods. (Note: A new discovery shows a sauropod in Thailand from the very end of the Triassic.)

SEXUAL DIMORPHISM:
The occurrence of two distinct male and female forms of the same species, especially visible differences in colouration, body shape, size and so on.

SPECIES:
A group of organisms that can breed with one another and produce fertile offspring.

THEROPOD ('beast-foot'):
A group of two-legged, primarily meat-eating, dinosaurs.

TITANOSAUR:
A group of advanced sauropods of the Late Jurassic and Cretaceous, including some very large forms. Some titanosaurs were armoured.

TRIASSIC ('three parts'):
The first geological period in the Age of Dinosaurs, from 251 to 200 million years ago.

TROODONTS:
A group of advanced bird-like theropods with large brains and very long, slender legs.

TYPE SPECIMEN:
The original specimen that is designated as the first example, and 'name bearer', of a given species or other group of organisms, and that is used as the basis for describing the group; the actual individual specimen first used to name a new species.

ABOUT THE AUTHORS

courtesy of Dr Thomas R. Holtz, Jr.

DR THOMAS R. HOLTZ, JR.

Realising he could not grow up to be a dinosaur, **Dr Thomas R. Holtz, Jr.**, did the next best thing and became a vertebrate paleontologist. His specialty is *Tyrannosaurus rex*, and his work on carnivorous dinosaurs has become the standard in several textbooks. In addition to his many scientific papers, he has been involved in the making of several documentaries, including the award-winning *Walking with Dinosaurs* and *Dinosaur Revolution* for The Discovery Channel. Dr Holtz is a senior lecturer in the Department of Geology at the University of Maryland, College Park.

To learn more about him, visit his website at geol.umd.edu/~tholtz/.

courtesy of Dr Micheal Brett-Surman

DR MICHAEL BRETT-SURMAN

As a child, **Dr Michael Brett-Surman** was deeply, deeply influenced by the two dinosaur halls at the American Museum of Natural History in New York. He went on to name two dinosaurs in early 1979, *Secernosaurus* and *Gilmoreosaurus*. Later that year he joined the staff of the National Museum of Natural History in Washington, D.C. He has been employed there ever since.

ABOUT THE ILLUSTRATOR

ROBERT WALTERS

Inspired by Rudolph Zallinger's mural *The Age of Reptiles*, young Robert Walters started drawing dinosaurs—and never stopped. He went on to study art at the Academy of the Fine Arts in Philadelphia and has been a professional dinosaur life restoration artist for more than twenty years. His work is on permanent display at museums across the United States, including the National Museum of Natural History and the Academy of Natural Sciences. He has illustrated more than twenty dinosaur books and countless magazine articles and has worked on documentaries for PBS and The Discovery Channel.

You can visit him online at dinoart.com.

courtesy of Robert Walters